MISS FLOSSIE'S WORLD

*Coping with Adversity During
The Great Depression Then
and the Recession Now*

Floriana Hall

PublishAmerica
Baltimore

Hardcover 978-1-4560-0734-8
Softcover 978-1-4560-0735-5
PUBLISHED BY PUBLISHAMERICA, LLLP
www.publishamerica.com
Baltimore

Printed in the United States of America

The names of some of the people and relatives in this book have been changed. However, Francis Benedict was my father's given name. His last name, Hanocek, is one I made up. The last name of my maternal Grandmother and Grandfather was 'Schmitt.' Most of the first names are correct except there are some false names used as a protection from being sued.

Floriana Hall

To Marie:
Enjoy each day and all its blessings.
Love,
Floriana Hall
6/5/12

The Lord is my strength and my shield, in whom my heart trusted and found help. So my heart rejoices; with my song I praise my God. Psalm 28.7

HOPE IN GOD'S GRACE

Only God's grace keeps me strong
I feel His presence all day long
When I feel ill or in pain
He gives me hope not in vain.

Only God's grace keeps me strong
He forgives me all my wrongs
I thank Him daily for any favors
He strengthens my faith which never waivers.

Only God's grace keeps me strong
In His hands I know I belong
Following his footsteps I walk behind
Keeping me hopeful and strong, I find.

Only God's grace keeps me strong
I pray and sing my heartfelt song
Of praise to our Blessed Lord
Who protects me from the sword.

Only God's grace keeps me strong
When I am alone or something goes wrong
He gives me strength to cope
He surrounds me with hope.

Floriana Hall

THE WORLD ACCORDING TO FLOSSIE

Flossie is a carefree girl who tosses her flaxen hair
She uses her hands as she talks, sometimes unaware.

Flossie is the lighter side of the person that is me
She has only laughter in her life, goes through life with glee.

She tiptoes through each bit of strife, bypasses turns in the road
Her laughter is heard by everyone, and her smile is her usual mode.

Though she may be old and wrinkled now, she still feels young at heart
She enjoys watching little babies and children play their part.

Flossie has always been confident and caring,
She has been called courageous, sometimes is daring.

Flossie continues to love herself and others
And likes to help all her sisters and brothers.

Flossie, my alter ego, my pseudonym for writing poetry and books
Is as real as she can be, for the little girl she always looks.

No matter how old she will finally be, there is some child remaining
That's the way it's supposed to be, Flossie's world is entertaining.

Floriana Hall

PROLOGUE:

I will be eighty-three years old on October 2, 2010. I have written thirteen books so far since the age of sixty-eight. Perhaps that is not too unusual except that I was inspired in church to write my first published poem which suddenly popped into my head. I called the poem *LOVE NEVER DIES*, entered it in a contest and it won the National Library of Poetry's Editor's Choice Award. Before that, I had not entered any poetry contests even though I had written poetry as a child and always had a passion for it. This poem was a gift from God because since that day poetry has come to me in the wee hours of the morning. It is said that is when the angels visit. This muse has created over 700 poems which are all inspirational in some form or other and are published all over the world.

A few weeks after the poetry suddenly zapped me, my daughter who taught fifth grade in Kansas asked me to write my adventures as a child during The Great Depression. The story just flowed in front of me like images on a television screen. At the time, I did not know where I might obtain the extra money to publish the book but I happened to win a sports contest at church in which Bingo balls were placed. My number 64 was picked (my mother's favorite number) and I won $100 two months in a row plus I won some poetry contests. I accumulated $400, enough to publish 100 books. I actually type set the book myself and that was a project in itself. It took me a year to write and typeset the first version titled *SMALL CHANGE*. The printer passed away at a young age after publishing five editions for me.It sold so well I decided to publish it again but changed the title to *THE ADVENTURES OF FLOSSIE, ROBBIE, AND JUNEY* During The Great Depression. It is read in many local schools; afterwards I visit some of the classes and talk about the book and answer many questions asked by the students. They are always eager to learn more. After all, the Great Depression is a part of history and every one who has lived in any era is a part of history.

I was asked by many readers to write the adult sequel to *THE ADVENTURES OF FLOSSIE, ROBBIE AND JUNEY* During The Great Depression which I called *FRANCIS, NOT THE SAINT*, subsequently translated into Spanish, *FRANCISO, NO EL SANTO*.

Twelve years have passed since the memoir was written and much has happened since my husband Robert and I celebrated our fiftieth wedding anniversary on December 31, 1990 which concluded the book *FRANCIS, NOT THE SAINT*.

This book, *MISS FLOSSIE'S WORLD*, is timely because right now the United States and other parts of the world are experiencing a recession. What goes around, comes around. People do not always learn by past mistakes and the same types of mistakes tend to be made again and again in the history of the world. Hopefully, this book will help readers. If it helps at least one person to understand coping with circumstances beyond one's control, I will be happy. If it helps adults not to blame their parents and past for their mistakes, that will be a plus. If it helps young women to carefully choose their partners to marry, that will be a bonus. And if it helps any reader to learn to cope with adversity, that will be my ultimate goal.

Table of Contents

CHAPTER 1—The Birth of Flossie

Last night I watched a movie called *THE INVENTION OF LYING*. It was a fantasy movie about a world where everyone told the absolute truth which really caused many people anguish. The main character was in a bind when he needed to pay his rent of $800 and knew he only had $300 in his account. The bank's computers were down and he suddenly blurted out that he had $800 in his account instead of $300 and that was supposed to be the invention of lying. The teller gave him $800. After that, he made a fortune telling tall tales but in the process he was regarded as a very respectful person and friend.

What has that got to do with my story? Well, I believe when it comes to lying, my father, Francis Benedict Hanocek was a better liar than anyone I have ever known. He lied about everything so much that no one knew when to believe him. When my two brothers and I were young children, he rarely lived up to his promises and it did not take us long to figure out that we should not expect him to follow through with his promises..

The first five years of my life, I felt loved by both my parents. I cannot say I remember the first two years but I know I enjoyed life from the age of three with my sweet mother and doting father.

I was born in the early morning of October 2, 1927, in Pittsburgh, Pennsylvania after a rainy and stormy night. My mother, Florrie, was in labor all night. My dad summoned the doctor who lived close by on Troy Hill on the north side of Pittsburgh, Pennsylvania, in the middle of the night. He was inebriated but delivered me with the aid of forceps. Florrie was a very tiny woman who weighed about 116 pounds. She was five feet, three inches tall. I weighed nine pounds and caused a lot of tearing during delivery. The doctor sewed my mother up but in so doing stitched her main nerve to her womb. That was the story I was told all my life by my parents.

My dad took one look at me and knew he wanted to name me after my mother. She wanted to name me 'Virginia' but dad insisted that I be named 'Floriana' (mother was called Florrie all of her life) because he thought I looked like my mother. Florrie had a ruddy complexion, thick dark hair and big blue eyes. I was very fair with blonde hair and I had smaller blue green eyes. Mother let him have his way. They decided to call me 'Flossie' so that there would not be too much confusion in the coming years. During the course of my lifetime, I was also addressed by many other names. My brothers and some relatives called me 'Sissie' and my Dad called me 'Dearie'. My friends have called me 'Floriana', 'Flo', 'Flossie' and many people have mistakenly called me 'Florence'. I prefer 'Flossie' and use it as my pen name.

My parents were at a loss to explain why I did not sleep much during the first year of my life. I did not seem to have colic nor cry much but was awake most of the time with a smile on my face. I guess I was just born that way and wanted to see what was going on. I sat up at five months, crawled at six months and walked at nine months. I started talking by the time I was a year old. Talk about a precocious baby!

One day soon after I turned one year old, my mother and dad took me to a movie with them and my Uncle Jim, who was my mother's younger brother. While watching the movie, I started calling out "Chop ice, Chop ice" when I saw an ice truck delivering ice to a neighborhood scene. Everyone in the theatre started laughing. Uncle Jim talked about that day to me many times throughout his life.

My brother, Robert Florian, was born on October 23, 1929. He weighed eleven pounds at birth and we called him Robbie. On

September 24, 1931, Juney was born. His name was Francis Philip but we always called him Juney when he was growing up.

We moved a few times while in Pittsburgh because we needed more room. We had fun roller skating on the sidewalk of one of the homes in Mount Troy. One day, when I was five years old, Robbie picked up a brick and threw it at me because I did not want to play house. I was wearing a blue velvet coat and hat which our maternal grandmother Schmitt had bought for me. Even at that young age I loved clothes so I did not want to get the coat dirty. Blood streamed down from my forehead where the brick hit me and it ruined my coat. My parents took me to the drug store where a bandage was applied to the injury. There was an inch scar above my eye which faded as the years flew by. I felt sad about my coat being ruined but did not cry. It was just a material thing and I did not dwell on it.

CHAPTER 2—Family and Early Trauma

Our mother kept losing weight after Juney was born which is what we were told. She was sent to recuperate at a rest home in Valencia, Pa. She lived there for a year and we children missed her terribly. She did not seem to be nervous but must have been somewhat depressed because she did not want to eat. It was discovered that the mistake in my delivery by the inebriated doctor caused her to have this problem. Our dad told us that someday there would be a surgery to correct the condition.

While mother was gone for the year, Robbie and I lived with our paternal grandfather, John Hanocek, and Juney lived with Grandma and Grandpa Schmitt. John Hanocek was very mean to Robbie and me although he provided us with food and shelter for a year. One day when Robbie was three years old and we were playing outside Grandpa's house, Robbie started running around in circles with other young boys and they all began calling out God's name in vain. Grandpa heard them and came running out from the house. He grabbed Robbie and called me to follow them. After we arrived in the living room, he forced us both to kneel on clothespins on a hard chair for fifteen minutes while he played the violin.

I did not think that was fair because I did nothing wrong. When he allowed us to get up, our knees and legs were shaking with pain. We both were sent to our bedrooms. His second wife was very kind to us, although she did not reprimand her husband. We loved her peach and plum dumplings and all the good food she cooked.

Our grandfather was not an easy man with whom to live. He had lost his beloved first wife, the mother of his six children, when his eldest child, Anna, was thirteen years old. He did not marry for years while Anna took care of her five brothers which must have been difficult for a young girl. John was kind to Anna but very strict with all the boys. Francis was next to the youngest of the brothers – there was John, Albert, Eddie, Francis and Anthony.

When Francis was six years old, John, his father, told him to jump off the Allegheny River bridge so that he could learn to swim. Francis, although very bold, did not want to jump. So John picked him up and threw him off the bridge and yelled "Sink or swim." John's father, Anton Hanocek who was born in Bohemia, now Czechoslovakia, had thrown John off the same bridge when he was six years old and he did learn to swim. As did Francis!

Francis became a handful for the nuns at Holy Name Catholic School which was located about a mile from Goettman Street where his family lived. When he was in the fourth grade, the nuns felt like they could not do anything about his atrocious behavior in class, his talking back, skipping school, teasing the girls and fighting with the boys so they literally kicked him out of school. He had made his First Communion in the second grade but found it difficult to follow any of the Ten Commandments, especially 'Honor thy father and thy mother.' John could not seem to do much about his behavior and gave up spanking Francis. Perhaps since Francis lost his mother at such a tender age, he resented anyone else trying to tell him what to do.

As he continued to grow, he delivered newspapers to make some money and did odd jobs for people. John was able to get him a paper delivery job because he wrote articles for The Pittsburgh Press besides working at Kaufman's as a tailor. Francis saved the money he earned and bought a motorcycle.

He won many motorcycle races but also had some life endangering spills. His sister, Anna, worried about him after a terrible accident when he was seventeen while pit driving his motorcycle. She did not think he would live and prayed for his recovery. She hoped he would not have brain damage.

Francis later obtained a job at Armour & Company selling meat to local butcher shops. He dated many girls and bragged about his conquests, saying "Just doing what comes naturally."

When he was walking down Lowrie street one day with a girlfriend named Martha Dill, he noticed a friend, Katie Schmitt, walking with a beautiful raven haired girl. As they approached, Francis exchanged pleasantries. He said to Katie,

"Hellooo, how are you? Who is the lovely girl with you?

Katie answered, "Oh, hello, Francis. This is my sister, Florrie."

Francis was dazzled by Florrie's beauty and knew he wanted to date her. He said,

"Oh, Florrie, it is so nice to meet you. Perhaps we could get together sometime."

Florrie was struck by Francis' good looks, sturdy shoulders and mannerisms. It was a case of love at first sight for both of them. Florrie replied,

"Yes, it is nice to meet you, too. Perhaps we could get together."

The girls went on their merry way. They were good friends besides being sisters from a very religious family. Florrie asked Katie,

"Is that the Francis you told me about who is known as a 'ladies man'? Katie replied,

"Yes, Francis has a reputation so I would be careful if you do decide to date him."

Francis was captivated by Florrie and could not stop thinking about her. A week later he walked past the Schmitt's home several times before knocking on the door to ask Florrie for a date. He finally knocked on the door and was invited in to meet her parents, Joseph and Catherine Schmitt. Florrie was not too surprised to see him. However, she remembered what her sister had told her about Francis and his escapades.

Francis asked Joseph, "Would you permit your daughter to go out on a date with me next Saturday? I promise to have her home by ten PM."

Joseph replied, "Yes, but make sure you bring her home by ten."

Joseph and Catherine were both very religious Catholics. His family included three sisters who were nuns and a cousin who was a priest and another cousin who was a nun. The Schmitt's had six children, three girls and three boys. Florrie was the eldest girl, Joe the eldest boy and Katie, Jim, Phil and Betty followed in that order.

Joseph was postmaster of Pittsburgh so the family always had enough money. They lived in a three story brick home across the street from a cemetery on Lowrie Street. Catherine took good care of her children, but banned Joseph from her bedroom after Betty was born. Joseph began visiting a local bar to drown his sorrow about the situation. He did not get drunk often nor was he mean when drinking. He was always a good father and they both went to church at Most Holy Name Church every Sunday with their children.

Catherine favored Florrie, her first daughter, because Florrie was extremely bright and sweet at the same time. She always excelled at school and was as honest as the day is long. Florrie graduated from the eighth grade at Holy Name School at the top of her class and went to two years of commercial school where she mastered typing and shorthand. She was hired as a secretary at a respected firm in downtown Pittsburgh.

One day while walking home across the Allegheny Bridge, Florrie noticed a strange looking gum wrapper on the sidewalk. She picked it up and found $100 bundled inside. She turned the money in to the Pittsburgh newspaper. After an ad was placed and no one claimed the money, Florrie decided to save the money for the future.

Florrie and Francis enjoyed their first date to a movie. They walked up Lowrie Street to the local theater. Francis wanted to kiss her goodnight but thought he should take it slow with Florrie because he knew of her background. They kept dating and falling more in love. Francis asked Florrie to marry him and reluctantly she said "Yes."

The reason she was hesitant is because she had seen how her Uncle Oscar mistreated her Aunt Anna, her mother Catherine's sister. While Florrie was helping Aunt Anna, Uncle Oscar demanded Anna get out of bed the same day she delivered a baby and bake him a cake even though Florrie offered to bake the cake. He also ate most of the pancakes at breakfast while his children were only permitted to eat one each. That left a bad impression on Florrie. I wonder if later on she ever thought she should have listened to her instincts.

The young couple was married on November 24, 1926, in Most Holy Name Church. They had a small breakfast reception with most of the relatives invited.

CHAPTER 3—Francis' Infidelity

While mother was in Valencia, Dad worked for Armour & Company selling meat to local butcher shops. One day when he was delivering meat to a butcher shop on Troy Hill, north side Pittsburgh, he was hit by a streetcar and his head hit the curb of the sidewalk. He did not go to the doctor, but may have had a concussion or damaged his brain.

Shortly after that incident, he met a girl who caught his eye at a butcher shop in another section of Pittsburgh. Her name was Pearl and she was extremely friendly toward him. Pearl had accidentally sliced off three of her fingers while slicing meat, but held her hand in such a way that people did not notice. She was pretty with dark hair, brown eyes and an ample figure.

Francis spoke to her in Hebrew and that caught her by surprise. Francis could speak seven languages, although not fluently, but enough to impress all the owners of ethnic butcher shops. He seemed to have a natural instinct for picking up languages and knew some Bohemian, Polish, German, Italian, Greek and Hebrew. He flattered everyone and that helped his prowess as a salesman. The owners of the shops were always happy to see and converse with 'Hans' as they called him, short for Hanocek.

Pearl became a prominent figure in our lives for many years. Florrie had no idea that Francis was secretly dating Pearl while she was at Valencia. Our mother had regained her weight and felt like herself again after a year. She was looking forward to her reunion with her children.

We, of course, could hardly wait for the return of our sweet mother. We all shouted, "Mommy, Mommy, we missed you so much. Florrie had tears in her eyes as she hugged each one of us and replied, "I missed all of you so much, too, more than you know and am so happy to be home again. You've all grown so much."

A few weeks after our mother returned home, our dad announced, "I lost my job at Armour & Company, but have found another selling job near Midway, Pa. We will be moving in a week to Midway and I think you will all like it there for it is in the country.

At that time, the economy was spiraling downward because of The Great Depression. Francis was fortunate to have found another job immediately because many people were unable to find jobs during the Depression Years.

CHAPTER 4 —
Moving During The Great Depression

It was in the summer of 1933 that we moved to Midway. The new house was a white frame home with a front porch. Francis did not make as much money as he did before but we still had enough to eat most of the time.

We children were unaware of all of the details of The Great Depression but were told later on about the stock market failure on Black Thursday, October 24, 1929, when falling prices sent panicky stockholders on a selling spree. It was the beginning of the massive economic crises that changed millions of lives for ten years. Our lives changed drastically along with most everyone else.

I do remember that people talked negatively about President Herbert Hoover who believed that government should not interfere with business. Many people blamed him for the growing problems. Families lost their homes and farms were taken over by banks and auctioned off to the highest bidder. In some cities, there were block long lines of people waiting for hours to receive free food from missions and welfare agencies. These lines were called 'breadlines'.

Bread was only a nickel a loaf but if they ate, some people could not pay their electric bill of $1 per month. When they did have bread, they smeared it with lard and sprinkled it with sugar. Sometimes we ate bread spread with lard as did the next door neighbor's children. We played that summer with the girl and boy who lived next to us.

People who lived on farms fared better than those who did not. They always had their own produce to eat along with poultry and meat. We never lived anywhere long enough to grow a garden or there was no space to grow it.

Our dad was gone a lot that summer, supposedly to make a living but that was only a part of his absence. He spent a lot of time with Pearl, unbeknownst to our mother.

He told Pearl that he was not allowed to have relations with our mother because it could be fatal if she were to get pregnant again.

I do remember my mother and father cuddling but I did not know what was really going on because no one explained much of anything to children in those days.

While in Midway, I remember that Uncle Joe, Mom's brother, came to visit us by train most weekends. One of the reasons he traveled to see us so often was that he met a girlfriend on his first visit to see us. She was our mother's friend, Lila, who visited us often. We found out later on that Uncle Joe wanted to marry Lila. Shortly after the proposal, he found out that he would eventually go blind. Uncle Joe did not want to burden her and never married. He wore thick glasses the rest of his life but never completely lost his eyesight.

Summer days dwindled into fall. It was time for school to start. My parents wanted to send me to a Catholic school, but there was none close by. They asked Grandma Schmitt if she would be willing to let me live with her, Grandpa, Uncle Joe and Aunt Betty. Grandma always doted on me and immediately approved. I thought it would be fun living with them and it was. Grandma bought me pretty new dresses and walked me to Most Holy Name school the first day.

I loved school, especially learning to read, write and do math. It was not long before I realized I was at the top of the class, the teacher liked me and I made friends easily. Aunt Betty was only eight years older than I was and was always good to me. What more could a child want!

Each Saturday, I got up early and scrubbed down Grandma's hallway steps before Uncle Joe and I left for Midway. I did not mind helping Grandma because she was always so good to me. She took me with her to Bingo on Friday nights at the church hall. It was fun winning embroidered pillow cases, baskets of food or money.

There was only one glitch, the sleeping arrangements. I did not sleep well scrunched in between Grandma and Aunt Betty in the double bed.

The first weekend in October, when Uncle Joe and I returned to Midway, my mother and Lila held a surprise birthday party for me. Mother made her famous banana cake which had been a tradition for generations in the Schmitt family. Lila made party favors, small paper baskets filled with chocolate candy. There were seven neighborhood children invited. I was so surprised and happy.

We played games, pin-the-tail on the donkey, guessing games such as how many marbles were in the bottle and spin-the-bottle. I did not really want to kiss the boys when the bottle stopped spinning in front of one of them, but did so just to make everyone happy.

The seventh birthday party was to be the only birthday party in my young life. I thanked everyone for their gifts, hair ribbons, games, books and clothing. I thanked Mother and Lila for the wonderful party I would always remember.

Florrie had taught her children well. Manners were important as well as prayer. She had told us, "Always say please and thank you, excuse me and I'm sorry when the occasion arises. When you set the table, put the fork on the left side of the dish and the knife and spoon on the right."

"Yes, mother, we will remember," and we did.

Mother also taught us to say our prayers before meals and before bedtime. We all knelt down together in front of one of our beds before she tucked us in for the night. We prayed the Our Father, the Hail Mary and Dear Angel of God. To this very day, I still pray the same prayers each night.

Grandma did everything to please me the three months I lived with her in Pittsburgh. Everything was going great at school but I started to have a sick feeling in the pit of my stomach, an ache to be with my immediate family full time. One day when I was not eating my dinner,

Grandma asked me, "What is wrong, sweetheart, I have noticed you have not been eating much?

"I am sorry, Grandma, but I just do not feel like eating because I miss my mother and brothers so much."

Grandma hugged me and told me she would tell my parents about my feelings and solve the dilemma. It all worked out because when Uncle Joe and I arrived in Midway the next weekend, my dad announced that he had a new meat selling route in McKees Rocks, Pa., and we would be moving there in a week.

God had answered my prayers and I learned at an early age that He is always there for me.

The Hanocek Family in McKees Rocks —
Florrie, Francis, holding Juney, Robbie and Flossie

CHAPTER 5—Moving Again

Anyone who has been to Pittsburgh knows how majestic the hills are to view. Some are so steep that one wonders how cars can navigate up the precipices, or how houses could be built alongside. One glance at the hills of McKees Rocks made the hills of Pittsburgh pale in color, especially the hill we lived on top of, the steepest one in that small city.

We had a large apartment on the first floor that we thought was unique because of the sliding doors between rooms. We were reprimanded verbally many times for playing with the doors. There was an outhouse behind the house just like in Midway.

Forest Hill Public School was just a few blocks away, so my mother enrolled me there. Miss Miller, my first-grade teacher, and I became friends immediately. She had such a jolly expression on her face that I felt at ease and returned her smiles. When she saw the transcript of my grades, her eyes lit up. Within a few days, she realized that I was ahead of her other students. I always raised my hand to answer her questions, and she called on me constantly.

I really loved her, the school, and the new friends I met. I walked home with Bernice and Alice after school and spent time at each of their homes. Bernice was a little on the plump side, but one of the nicest girls in the class. No one ever teased her about her weight. Alice was darling with her long blonde curls and happy personality. Everyone in the class was friendly and cordial to each other.

Walter Hart, one of the boys in my class, kept talking to me and brought me candy which I ate at recess every day. Walter was kind to all his classmates, but took a fancy to me, and asked me to jump rope with him and some of the other boys and girls. We chanted little ditties such as "Mabel, Mabel, set the table," and I always took such delight in the rhythm. From the time I was a toddler, I loved to hear all the nursery rhymes our mother would read to us. Now that I could read and write, I started to write short poems. Some of them were very simple, and were variations of "Roses are red, violets are blue, sugar is sweet, and so are you." I superimposed, "You love me and I love you." Or, "God knows everything we do."

Miss Miller and the children in that class made me feel like I belonged, and I thought I'd never want to leave McKees Rocks.

Robbie, Juney, and I had fun the three months we lived there. Dad brought home a little green pedal car for the boys, and they went speeding down the slope around the corner. He brought home a doll that he bought for $1.50. The name on the newborn size doll was "Snoozie," but I decided to rename her "Phronsie" because I saw that name in a book I read, and liked it. I spent time rocking the only doll I ever had in the small wicker rocking chair that Grandma Schmitt bought me for Christmas.

Dad was home most of the time while we lived in McKees Rocks, and our family seemed intact. However, he was still visiting Pearl occasionally while he was on his route. They always found time to be alone and their romance was heating up.

When I heard that my dad was changing jobs again after only three months in McKees Rocks, I was very disappointed. I didn't want to leave there, and although I had no say-so in my parents' affairs, I complained. Mother said she was sorry, but that's the way life is.

I told Miss Miller and my friends there that I would be leaving, and they were surprised and told me that they were sorry and would miss me.

"I will never forget you," I remarked as I said my goodbyes.

Dad saw that I looked sad while I was helping pack our belongings, and tried to console me,

"You will like Turtle Creek, for it's in the country. There will be room to have a dog, and meadows in which to romp and play."

So we moved again. When we unpacked, we realized that all of our baby pictures were missing except for a few of Robbie's and Juney's. Dad did not go back to McKees Rocks to retrieve them, if indeed, we left them there. He mentioned that the box may have fallen off the moving van. For Mother, and for me, that was a precious memory to lose that could never be replaced.

I quickly accepted Turtle Creek, even though there was trauma in moving from a place I really liked to start over again. I started smiling and wondered what adventure this new home and school would bring.

CHAPTER 6—The Angel Experience

Our new home was a large white frame house that had a water pump over the kitchen sink, and an outhouse. It was grand to see the lush green grass in the spacious front yard, and the variety of trees in the back yard as we stood on the back porch. There were oaks, maples, firs, and crabapple; and also rose bushes. Roses were the favorite flowers of most people in our family. Grandma Schmitt had a trellis of roses in her small back yard every year. The fragrance of a rose is always comforting and intoxicating, and tends to saturate the senses. The meadow up the hill from the back yard was so enticing that my brothers and I ran around in the tracks made by a neighbor's tractor the first thing after getting settled. My dad was right, I was going to enjoy the country.

However, there were some drawbacks. The water that flowed from the pump in the kitchen tasted like sulfur and smelled like rotten eggs. Robbie and I were assigned the chore of carrying buckets of good well water from the neighbor's across the dirt road. Dad asked them if they would share their water with us, and they kindly accommodated.

The buckets were so heavy that we spilled some of the water as we trudged up the long path from the well and across the dirt road. Some days we had to fetch water twice because we all drank a lot of water, and Mom made iced tea.

We used the water from the pump to wash dishes, clothing, and for bathing. I helped with the dishes and the laundry. Mom filled a large round tub with buckets of heated water and we took turns scrubbing the clothing on a scrub board. We often scraped our knuckles on the ridges of the scrub board trying to get socks clean, and our hands looked like prunes from the lye soap. I never minded helping with the chores because I wanted to please my mom and I liked being clean.

I always looked forward to Saturdays when my mom filled the big washtubs with warm water and let me get in first to bathe. Robbie then bathed himself and Mom helped Juney. Being the eldest, I did get special favors.

School was no problem, and it was exciting taking a bus to the Catholic school. Grandma Schmitt bought me a white dress with a veil for my First Communion. After the ceremony, our relatives gathered at our home to celebrate with good food, games, and laughter. Two weeks later, the teacher chose me to crown Mary Queen of May, and I felt so honored. All the girls were hoping to be chosen for that celebration, and I was delighted that the teacher picked me. I walked slowly and solemnly up the church aisle with my hands folded, climbed up two steps, and put the crown on Mary's head while the choir sang "Hail, Holy Queen Enthroned Above, Oh, Maria." Of course, I understood that the statue was just to remind everyone of Mary, and Catholics didn't worship statues.

Suddenly it was summer. Dad brought home a female part-shepherd dog. There was already a big doghouse in the back yard for her. We named her Shep and we ran and played in the fields and meadows with her. Later, Shep had seven pups and we each were allowed to keep one of them. I picked a black and white one that I called "Trixie." Dad gave the other four to the neighbors.

Unfortunately, a few weeks later, Trixie ran into the road and was run over by a car, a hit and run. We felt sad to lose Trixie, for she was so cute and friendly. I didn't cry and as I grew older, kept my feelings inside. For some reason, I never dwelled on misfortune and quickly resumed my happy nature.

Our family drove to Pittsburgh some weekends to see the grandparents. Dad had a green car with a rumble seat. We took turns sitting in the rumble seat enjoying the breeze blowing our hair.

We always had a feast when we returned to Pittsburgh. Grandma seemed to derive pleasure from serving her nutritious meals. It was crowded in the kitchen, but we all managed to fit around the table.

On the way home, we took turns sleeping on top of the back seat. I thought it was cozy after a long day to watch the stars as I drifted into slumber.

During the summer, my dad asked me, "Flossie, would you like to drive the car?"

"I guess so," I replied. I wasn't sure I'd like driving, even though I was adventurous. We drove down a side road that wasn't traveled, and, while sitting on his lap, I went zigzagging along the road, scaring Robbie and myself. Robbie took his turn and he kept a straight path. Dad helped Juney, who was delighted since he loved cars. A partly submerged pink junk car down the creek fascinated him. He called it the "crashin' car" and became excited every time we passed junkyards calling out, "Crashin' cars, crashin' cars." One day when we stopped, I took Juney to sit in one of the damaged cars and he pretended to drive.

Dad was gone sometimes during the week, but was home most weekends. He began to have a guilty conscience about his trysts with Pearl. He cared about her but did not understand how he could be in love with two women at the same time. Months went by and Pearl was in love with him and wanted to be with him more often.

Francis was bewildered when she began making demands. He did not want to hurt Florrie who was so sweet and easy to get along with, one of the kindest persons he had ever known. He felt trapped by his own sexual feelings. Florrie would be in danger if she became pregnant again and they took chances when they thought it was safe, but that was not enough for him, though he prayed it would be.

I spent a weekend that summer with Grandma and Grandpa Schmitt and all the relatives. They had a family picnic in the park that had a creek for swimming. I asked permission to swim in the creek. Little did I realize that I was about to experience one of the most influential happenings of my entire life, one that molded and shaped me spiritually. As a young adventurous child, I thought that I could swim, but was wrong.

32

I removed my outer clothing and waded in the cool water clad only in my one-piece underwear. I lunged forward as if to swim. I was always a positive child, but perhaps at seven years old, I just didn't think of the consequences. All of a sudden I was spiraling through a tunnel of light, shaped somewhat like a cornucopia. It was without a doubt the most peaceful moments of my life. Words cannot describe the incredible feeling of utter contentment that enveloped me. I don't remember struggling to come up for air, just feeling completely relaxed. I could see the opening of the tunnel and people in white with outstretched hands waiting to greet me. No, they are angels, I thought, as I willingly extended my hand toward them.

The next thing I remember was throwing up water as I lay on the grass beside the stream. A sixteen-year-old girl had pulled me out of the water downstream.

"Where am I?" I asked, still choking. At first I thought I may have been dreaming, so didn't tell anyone what I saw and felt. But then my relatives made me promise not to tell anyone, especially my parents, about the near drowning. They didn't want to get in trouble. So I kept this secret for many years, but it had a definite effect on my approach to life. I became more devout in my beliefs, felt closer to God, and was aware a young age not to be afraid of death. I felt that God and His angels were always there protecting me. I still do.

Later that autumn, I developed a kidney infection, accompanied by a high fever, and found it necessary to run to the outhouse constantly. Mom put an old bucket beside my bed at night and told me to drink extra water. I drank, prayed, was not afraid and finally the infection ceased.

Uncle Joe visited most weekends. He taught me how to play the card game of "66," a German bidding game. It felt great to be able to play at a level with the grownups.

Robbie, Juney and I spent days running through the upper meadow with Shep and the pups. I broke out with milkweed poisoning. I had a rash all over me and could not stop scratching. Mom applied calamine lotion but the itching was so intense that I prayed I would never get anything like that again. Robbie caught it, too, and we both looked like pink bunnies. I liked living in the country, but thought perhaps it didn't agree with us.

Our dad treated us rather kindly while living in Turtle Creek. All summer I had pleaded with him to take me to Kennywood Park, an amusement park not far from where we lived, but actually closer to Pittsburgh.

"Dad, please, pretty please, take me to ride the roller coaster," I pleaded.

His answer was always, "We'll see, Dearie."

One Sunday in August he did just that and he and I rode the roller coaster thirteen times in a row! I was so happy and thanked him many times. I loved the thrill of the steep track and fast curves while the wind exhilarated me. He bought me a candied apple which I thought was the ultimate treat. I enjoyed being with him that day.

My dad brought home a live chicken for dinner one day, took it down the basement, and cut off its head. I went down the stairs to see what the commotion was about and much to my chagrin, watched the chicken run around in circles with its head cut off. I screamed (I was always finicky) and ran back upstairs. It was hard to eat the chicken that evening.

Right before school started, Dad lost his selling job, but was able to get another meat selling job near Wilmerding, Pennsylvania. He had the charisma to convince employers he was the one for the job.

The only thing that was difficult about moving from Turtle Creek was leaving our dogs with the neighbors. We would miss them so!

Packing was always a chore, especially since we did this so many times. We wrapped all the tableware in paper, along with other breakables, and labeled all the boxes. Then we cleaned the whole house for the new occupants. When we arrived at our destination, we scrubbed our new surroundings from top to bottom before unpacking again. Aside from all this, moving seemed like an adventure for my brothers and me. I started looking forward to seeing new places and meeting new friends. I had no idea that Wilmerding would forever be my favorite city to live in Pennsylvania, and that life would be more difficult in the moves to follow.

CHAPTER 7—The Best of Times

We moved to Wilmerding before school started. We were all delighted with the new home and surroundings. The two-story house our dad rented had a large brick exterior with a big front porch. There was a good-sized kitchen, dining room, living room, four bedrooms, a bathroom, and a basement. We were especially enthused with the modern facilities so we could bathe more often. Behind the house was a babbling brook and woods where we could hike and play.

Life was wonderful. We picked violets in the woods and presented them to our darling mother. She always seemed so happy that we thought of her.

She said to our dad, "Francis, I am glad you found us such an appropriate home. I hope we can stay here for a long time."

My mother enrolled me at St. Aloysius Catholic School, which was within walking distance. The second grade teacher, Sister Lucy, took an immediate liking to me and vice versa. She was without a doubt the sweetest nun I had ever met. She was very young and pretty in her black habit with the stiff white collar.

I just loved and enjoyed school in Wilmerding, especially with Sister Lucy doting on me. It was as positive a reaction as was McKees Rocks with Miss Miller.

One day, Sister Lucy asked me, "Flossie, would you like to learn how to play the piano? I could give you free lessons after school."

I answered excitedly, "I would love that—thank you, Sister, but we don't have a piano at home."

"You could practice here every day after school."

"That would be great."

Sr. Lucy spent a half hour once a week teaching me the fundamentals of playing the piano, and I practiced half an hour the other four days. I felt very fortunate and wanted to excel at the ivories. I had tried to play Grandma Schmitt's player piano by ear like Uncle Jim could, but that natural talent did not come naturally to me.

Aunt Betty had been taking piano lessons, but when she was fifteen years old she decided she wasn't interested any more. Grandma gave us her piano. I was elated to have the piano at home and practiced an hour every day after school. My goal was to someday play "Edelweiss" as lovely as Aunt Betty but I do not believe I really achieved that goal. I was just a 'mediocre' piano player. One either has the talent or they do not!

In school, we were introduced to a catechism book which helped us to understand the Catholic religion. I remember memorizing it quickly. Sister Lucy would ask the class, "Why did God make you?" I raised my hand, and when Sister called on me, I answered, "God made me to know Him, to love Him, to serve Him in this world, and to be happy with Him forever in the next." That is something I have believed all my life.

Since Christmas was approaching and everything seemed to be going well, I thought I'd ask for some special gifts that year. I mentioned to my mother, "I would like to have a sled and a roll-top desk for Christmas."

She responded with a smile, "Santa just might bring you what you want, because you've been a good girl."

I had suspected for a while that my parents were "Santa Claus," and my suspicions were confirmed when I peeked through the keyhole of an upstairs locked door and could see part of a sled and a desk. I knew not to tell my brothers because believing in a fantasy is fun for youngsters and I did not want to spoil that.

Christmas in Wilmerding was a joyous occasion. Dad brought home a large pine tree which we trimmed with pretty colored balls and homemade decorations. We strung popcorn and pasted colored strips of paper together to encircle the tree which we decorated on Christmas Eve, a tradition in the family. We also drank eggnog. It tasted so delicious, sweet, thick, and syrupy.

On Christmas morning, the sleds, one for each child, were sitting under the tree with bows wrapped around them along with other gifts. When I saw the desk was a roll-top, just what I wanted, I jumped up and down with glee. There were under clothes from Grandma and two lovely dresses. One was red but my favorite was a beautiful blue plaid dress which I wore many times to church and school.

We attended Mass, and had a big turkey dinner with all the trimmings in the afternoon. Mom made sweet potatoes, homemade cranberry sauce, mashed potatoes, gravy, stuffing, and pumpkin pie. We wondered how life could get any better. But we had already learned not to take the good times for granted and to just be thankful for them.

Shortly after the holidays, Francis asked Florrie, "Would you like someone to help you with the cooking and the housework? I know someone who is looking for a housekeeping job."

Florrie replied, "No, Francis, that's not necessary. I can handle everything myself."

Francis was in a dither. Pearl had been crying and begging him to stay with her, but he didn't want to leave his family. Pearl knew she was wrong to try to break up a marriage, especially where there were children involved, but it was as if Francis had cast a spell on her and she couldn't think coherently. She was so happy to hear that he wanted her to come into the Hanocek home as a maid so they could be near each other. It would be easier for him than traveling back and forth.

Against our mother's protests, he brought Pearl to our home and she moved into the spare bedroom. We thought she was our maid. Actually, she was very good to us and helped mom with all the chores. I could tell she liked us children.

Mom was a little suspicious of Francis' motives from the beginning, since he was so insistent that they hire Pearl. She soon noticed signs of his interest in Pearl and caught them kissing one day behind her back. She complained to Francis, "I want Pearl out of this house immediately."

Dad begged her forgiveness and said it wouldn't happen again. I didn't understand exactly what was going on, but sided secretly with my mom because she always seemed to know all the answers to everything.

Mom did not get her way this time. We heard our parents arguing and shouting, especially Dad, in a loud voice, practically every evening after we had retired. That was very upsetting for us, but mother was very hurt that dad betrayed her and their marriage vows. She didn't want to hear how hard it was for him not to have sex constantly and that he was also in love with Pearl. Much to my mother's dismay, Pearl remained.

My parents were called into my school for a conference with the principal and Sister Lucy regarding promoting me to the third grade. I had been tested with long division and multiplication problems the day before and they found out that I was able to do third-grade and fourth-grade math. Mom and Dad agreed to the promotion, so I was advanced to the third grade in March 1936. I didn't mind moving up, although I was never bored in school, just as I was never bored in all my life. No one thought about that word then, just kept busy.

I was surprised and pleased that I was again chosen to crown Mary May Queen. I wore my communion dress which still fit me, and felt honored as I once again climbed the steps to put the wreath of flowers on the head of the statue of Mary. I started saying the Rosary that year, and have always felt close to Mary, the mother of Jesus.

As far as school was concerned, I had the third highest grades in the third grade after only three months in that class. I missed Sister Lucy when school was dismissed for the summer.

Pearl left right after school was dismissed, and once again life was peaceful and comfortable. Perhaps, like a broken record, they all got sick and tired of quarreling and felt that it could affect us. Young children tend to react negatively when their parents argue. Mother suspected that wasn't the end of Pearl, though.

Pearl returned to Pittsburgh. Our dad was absent most of that summer. He interviewed for a job back at Armour & Co., and because of his previous success in selling meat, was rehired. He wanted to be close to Pearl again.

He looked for a decent house for us because he was now supporting two families. Since he could not find one that was suitable for the amount he could afford, he rented a small apartment in Etna. Etna was a suburb of Pittsburgh surrounded by industry. It was not an appealing place to anyone's eyes.

In August, when my dad announced, "We will be moving soon," I thought Oh, no, not again. I didn't want to leave Wilmerding and Sister Lucy and my friends at school. But we had to cope with what life handed us, and couldn't change a thing. The fact that our dad could always seem to get jobs helped, but we didn't foresee what Etna would bring.

CHAPTER 8—The Worst of Times

I didn't like Etna from the moment I saw the congested area and our apartment next to an alley. There was no yard, and the rooms were rather small. Our furniture had to be stored in the living room, so we lived in the kitchen and one bedroom. The only redeeming factor about the apartment was that it had a bathroom. We could scarcely walk in the bedroom which was crowded with three separate beds and a dresser. We each had a drawer in the dresser to keep our personal belongings and our clothing which was minimal.

When our dad noticed that our mother looked somewhat disgruntled with the living arrangements, he told her "This is only temporary."

Temporary turned into a year. Dad earned a little more than the average wages of $500.00 per year, but because he had been having a pain in his right side, only worked for approximately two months. He did not choose to go to a doctor. Since he was gone most of the time, I started wondering where he was and suspected he was with Pearl. Mother knew he was with her, and had given up protesting too much.

One day the pain in his side became so intense he drove to Allegheny General Hospital in Pittsburgh. His appendix had burst and he had an emergency appendectomy. It was a close call. His recovery took almost a year, during which time we hardly saw him.

Mom never complained to us about his absence. She, like us, was dwelling on how empty our stomachs were that year. When we first moved to Etna, Dad had bought us fifty pounds of potatoes and tea, flour and canned tomatoes. Mom baked homemade bread every

40

other day. Homemade bread fresh from the oven is very satisfying and quelled our hunger. Our diet consisted of hot tea and bread for breakfast, a slice of bread for lunch, and fried potatoes covered with some canned tomatoes, bread and hot tea for dinner.

Despite having little variety in our diet, we were healthy children. Robbie and I walked about a mile to the Catholic school through busy intersections and across railroad tracks. Naturally, I excelled in school and made a few friends who always asked me to join them in the milk line at lunch. Although my mouth was watering for milk, I told them, "That's okay, I'd rather drink water."

When I complained to Mom, "I wish I could have milk to drink for lunch at school," she responded, "I'm sorry, but you will have to make do because we just don't have any money for milk. Things will get better eventually, and then you will have all the milk you can drink."

Mom's optimism rubbed off on me like positive thinking and hope usually do, so I didn't mention the lack of milk for lunch anymore.

We all missed Wilmerding, the green grass, the school, the food, and happier days. However, we felt close to one another even with adversity. We knew Mom loved us, and we loved her. We had empathy for each other. Mom didn't kiss and hug us very often, which happened to be the custom of most parents at that time, but we felt loved and respected our parents. Most children were not the center of attention and respected their parents and elders. As I look back, I wouldn't change a thing about our relationship with our mother, except maybe she could have hugged us just a tad more. I'm sure there are others my age who think the same.

Since Etna was a suburb of Pittsburgh, we took the streetcar or the incline to Troy Hill to visit our grandparents, Aunt Betty and Uncle Joe. We walked to the incline car that crawled up the large hill at a nail-biting forty-seven degree angle. All the other Schmitt children were married by now. Aunt Katie married Donald Strickland, a policeman from Wisconsin, and they had two sons, Bobby and Don. Every time I saw Bobby at Grandma's house throughout our young years, he was always carrying a toy trumpet or a real trumpet with him. He was born with a definite musical talent.

Uncle Jim married Emma Shindler and they lived on the second floor of Grandma's house. Uncle Phil married Meryl Maher and they lived in an upstairs apartment across the street from his parents.

Sometimes I stayed overnight at Grandma's. The next day she would take Aunt Betty and me to Michael's, the small department store on Troy Hill, and buy me needed clothing, especially coats, hats, and shoes. Robbie and Juney felt a little left out because Grandma paid so much attention to me besides buying me clothing. However, Grandma occasionally purchased shoes for the boys for a dollar. I felt good about how wonderful Grandma treated me, but at the same time, felt sorry that my brothers didn't get as much as I did. At the age of nine, I didn't know what to do about it. There was probably nothing I could do. Hardly anyone then talked about feelings, especially children. We were, more or less, seen and not heard, and knew it.

Grandma, Grandpa and Aunt Betty were not fully aware of the dire circumstances in which we were living. They knew that our dad had the appendectomy, but Mom never told her parents all the facts, or how bad the financial situation had become. Perhaps Grandma had some inkling, because she made us good, filling lunches when we visited. She sent Robbie and me to the stores for extra food so there would be plenty for everyone.

Uncle Joe worked at a factory near Etna where we lived and occasionally stopped to see us after work. He handed us a dime or a quarter to buy an ice cream cone or a banana split. We loved Uncle Joe, as did all the Schmitt grandchildren, for he passed money out to all of them. He may have suspected that we were in financial trouble.

That winter, on December 20, Grandpa Schmitt contracted pneumonia and passed away. Our whole family attended his funeral. I imagined Grandpa in heaven, because he was basically a good person and practiced his religion. Exactly one week later, Grandpa Hanocek had a heart attack in church and keeled over. It seemed strange to all of us, that he would die in church, and we wondered if he would be worthy of heaven.

John Hanocek left all of his children a small inheritance. Francis had a brainstorm: he would start his own meat packing business with the money. He left Etna to search for a suitable building he could afford. While he was gone, Mom took us to visit the Schmitts on the incline. That was exciting, and the excitement continued after we arrived at Grandma's. She asked us to check the furnace to see if it needed more coal. Juney started screaming when he saw Grandpa's overalls hanging on the clothesline in the basement. Grandma hadn't as yet put Grandpa's belongings away.

Mom calmed Juney, but Robbie and I thought of a plan to keep scaring him. We put sheets over our heads and chased him up and down the hall stairway, yelling "Boo, Boo.!" He kept screaming, so Mom reprimanded us for tormenting our little brother. He hid behind our mother's skirts even more after that taunting. We finally listened to our mother and stopped trying to frighten him. We, like most young children, didn't realize how traumatizing teasing can be.

Francis arrived home a couple of weeks later and told us he had found a suitable building for his business near Kittanning, Pennsylvania.

"Start packing, and we will move in two weeks," he informed us. We were all more than happy to be able to leave Etna, and looked forward to something better. We couldn't imagine it being any worse.

A poem I wrote years later encompasses how I felt about the lack of having milk to drink at lunch while we barely existed in Etna:

THE MILK LINE

The children at lunchtime standing in line
To buy a pint of elixir from heaven —
That pleasure one year would never be hers,
Bread, not milk, her only leaven.

"Come join us," they beckoned —
She, with her clean skirt and blouse,

They never reckoned
She didn't live in a prosperous house.

She yearned to take her place in the line,
Mouth dry after eating plain white bread,
Salivating for milk to wash it down —
To the water fountain she headed instead.

A bright nine year old, head of the class,
Depression, father not working, appendix burst,
Kept this all to herself, a comely young lass,
Wondering how it could get any worse.

The year passed, she learned to accept,
Playing at recess, smiling, a caregiver —
Somehow, someday, she knew she'd overstep
The poverty and drink of the milk river.

CHAPTER 9—A Learning Experience

Kittanning wasn't worse, at least not at first. As our family drove down the hill and across the bridge, a sense of relief overwhelmed us and we viewed the sprawling city built on hills. The main street had many shops, grocery stores, theaters, and an Isaly's, an ice cream store.

We continued up the hill, turning left at the top, and drove a short distance to our new apartment on the left of the highway. The brick structure had large garages underneath and a small apartment on the right side that housed an elderly woman who owned many cats.

Dad called out, "We have rented the apartment upstairs. Everyone pitch in to carry up the furniture and the boxes," and we did. We were pleasantly surprised to see how large this apartment was, with a kitchen, a combined living and dining room, three bedrooms and a bath—a great improvement on Etna's accommodations.

Dad set up a cot for me to sleep on in my parents' room until he could buy me a new double bed. But I couldn't seem to sleep because I started itching all over. I thought something was biting me, but when the lights were turned on, we didn't see anything. Bedbugs were the culprit, probably coming from the old woman's cluttered apartment downstairs.

Dad tore out the framework and baseboards in the bedroom and sprayed them with insecticide. He also sprayed the mattresses, and it really worked. We had no bedbugs ever after that episode. I didn't like bugs of any kind, but of course the boys did and teased me occasionally with different species.

A week later, Dad brought home a new double bed and I enjoyed my bedroom for awhile. I used my roll-top desk to write poetry and stories and to do homework. In my room was the rocking chair that Grandma Schmitt had bought me, upon which sat my doll, Phronsie. I really didn't play with her anymore. I was ready for other things, such as school and friends at St. Mary's Catholic School.

I discovered that Mary Colucci lived a couple of blocks away, and we started walking to school together and became best friends. We talked and laughed the entire mile. Mary had the best sense of humor, and made light about school and every day family happenings. I also became best friends with Jean Moore, who lived close to St. Mary's. I excelled in every subject at school and had high self-esteem. Robbie also did well in his subjects, and was well-liked.

Francis worked diligently at building his meat-packing business and had high hopes of being successful. He had used all of his inheritance money to get started. However, because of the Depression, not many people had much money, and as a result, Francis extended too much credit. The business floundered, and, after a few months, failed. Contributing to the demise was the fact that a burglar broke into our apartment one day when no one was at home and stole cash and checks which were never recovered.

Francis then obtained a job working for the WPA, the Works Progress Administration originated by President Franklin D. Roosevelt to place two million workers on projects such as construction of school and hospital buildings, slum clearance, flood control, roads, etc. The job building roads through Pennsylvania and Ohio didn't pay much, and Dad was gone most of the time again. He stopped in Pittsburgh to see Pearl and asked her to rejoin the family—it would be easier for him financially. She was somewhat hesitant and asked, "Wouldn't that be hard on Florrie?"

He replied, "Perhaps, but it's the only way we can manage, and I miss you. I'll pick you up in a couple of weeks."

Meanwhile, we walked to the store with Mom to get the few groceries we could afford. There was a jailhouse at the top of the hill, and some prisoners yelled out vulgar remarks as we passed. Mom said emphatically, "Close your ears to all of that."

After a week, there was little to eat in the apartment. Mom sent me to the gas station across the dirt road to ask for a loaf of bread on credit. It wasn't something that I wanted to do, but had to if I wanted anything to eat. Mom always paid the attendant later on.

In the evenings toward spring, we started playing kick-the-can with neighbor children down the dirt road. We played almost every day after school until dusk. Some days when we were tired of playing kick-the-can, we dressed up in our family's old clothing and tried to put on plays. I always enjoyed playing the mother or the teacher and the other children seemed to want me to play those roles.

When Dad returned home, Pearl accompanied him. Mother was devastated when she saw Pearl, and asked, "What are you doing here again?"

"Francis insisted that I live with you and help out."

At this point, we, as children, did not understand what was going on but we cringed at the ensuing arguments when our dad was home. Pearl was sleeping with me, but I liked sleeping alone and having the bed and room to myself. One night when my dad thought I was sound asleep, he crawled into the bed, and I wasn't sure what went on, but heard Pearl and him whispering and moving around. I was too petrified to speak.

The next day, my mom and dad got into a terrible argument. I'm sure Mom was protesting the fact that he snuck out of their bed during the night. He became violent, hit Mom in the face, and knocked her across the room. Mom was crying, and we children were very frightened. We had never seen him in such a rage. Luckily, Mom wasn't hurt badly. They didn't argue much after that because Mom was afraid of him, also.

He never crawled into my bed again, but I'm sure he and Pearl found time to be alone elsewhere. He was absent most of the time, supposedly working out of town working for the WPA.

When summer arrived, we kids had fun playing across the highway on the mammoth hills that had small caves and large meadows above. The boys picked crabapples and ate enough to satisfy their hunger. I had an intestinal reaction when I ate them, so avoided them most of the time.

Once in awhile, when Dad returned home, my mom and Pearl baked homemade doughnuts, or rather fried them in grease. They sprinkled powdered sugar on them, and we children thought we had died and gone to heaven, they were so delicious. Mom and Pearl seemed to get along better when Dad was away from home. After he returned, the arguing started all over again.

Our dad had copied from his father the notion that all the children should be spanked if one of them disobeyed. It seemed that I was always getting spanked for something my brothers did, and I resented that, especially since he put me across his lap and pulled my underpants down so he could pound me with his slipper. At the age of nine, that was so embarrassing. I'm sure Robbie and Juney felt the same.

I never liked condiments, especially mayonnaise, and Dad teased me about that. One day, he chased me around the table saying, "Flossie, you have to try mayonnaise on your sandwich." The knife was covered with mayonnaise which I didn't want to be forced to eat, so being a faster runner than Dad, I escaped out the door and down the stairs, across the highway, and into a cave where I hid all afternoon. It was twilight when I thought I'd better get home, or Dad would pull down my pants again and spank me and my brothers.

While I was gone, my Mom had a serious discussion about Dad's method of punishment. She somehow convinced him not to punish us in this distressing manner, especially since I was getting older. She knew I was very perturbed about this situation.

When I cautiously returned home, slowly creeping up the staircase, apprehension at its highest level, I was surprised that he didn't grab me and punish me in the usual cruel manner. I was so thankful that he quit this demeaning practice, for I was beginning to understand that my body was my private property and I didn't want to be on display to anyone.

Shortly after that incident, Dad took me aside and tried to explain the facts of life to me. He noticed that I was beginning to develop in the breasts. I really wasn't interested in hearing about bodily functions and was very nonchalant about becoming a woman. I wondered why he approached the subject instead of my mom. When my menstrual period started years later, I wasn't afraid to see the blood. He hadn't explained too much about the function, but enough for me to know that it was a normal occurrence with females.

My mom hadn't even told Aunt Betty about menstruating—in fact, no one had told her what to expect. When she did experience her first period, she thought she had cut herself, so she took an ice cold bath. That sent her body into a hormonal tailspin, and she felt ill for a week, shaky and anxious, probably what the modern day female says is PMS, premenstrual syndrome. I'm not sure who told her about the facts of life that next week, but she finally experienced normal menstruation.

When Dad arrived home after the usual absences, he gave Mom a small amount of money so she could pay the rent, etc., and there was a little left over for food. She sent my brothers and me to the A&P grocery store where I bought the bargains—food for a nickel—such as rice, soups, beans, spaghetti, carrots, bread, noodles, salt, macaroni and toilet tissue. I also bought Nutley oleo, two pounds for twenty-nine cents, flour, twenty-five pounds for eight-five cents, and once in awhile a few bananas, six pounds for a quarter.

It was fun mixing the yellow oil and flavoring with the white portion of the Nutley oleo, and it tasted so scrumptious with homemade bread, or store bought bread when the flour was gone.

One day, Dad brought a dog home and we named him "Rover." It was great to have another dog! Unfortunately, Rover began foaming at the mouth that summer. Dad isolated him on the balcony of our apartment, and called the police. The policeman shot Rover with a pistol while we all watched. What a chilling event to witness. I always was frightened of guns after that.

Another traumatic thing happened that summer. We children always enjoyed climbing the tree on the hill to the left of our apartment. One pleasant summer day, Juney and I were sitting on the limb when it cracked, sending me rolling downward, while catching Juney's collarbone in the split branch. Juney started screaming and crying and I felt terrible when I found out he had broken his collarbone. Dad blamed me for the accident, and I cried, also, sobbing, "I'm sorry, I didn't know the branch would break, but I should have taken better care of Juney."

For the first time, my parents took one of us to the doctor. The doctor put a cast on Juney's arm to stabilize the collarbone, and it remained there for six weeks. He was in absolute torture because he developed eczema, an unbearably itchy skin disease, under the cast.

My dad eventually became sensitive to the fact that Pearl's presence caused my mom so much unhappiness, and when he realized we were all being affected, he decided to drive Pearl back to Pittsburgh. Of course, he still planned to keep seeing her.

I washed and dried the dishes every day after dinner. Mom cooked meager meals on the coal stove, and the hot stovepipe remained scorching for a while. One late fall evening, as I was hanging up the dishpan behind the stove, I tripped over my own feet and landed with my left arm against the stovepipe. I screamed as the heat took off all the skin on my arm. The pain was excruciating. Mom put Vaseline all over the burn, but did not take me to the doctor. Sleep was hard to come by that night. Mom kept wrapping my arm in bandages—I looked like a mummy—and I went to school two days later. Each day the pain became less intense and to everyone's surprise, my arm healed without leaving a trace of a scar. I had prayed a lot, so figured my prayers were answered. That's what always seemed to happen when I prayed fervently and it made me want to pray and to thank God for all his blessings. I believed!

It was almost Christmas when Dad asked me if I would like to go to a friend's house to play with her daughter's toys. I was delighted. I'm not sure what he told Mom. The next day, Saturday, we drove to Squirrel Hill, a rich suburb of Pittsburgh.

As we entered the house by the side entrance, we noticed some clothing on the floor by the stairway leading upstairs. Dad mentioned,

"Oh, the maid picks up the clothes that the kids throw down the stairs and launders them." I didn't see anyone, though, and he led me down to the basement which was cluttered with all kinds of toys. There was a table and chairs, china dishes, a tea set, dolls, games, cars, trucks, an archery set, train, stuffed animals, and some cookies and lemonade for me on the table.

He left me alone there and I had a lot of fun playing with all the exciting new toys; new to me, that is. When he returned after about an hour, he had to pry me away from the scene to return home. As we drove away, I asked him, "Dad, do you think I could have a table and chair set and dishes or a tea set for Christmas?" He promised me I would get them. I was afraid to ask him if the maid was Pearl but assumed that it was.

A short time later, Dad took Juney to visit another friend who lived above a funeral home. He left Juney in a room with the empty caskets while he went upstairs. Poor Juney was shaking in his boots because it was dark in the room. That was a cruel thing to do to a small boy who was afraid of most everything. Juney was so glad to see Dad when he came downstairs after about half an hour to take him home. We never found out who Dad visited—did he have another woman friend?

When Christmas came, I thought, maybe once my dad would keep his promise. The year before, all we received in our stockings was coal, an orange, candy, and nuts. Of course, we had asked for some toys, too. The stockings this year were filled with coal and an orange. As a child, I always wondered why the coal, because we were basically well-behaved children. Coal was supposed to indicate that we were not good children. Later on, I figured out that it was just a filler. There was no money for toys, or candy and nuts that Christmas. I longed for a tea set so that I could have a tea party with my friends. Years later, I wrote this poem which is included in a children's winning poetry book which I assembled for THE POET'S NOOK, a group that I founded and coordinate once a month at Cuyahoga Falls Library.

THE TEA PARTY

How I longed for a tea set when I was eight years old
It didn't have to be elaborate or crystal, silver, or gold.
Just a simple little tea set
With a teapot, saucers and cups -
I'd pretend I was a grown up, extended pinkie pointed up.
I'd invite my best friends to tea,
We would dress up accordingly
Our Mom's old high heels, dress and hat
And slowly sip hot tea and chat.
I'd say, "May I pour more tea?"
While tales told drew laughter or sympathy -
Even though it's just pretend,
It would have been nice with just one friend.
I never received the tea set on my birthday, or Christmas, yet
I bought them for all my children and grandkids
So they would never fret.
Now I get such satisfaction
Seeing the youngsters play with glee
That I join in their celebration
Fantasizing the wee girl who finally came to tea.

Floriana Hall

My brothers and I enjoyed winters in Kittanning. After school and on weekends, we sledded down the steep hill a short block from our home. There wasn't much traffic and we loved the speed we traveled down the hill. The boys even tried standing on their sleds—what daredevils! I particularly liked the wind blowing my hair and the snow blowing in my eyes as I lay down on the sled and sped down the hill. It stimulated my senses at a young age. Even with a gentle breeze, I felt God's presence. It was as if He was embracing me.

After school, I went home with Jean at least once a week. We had a snack, and then went out to play. We tried skiing down small hills near her house. She shared her skis with me. Other times, we enjoyed walking in the rain with umbrellas, and jumping off tree trunks to get the illusion of flying just like Mary Poppins.

Juney was attending St. Mary's now. One day he raised his hand to ask to go to the bathroom, but his teacher ignored him at first. When he finally got her attention, she told him, "No, you must wait a few minutes until recess." She then called him up to the board to answer a few addition problems. While he was standing there, his bladder exploded and he wet himself. The kids noticed and started laughing. He had to sit the rest of the afternoon in wet pants which was very uncomfortable. He was mortified about the whole incident and told Dad when he arrived home.

Francis was furious that his son was so embarrassed. He went first thing in the morning to complain. The nun did apologize because she was intimidated by Francis's attitude. After that, she always let Juney go to the bathroom whenever he asked.

I was a rather skinny child at ten years old, but no one ever made fun of me except for my dad. He called me "Beanpoles" because I had such thin legs. I thought it was mean that he called me any name—it wasn't my fault we didn't have much to eat. At least no one else ever called me names.

Even though I was the head of the class, I was well-liked at school. No one seemed jealous. I loved my classmates and they knew it. Smiling and laughing were part of my nature, and I loved talking to everyone and could sense they felt as comfortable with me as I did with them. I liked to ask them questions about themselves and made them feel important. I never really wanted to talk about our family situation, although I may have talked about myself to some extent.

In the spring, we were all in for a special treat. Robbie had a friend in his class whose father managed one of the movie theaters downtown. He invited the whole school to view the children's classics free of charge. Each week, we were treated to a different movie, such as Tom Sawyer, Rebecca of Sunnybrook Farm, Snow White, and many more. The movies were uplifting because for awhile we could escape into a magic world of make-believe. I imagined myself as Becky Thatcher in Tom Sawyer, or Rebecca in Rebecca of Sunnybrook Farm, starring Shirley Temple. Shirley Temple was just about my age and she was so cute. Her movies were my favorites, and she could sing and tap dance like no other child I ever saw.

One day after a movie, my brothers and I bought ice cream cones at Isaly's for a dime. I bit into a large piece of glass, and just threw it in the trash. I didn't tell my dad because he often talked about suing someone for the least offense. It sounded like a waste of money to me.

After another movie, we heard sirens as we exited the theater. I said to my brothers,

"Let's go see what's happening." Crowds of people were running around the corner and we followed them. As we turned the corner, we saw smoke billowing from the hotel across the street. This was the same hotel where we had watched performers walk a tightrope from the roof to the roof of a building across the street. It was frightening to see the fire, and yet somehow fascinating to see the firemen rescue the guests from the third floor window. I prayed they wouldn't fall down the ladder. Fortunately, no one was injured.

The lazy summer days approached once more. Mom skipped her portion of food many times so we children would have something to sustain us. Robbie and Juney filled up on crabapples.

I was interested in learning to ride a two-wheel bike. While I was visiting Jean, her next door neighbor, Steve, rode over on his twenty-six inch bike. I asked him, "Steve, may I please ride your bike?"

"Sure, Flossie, just be careful," he answered.

"I will," I said gratefully.

With my usual self-confidence, I took off on the bike, balancing it as though I'd ridden before. I had pedaled up the next street when suddenly I realized I didn't know how to stop the bike. There was a car approaching behind me, and in front of me were two parked cars. I decided to ram into the parked car in front of me. I hit the bumper, and literally went flying off the bike. Luckily, I didn't get seriously hurt and Steve's bike was not scratched or dented. I was unaware that I was bleeding from my private parts when I hit the bar before falling off.

I ran home after returning Steve's bike, and I couldn't quite understand the fuss my mom made about the bleeding. I decided to spend the rest of the summer playing jacks, jumping rope and playing hopscotch with the neighbor girl downstairs. Robbie, Juney and I played marbles and they also collected them. Somehow I knew how to execute gymnastics, walk on my hands and stand on my head. I loved to pretend that I was Shirley Temple and tried to imitate her tap dancing.

We kept busy doing chores, playing, reading, or polishing shoes. Some Saturdays, Mom gave us a penny to buy candy at the candy store about a mile away. We bought ten caramels for a penny, large strings of licorice, gumballs, chocolate-covered suckers and other goodies.

We had extra fun when Aunt Katie and her sons, Bob and Don (Buddy), visited us that summer. Aunt Katie joked all the time and was such fun to be around. We had a picnic in the meadow across the street, and laughed a lot the week they were with us.

Occasionally, when dad came home, we drove to Pittsburgh to visit Aunt Betty, Uncle Joe, Uncle Jim and Aunt Emma, and their children, Shirley and Jimmy. They lived upstairs in Grandma's house. Visiting them was certainly a pleasure since Uncle Jim always paid me compliments, such as "You look pretty, Flossie," or, "You are so smart." I really felt loved when I was in his company and loved him in return.

When I stayed over the week-end at Grandma's, Aunt Betty, whom I always admired and loved, took me downtown on the streetcar to shop at Kaufmann's, Boggs & Buhl, or other shops. Aunt Betty was so beautiful at eighteen with her blonde hair, big blue eyes and sweet personality. As we were walking around downtown, a photographer took our picture one day and she purchased it and gave it to me.

Somehow, I never mentioned the dreadful circumstances we were caught up in when I talked to Aunt Betty. I'm sure Grandma would have helped us more had she known. Everybody was so tight-lipped then. Although Mom and Dad did not tell us to keep our poverty a secret, we probably were too disconcerted or too proud to mention it.

It was in Kittanning that I first noticed that Dad was constantly drinking baking soda water. He said he had dyspepsia. I wasn't exactly sure what that meant, but figured it was like an upset stomach and gas since he was always making bodily noises. He sometimes said, as I walked away from him with a disgusted look, "Better out than in." He is so gross, I thought. Every day while home, he asked me, "Get me some baking soda, Dearie." I stirred one teaspoon of baking soda in a glass of water and handed it to him. I didn't realize then that most human beings at some time have problems with gastritis, but women don't make a big deal out of it. Perhaps boys and men do!

I remember him crying a lot, especially when returning home. He begged forgiveness for all his sins of the flesh, crying, "I'm so sorry, Florrie, I'm so sorry, please forgive me. I won't do it again." Mom forgave him seventy times seven, probably because she couldn't bear to see him sobbing—I'm sure she didn't really believe him. Divorce was unheard of at that time, a devout Catholic woman especially wouldn't think of it. Oh, the shame of it all!

Francis really wished he could be faithful, and even thought he was a good Catholic. He went to church and confession. But what good is it if one commits the same sins over and over and receives absolution by reciting twenty Our Fathers and Hail Mary's? Confession is good for the soul, but it should be sincere.

Was Dad sincere about his feelings for his children? In his own way, he tried to show love for us. He hugged me occasionally, never in a sexual manner. I thought he may have felt affection for us, but it wasn't enough to keep him from other women. Does any man really think of his children when he has an affair with another woman? I doubt it, for at the time they only think of their own satisfaction. Dad also said years later, "If I am aroused by a woman, I have no conscience."

However, I can't say that Dad never had compassion for people. He stopped in to see his brothers and sister, Anna, when he drove to Pittsburgh. Anna told him that their brother's wife was exhibiting signs of mental illness. Her behavior got out of hand one day when she started chasing her three young children around the kitchen table with a carving knife. There was no choice but to put her in a mental asylum.

Francis felt so sorry for all of them, and visited his sister-in-law in the institution. He told us that no one else visited her, so he would try to visit her once in awhile.

He stopped to see his sister Anna and her husband and children, more than he saw anyone else, except Pearl, in Pittsburgh. He felt closer to his sister because she had always been a mother figure to him. He discussed his money problems with her and borrowed money from her when he felt desperate. Anna was a kind person and listened attentively to Francis' problems. He was careful not to mention Pearl lest she disapprove and lecture him.

What makes one child a black sheep of the family? The only one who strayed from his marriage vows, left his children without enough food to eat? Is it because the particular child is more sensitive to what occurs around him or her? I believe we are all born with certain genes, some with a tendency to be more sensitive and to respond in a negative way to the circumstances they were born into, good or bad. Losing his mother at the tender age of four may have affected Francis more than his siblings.

Although Francis didn't smoke, he tried it as a youngster but didn't enjoy it. He rarely drank alcoholic beverages, or cussed, or took the Lord's name in vain. He told some off-color jokes, but nothing like today's generation. He really didn't want to offend Florrie—it was enough that Pearl was in the picture. He didn't realize that that was the worst joke of all, and not a funny one. Men should be monogamous, but unfortunately, not all of them are. Perhaps they can love two or more women at a time.

And perhaps there are women who feel the same. I just never understood the "why" of it, but I already knew that I was glad I wasn't a man.

Francis kept on seeing Pearl when he was in Pittsburgh, and her family was appalled at the situation. They secretly hoped that he would make a choice and it would be Pearl. But he had trouble with that, since he loved both women. It bothered him a little that he had to sneak and lie, but he always managed to do that very thing.

We started school at St. Mary's once again, but a few weeks afterwards, Dad announced, "I have a new job selling bakery items in Pittsburgh, so we will be moving back soon."

Mom was rather happy to be able to move back to her roots and be closer to her family once more. Dad was also delighted since he could be close to both of his families living in the same city. Although we children were happy in Kittanning, and we would miss our friends and St. Mary's church and school, we accepted the move without complaint.

CHAPTER 10—Moving Back to Pittsburgh

Francis had located an upstairs apartment on Goettman Street, on the North Side. Goettman Street dead-ended near Grandpa Hanocek's former home. The apartment was directly across the street from Uncle Eddie Hanocek's family. Eddie lived in the first floor apartment with his wife Rose, and children Rosemary and Edward, Jr. We played with our cousins in the street because our apartment had no yard, just a brick alley between houses. The people who lived downstairs had a daughter, Gertrude, five years older than I was. Gertrude and I became friendly immediately. We sat on the front steps in the evenings and talked about school, movies, and just about everything else.

Francis continued to see Pearl. Her family was appalled at the situation but they secretly hoped that he would make a choice and it would be Pearl. Francis had trouble with that since he loved both women. It bothered him that he had to sneak and lie but he always managed to do that very thing.

We children were enrolled in Most Holy Name School. I was in the sixth grade, Robbie in third, and Juney in first grade. Sister Floriana, Mom's aunt, who belonged to the order of Notre Dame, taught the eighth grade there. She kept an eye on us, checking our grades, and we liked her even though she was rather stringent. She was only about five feet tall, but had a commanding voice. Some weekends we visited her at the convent and her manner softened during our visits. She often gave us chocolate candy which she had stored in her dresser drawer along with mothballs which she used to keep moths away. Although we craved the chocolates, we couldn't eat them since they smelled and tasted like mothballs. We pretended to be thankful for the candy so as not to hurt our aunt's feelings, but threw it away after arriving home. As knowledgeable as Sister Floriana seemed to be, we wondered why she didn't know not to put mothballs in the same drawer as candy. We also wondered why our mom didn't tell her—she probably did not want to cause her aunt embarrassment.

Our dad drove a van for a prominent bakery company, selling cakes, pies, cupcakes, rolls, bread, and cookies. He explained his frequent absences due to a large route in Pennsylvania. Mom must have known that part of the time he was staying with Pearl. She never discussed her concerns with us, but looked hurt and worried most of the time, especially when the pittance Dad gave her was gone and he was nowhere in sight.

When she confronted him upon his arrival home, he either denied the affair, or begged her for forgiveness. He still cried and promised not to see Pearl again. What a farce!

Meanwhile, Robbie, Juney, and I walked to Most Holy Name School and Church about a mile from our apartment, crossing the field to Goettman Street where we passed dad's brother John's house. John and his wife, Flora, had two daughters, Catherine and Mary Ann. Catherine was one year older, and Mary Ann one year younger than I was. We stopped to see them some weekends.

I gradually became head of the class and was pleased with my new friends. I had never had a cold before, but started coughing nonstop that winter. The persistent coughing bothered me in school, but, of course, no one made a doctor's appointment. Mom boiled onions with sugar and gave us the syrup for curtailing the cough to a certain extent.

When Christmas came to Troy Hill, our reward was a new diet of fruitcake and anise cookies that Francis did not sell. As time went on, the fruitcake became harder and harder to swallow, and we practically gagged on the anise cookies. Some days we did have spaghetti or lentils besides fruitcake and anise cookies, but other days not.

With spring approaching, we started roller-skating in the street after school and on weekends with our cousins Rosemary and Eddie.

At Most Holy Name school, we were required to attend Mass every school day. Speaking for myself, I didn't mind. I always enjoyed going to church even if it made me sleepy at times. I prayed for many things: for Mom to feel better, for Dad to stay home with us more, for food to eat, and for other people who were ill. I was happy and optimistic regardless of the situation. I thanked God for the blessings we had.

Francis did his best to stay away from Pearl for awhile, but succumbed to his lust once again by summer. It takes two to have an illicit relationship, and their desire for each other was not smothered by good intentions on either side.

Hot weather arrived, and with it a new electric washer from Sears for $35.00. What a wonder to be able to see the clothes becoming clean while the water became gray, the washer agitating the soil out instead of our hands scrubbing on the harsh wash boards! There were two hand rollers that squeezed the water out of the wet clothing. It was an easy chore to keep turning the handle, then rinsing the clothes, and once again wringing them out through the rollers. We hung the clothes to dry in the upstairs bathroom, which was spacious. We kept the washer in the corner of the large rectangular kitchen. The living room was more than adequate and had an entrance to the hallway and stairs down to the front door. However, we usually entered through the back stairs to the kitchen. There were three small bedrooms, so I had my own space.

On extremely hot days, Robbie, Juney and I walked to the fire department located off Lowrie Street, one block past Most Holy Name School, to join in the fun of running through many sprinklers to cool off. A whole block was cordoned off to entertain the children on Troy Hill.

Other days we walked down Lowrie Street to visit Grandma and Uncle Jim's family. Uncle Jim worked for Westinghouse, and Aunt Betty worked at the Arcade Theater. While we visited, our cute little cousin Shirley rode her tricycle in the small back yard. Shirley was only two years old and couldn't pronounce her last name 'Schmitt' properly, saying her name was 'Shirley Shit." We thought that was funny.

One day my brothers asked Aunt Emma if they could ride Shirley's tricycle because we never had one, but she replied, "You are too big to ride it, it could break." In reality, they were too big but were disappointed and always remembered that.

Some Saturdays when Mom had a dime for each of us children, we walked down many flights of steps to the Arcade Theater to see Aunt Betty working in the ticket booth. We also got to see a movie, a cartoon, and a sequel of The Little Rascals, plus the newsreel, and the best dividend of all, a candy bar. Imagine that, all for a dime!

We didn't often have a quarter to go swimming at the nearby pool, but when we did, we enjoyed it immensely. Both boys seemed a natural at swimming, and I wasn't too shabby.

Other summer frolic was going to North Park once each year for a family picnic. Dad did see to that even though we did not go to amusement parks. Mom made "Frickadelions" (hamburgers mixed with egg, onions, and bread crumbs, then fried to perfection). Dad bought a watermelon, and added the leftover anise cookies to the menu. Mom also sliced tomatoes to add to the delicacy of the sandwiches. That particular summer, Mom forgot the hamburger buns. Dad screamed at her nonstop, "You dummy, how could you forget the buns? This whole picnic is a waste."

I thought, You are the dummy, to yell at our sweet mother who puts up with you. My dislike for him was at its peak then, because I started to really understand what was and had been going on, the deceit, the abandonment, the constant begging for forgiveness, the broken promises. I wondered why he was the only dad I knew who was a sinner. My uncles were all kind to their wives, albeit there were facts I didn't know, but at least they stayed with them.

Aunt Betty became engaged to Pat Callahan, whom she had dated for two years. Pat was an ambitious, kind, soft-spoken young man who thought the world of Betty. He had blonde curly hair, a good build, and gentlemanly manners.

Betty rode the streetcar to work down on East Ohio Street, and met a conductor who started paying a lot of attention to her. He was a nice looking young man who finally asked her for a date. She was a little confused about her feelings, and decided to go out with him once. He seemed to be a very nice person who told her he was already going steady with another girl. When Betty didn't hear from him for a long time, she assumed he was with his steady. Later on, she discovered he had been in the hospital with rheumatoid arthritis.

It was time for school to start. I looked forward eagerly to school because I loved to learn and be with my classmates again. The challenge of being the head of the class was something to strive for, although I didn't think others would like me better if I was, but because it seemed to compensate for the lack of a stable family life. My mother was always there for us, but the constant turmoil associated with my dad loomed over the horizon.

After being absent for three weeks, he returned home with three dresses for me to wear to school. I asked him where he bought them, and he said Pearl picked them out for me. I absolutely needed clothing for school, but when I tried on the dresses, only one fit me properly. The other two were very tight across the chest. They weren't made for my expanding bosom. Mom tried altering one, but the pleats on top left marks that made the dress look awful, so I only wore the one dress that didn't have pleats, and the other one Mom didn't alter. I felt like I was suffocating with the unaltered dress.

I rather resented Pearl spending our money on dresses that didn't fit me properly, and expected to pick out my dresses myself. But I kept my thoughts to myself, as usual.

I was in the seventh grade and eager to learn cooking, and especially sewing at the public school so I could make myself dresses that fit me comfortably. To start, our sewing class made a cute apron. Cooking was a cinch because I already knew how to make the foods we had to eat. Twice a week, our class walked the short block to the public school.

In September and October, my brothers and I walked down the hill to downtown North Side from our home, passing the Heinz Company, which manufactured and sold pickles, ketchup, and other canned and bottled products. We shopped at the A & P grocery store, which sold every variety of food. Prices were still reasonable: for instance, peanut butter was seventeen cents a jar; oranges, twenty-three cents a dozen; macaroni, four packages for a quarter; and potatoes, five pounds for a quarter. Once in awhile, we bought hot pretzels from vendors on the streets, and sometimes a huge dill pickle for a nickel instead of the hot pretzels.

The Depression years were over and most people's lives were back to normal, although there wasn't any change in our style of living. Naturally, we ate better when Dad was home, as in the past, but food was scarce when he was gone.

Robbie's birthday was approaching. Robbie and I had been asking for a bike for our birthdays. Mine had already passed and I didn't receive one, although Dad had promised I would. We were accustomed to Dad's promises being broken; however, Dad did bring home a two-wheel bike Robbie. I was a little disappointed, especially after Dad agreed with Robbie that no one else could ride his new bike. A week later, I decided to ride the bike anyhow, when he wasn't home. I had pouted all week about the fact that I didn't get a bike, and needed to ride Robbie's to get it out of my system. Wrong thing to do!

It was exhilarating to feel the breeze as I headed down Lowrie Street, mostly on the sidewalk. Suddenly, a loud noise preceded a very flat front tire. I had accidentally ridden over an umbrella spike. I reprimanded myself, This is what I get for taking Robbie's bike without permission. I had to think fast. Since the accident happened right across the street from my friend and classmate, Charles (Chuck) Worthy, I thought I'd check with him as to my next move.

Chuck was home, and offered to fix the flat for me. He patched the two tears made by the umbrella spike. I asked Chuck, "Do you think anyone will be able to notice the repair?"

He replied, "It's unlikely, Flossie, unless there is another flat on the front tire."

"Thanks, Chuck, for helping me," I said gratefully. At the time, I didn't realize that he liked me and wanted to be my boyfriend.

With some hesitation, I arrived home to find that Robbie had not yet returned. I said a prayer of thanks.

The winter passed without much incident. I walked home from school with Wanda Kramer, a very nice friend who had had mastoid surgery. The hole beside her left ear drained a lot, and, although she was a bright and clean person, she had an odor about her from the mastoid drainage.

I also became fast friends with Barbara Hall who walked the other way home down Lowrie hill. She invited me to her upstairs apartment. I liked her mother, her sister Betsy, and little sister Yvonne. I don't recall ever meeting her father—seems he was gone most of the time, too.

In the evenings, after homework was finished, we spent some time as a family listening to radio programs. Our favorites were Jack Armstrong, the All-American Boy, Amos and Andy, Inner Sanctum, Fibber McGee and Molly, and a so-called soap opera, Ma Perkins. We all enjoyed Kate Smith's program with Kate singing her theme song 'When the Moon Comes Over the Mountain', and Rudy Vallee's program with Rudy singing his theme song, 'My Time is Your Time'. Major Bowes Amateur Hour was also a favorite.

In the spring, we lost our dear Grandmother Schmitt. Losing someone you love is never easy, but Grandma's death was not only sad but frightening. Grandma had been ill with pneumonia when her heart gave out at the age of sixty. We were called to her bedside, along with the priest who had lit all the Extreme Unction candles. As he administered the last rites to Grandma, we heard the pitter-patter of a gentle rain which suddenly accelerated to a storm, with lightning and thunder cracking simultaneously. As Grandma expired, lightning enveloped the room, and all the Extreme Unction candles blew out by themselves while the large statue of Mary sitting on the side table cracked in two.

Aunt Betty became hysterical, and I was too petrified to move. Mom followed Aunt Betty into the living room to try to console her. My brothers and I were in a state of shock, and I remained that way all through the funeral. No one ever figured out what exactly happened or why, but we remembered this unexplained happening all our lives. At the time, Robbie, Juney, and I had the fear of God in us that remained for many years. I learned later that God was not to be feared but to be loved because of His great goodness and love for us.

On the way to the cemetery, I sat with Aunt Betty in the back seat of the limo, feeling very sad, but still in shock. Aunt Betty seemed calm by this time but missed her mother terribly. I kept dreaming about Grandma for awhile and really missed her, too. Even as a child, I felt that she was looking down from heaven and watching her family. I always tried to make her proud of me, and hoped I could live up to what I thought would be her expectations.

That summer, when I was almost thirteen, Uncle Phil and Aunt Meryl invited our family to their summer cabin in the country which they had rented for two weeks. The cabin wasn't elaborate, but it stood beside a creek with water deep enough to swim in, and trees and woods to roam about. There was a large tree that had a rope tied to one of the branches, which we used to swing over the creek, imitating Tarzan. The boys and I climbed the tree, grabbed hold of the rope, jumped, and soared over the water dropping down into the water midway across the creek. We yelled Aayyee! like Tarzan.

Dad didn't join us, but Uncle Joe did. On Sunday, he and Robbie and I walked four miles to church and back. Uncle Joe gave us some candy on the way home. Time spent with him was memorable. Always joking, always caring!

There were some neighbor children at a farm near the cabin to play with, too. They took us into their barn, and I climbed up the ladder to the loft, which was approximately eleven feet high. As I reached the top and tried to pull myself up, somehow I grabbed just straw and went plummeting down, landing flat on my back. At first I couldn't get up, but finally rolled over. I had prayed as I was falling, and once again prayed as I struggled to get up. I had cracked my tail bone, but I learned to live with the pain, however, since no one took me to a doctor. It was uncomfortable to sit for long periods at a time, but I had also learned not to complain and to just get used to the pain, since it wasn't intense.

When we arrived back home, once again I realized country living didn't seem to be my forte.

Dad decided to take us on a trip to Baltimore, Maryland, to visit Florrie's other aunts, who were nuns. Sister Philip and Sister Anne, Grandpa's sisters, were very friendly and sweet, as was Sister Pamphilia, their cousin. The convent was beautiful, but the city of Baltimore was more congested than Pittsburgh, with houses directly connected to one another and no alleys in between. Our apartment looked rather cozy to me after viewing Baltimore.

CHAPTER 11—First Boyfriends

Eighth grade was a memorable experience for me since Sister Floriana was the teacher. I had looked forward without any trepidation to being in her class. It did not take me long to realize that she expected me to be perfect and to get perfect grades. Not that the grades were a problem, but no one is perfect in every way, or perhaps any way—only God.

I never had to exert myself studying until the eighth grade, when I had to really hit the books to get one hundred percent in geography, my least favorite subject. I memorized everything that I needed to know for the geography tests.

I still didn't have many clothes, and was enthusiastic about making myself a blue dress in sewing class. Until it was finished, I only owned one sweater and skirt, a black hand-me-down dress from Pearl, and a new sailor dress that faded the first time it was washed. I felt like crying when all the white brocade on the collar and skirt turned gray-blue. At that age, clothing and looking presentable was so important to me, as it is with most teens.

Sister Floriana was appalled that I wore a sweater to school because I was well-endowed. I didn't own a bra, so it was probably noticeable, and I didn't understand that the boys were reacting more than I realized—it did seem that most of the boys were paying a little extra attention to me. Sister told me never to wear the sweater again. That left me with two dresses to wear to school.

Robert (Bobby) Betts, a bright boy in my class to whom I had never given the time of day, began teasing me about the lack of pretty dresses, saying "One day you wear a black dress, the next day you wear a faded one."

I was embarrassed in front of my friends as we walked out of class into the hallway. I turned around and slapped Bobby across his cheek, retorting, "How dare you?"

After I slapped him, I felt gratified and dismayed at the same time, for I was not a violent person and deplored it in others. Shortly afterwards, Bobby became my friend, or, rather, boyfriend. I'm not sure why, but I also became attracted to him. He had a round face, was rather tall and wore glasses, and spoke gently to me. However, every time I saw him I became nervous, excited, and tongue-tied. I hoped he didn't notice. Then again, I suspected he felt the same.

One school day the whole class took a bus to the planetarium in downtown Pittsburgh. Bobby sat behind me while we watched the turning constellations. When he handed me my coat belt that was dragging on the floor, he touched my hand and I felt an electric shock. Being infatuated was crazy and I wasn't sure I liked it.

Bobby walked me home some days, and we roller-skated on the street. He told me, "I like you—I'm not sure why, but I do." That is exactly how I felt, but my tongue was frozen and I couldn't say a word.

Meanwhile, several other boys started following me around and some teased me about others. Andy kept repeating, "Tony Peck will give you another Peck." I tried to ignore him for the most part, but was offended by the crude remarks with sexual implications. I didn't understand why he didn't know I wouldn't do anything related to sex, let alone the act which I still couldn't quite picture.

Sister Floriana did not hear Andy's remarks, but Andy was a troublemaker in the class. Sister hit him on the knuckles with a ruler for any slight offense.

Previously, I had thought about becoming a nun, but after Sister Floriana hit Andy so often, I was not sure that I wanted to be in that situation. I thought that I would like to teach but was not sure that I would like to spend all my time trying to restore order to a class. Even at the age of thirteen, I knew that it was the parent's duty to teach their children how to act like a responsible person and to respect their teachers and others.

Chuck became our paper boy and also became friends with Robbie and Juney. After school he asked me if I wanted a ride home on his bike and I agreed. At first it wasn't clear to me that he also liked me and wanted to be my boyfriend. He visited us in the evening on pretense of seeing my brothers. As we sat on the living room couch listening to the radio, Chuck put his arm around me. I immediately got up and walked into the kitchen. I liked him as a friend. He was good looking with blonde curly hair, and a nice friendly personality. The magic just wasn't there for me.

At Christmas, Chuck bought me a box of chocolates, and Bobby gave me a beautiful blue rosary. I really appreciated the gifts because we didn't get much else.

As I was walking to school one morning by myself across the field to Goettman Street, a worrisome thing happened, although, thank heavens, no one was around to see it. I was on my period, and at that time we used white rags to catch the flow of menstrual blood—I had one pinned to my panties. The pins somehow came undone and there was the rag lying behind me as I walked. I quickly snatched it up, looked around to make sure no one was around, and stuck it back. What a fretful day that was, worrying that that could happen again. We didn't even have reliable safety pins!

Our eighth-grade class was preparing to make our Confirmation in the spring. The girls were instructed to wear light-colored dresses, and the boys black pants, white shirts and blue ties. Mom insisted that I should have a new dress. She didn't think the blue dress I made in class was dressy enough.

Barbara was making a sheer light blue dress. I wanted to make a pink dress to save money, but Mom took me downtown, a rare event, to look for a suitable dress for the occasion. She had worn a white satin dress for her Confirmation, and wanted me to look extra special like she did.

For Easter I had picked out a blue suit, with a white blouse, blue coat, and straw hat with blue satin ribbon. That was the first all new Easter outfit I ever had. Dad was probably trying to make up for never buying me a bike. When I asked Sister Floriana if I could wear my suit instead of a dress, she said that I should stick to the rules.

Mom and I shopped in several department stores but couldn't find a light-colored dress that was suitable. We found a coral rayon dress with white lace on the collar and white lace around heart-shaped pockets. We both liked it, and the way it fit, so Mom bought it with money that was supposed to be for food.

On Confirmation day, Sister Floriana gave me a discerning look with her eyes cast downward. I'm sure she thought the dress too bright. She must have bit her tongue, though, for she said nothing. Some of the other girls wore bright-colored dresses, too, but mine was probably the brightest. It seemed appropriate to me to look radiant on this special day.

After the ceremony, I stopped at Aunt Meryl and Uncle Phil's home on Lowrie Street, not far from Most Holy Name. Uncle Phil took a picture of me and Betty Lou, their adorable little girl, two years old who had blonde curls like Shirley Temple. Being with Betty Lou was fun. I wondered what it would be like to have children of my own someday after I was married.

Shortly afterward, Uncle Phil and family moved to Mount Troy, where they had a panoramic view of Troy Hill. Their home was three stories high, and to get to the front porch, one had to climb many steps.

Aunt Meryl had another girl, a darling little baby named Phyllis. They asked me to baby sit, and I really loved rocking Phyllis to sleep and making a little money.

As a result of studying so hard in the eighth grade, I received one hundred percent on all the exams and was awarded a full paid scholarship to Holy Ghost High School. I also was chosen to give a speech on stage before the entire school preceding graduation. I memorized a lengthy presentation about Frederick Ozanam, the founder of the St. Vincent de Paul Society. I was exceedingly nervous, but no one seemed to notice, and everyone congratulated me on the long speech.

Dad still came and left, sometimes on the same day, just giving Mom enough money to barely survive. On the day after graduation, he exclaimed, "We are moving to Carnegie, Pennsylvania, because it's central to my new meat selling route. I found a nice house with a large front yard."

We all replied, "That sounds good, but we'll miss our friends."

"It's not far away, so you could take a streetcar."

Somehow, I knew we wouldn't be coming back often, but at least that was the end of eating fruitcake and anise cookies. When Dad sold meat, he could bring home jars of pig's feet which I detested, or dreaded hot tamales, or bacon rind to suck on for fat content.

CHAPTER 12—One Too Many People

The house in Carnegie sat back away from the street and had a grassy green with several trees and a lilac bush. Mom and I enjoyed the fragrant aroma of the lilacs. Not far away was a river that ran through Carnegie. The setting was pleasing to the eyes. However, the unusual floor plan of the house caused a lot of privacy problems. The bathroom was situated between the kitchen and the living room, without any doors. I found it difficult at times to use the bathroom only when no one was in sight, but I always waited until that was the case. The rest of the family didn't seem to complain about it although they also had to wait. I never understood why our parents didn't at least hang curtains at the doorways.

Dad was home more than usual, especially after Pearl joined our family again a couple of weeks later. I was distressed when I saw her walk into the kitchen, and couldn't understand why Mom was not perturbed about her presence. However, Mom and Dad didn't argue about her staying with us this time, so it was rather peaceful living in Carnegie.

Robbie and Juney made some friends in the neighborhood that summer and played games in the street with them. I, on the other hand, did not get to know any girls my age. I started babysitting the little girl next door, and Mom became friendly with her mother. I have no idea how she explained Pearl living with us.

Mom, Pearl and I shared the chores. We actually had enough food to eat while in Carnegie. Pearl was kind to me, but I had so many unanswered questions. Why were all three sleeping in the same bed? I was happy that Pearl wasn't sleeping with me, but thought it unsuitable that she occupied my parents' bed, even though Mom was sleeping in the middle. I knew this because I walked into their room one morning when the door was open. I still didn't really comprehend the sexual act, and never told anyone what I saw.

Juney walked into our parents' room one day to see Pearl and Dad asleep and she was naked, at least on top. She awakened, jumped up and pulled the sheet over her. Juney was at an inquisitive age, and was secretly delighted to see Pearl naked.

On Saturdays, the boys and I walked to downtown Carnegie to buy one of the local newspapers, either the Pittsburgh Press or the Sun-Telegraph. After arriving home, we read the comics together. We especially got a kick out of 'The Katzenjammer Kids."

Dad bought a Ford for two hundred dollars. I assumed he would drive me to Holy Ghost High School in September when school resumed, but I was mistaken. He said he didn't have time to take me to school. I had to take two streetcars to get there, so the trip took about an hour each way. The rollicking motion of the streetcars for such a long time made me nauseous. I complained to Mom, "I can't ride the streetcar any more because it makes me ill."

Mom said, "You could board at the school, since the scholarship includes room and board."

I had a feeling I wasn't going to like living there because it was so straight-laced and I hadn't as yet become friends with anyone. The rules were rigid, everything on a schedule even after school hours. I felt lonely and missed my family, although I went home on weekends.

Our dad, in the meantime, was looking for a better paying job. He had been in the meat- packing business and a salesman for so many years; he now wanted a stationary type of job. He heard that the rubber industry was booming in Akron, Ohio. After traveling there and finding out that Firestone Tire & Rubber Company was hiring factory workers, he applied for a job and was hired on the spot to build tires.

Akron, Ohio, at that time, was called 'the rubber capital of the world'. It was the home of many companies: Goodyear, Seiberling, Mohawk, Monarch, Sun, General, and B. F. Goodrich Tire and Rubber companies. Benjamin Franklin Goodrich founded his company in 1870 in Akron, making tires, insulation, home, and many other products.

In 1941, there was a demand for all types of tires in Europe because of the war raging there. Germany, under the leadership of Adolph Hitler, was trying to take over other countries. There was much resistance and fighting in many countries. Hitler mesmerized the German population into trying to create a so-called master race by eliminating the Jewish people. Not all Germans agreed with his policy and some thought he was a crazed man. However, they were hesitant to disagree for fear of being turned in as a traitor.

The demand for tires helped Akron, Ohio, to prosper. Francis rather liked the city (he had been to Akron some years ago when he worked for the WPA) and thought his family would, also. He agreed to start working the next week.

Francis was bewildered that both Florrie and Pearl became cool to his advances while living in Carnegie. Pearl demanded he make a choice, but Florrie felt he really didn't have a choice if he were to take his children into consideration. Actually, he was probably once again thinking of himself. Perhaps he also wanted to move to Akron because of the fact that he had met a woman there years ago who liked him, and he figured she would give him what he wanted most.

CHAPTER 13—Akron, Ohio and
The Haunted House

We moved to Akron, Ohio on October 1, 1941, leaving Pearl behind with her parents.

I was so relieved to leave Holy Ghost High School, I was almost giddy when we arrived in Akron. The moving van followed behind us as we approached our new rented home on Penfield Avenue. It was a large white frame house with a front porch. As we entered the hallway, there were several steps that led upstairs, across a small hallway, then downstairs into the kitchen. A left turn took us upstairs where there were two bedrooms, one for me, and one for my brothers. We started running up and down in delight. Things were really looking up, in our estimation.

Mom and Dad used the dining room as their bedroom. The kitchen was large enough for comfortable dining, and the living room was spacious.

I was enrolled at Jennings Junior High School, and Robbie and Juney at St. Hedwig's Catholic School, where we also attended church on most Sundays. To get to St. Hedwig's we crossed Howard Street past Saint Thomas Hospital, crossed N. Main Street and walked two blocks. Jennings was on Tallmadge Avenue, about four blocks away. St. Martha's church was across the street from Jennings, so we attended services there some Sundays.

We all really liked Akron immediately. Dad made more money at Firestone and didn't mind the hard work lifting tires. Mom was glad

Pearl did not accompany us, and hoped that this time Dad would keep his promise to her to be faithful.

The boys and I started walking across the bridge to downtown Akron every Saturday. The scenic view from the bridge was breathtaking. After crossing it to Main Street, we loved to shop in the many department stores: Yeager's, Akron Dry Goods, Federmans, Polsky's, O'Neils, and other smaller stores and specialty shops. There were many restaurants, but we never ate at any of them, except once or twice we bought a hamburger at White Tower, a fast food restaurant, as we strolled up High Street to Broadway.

. We saw many movies at the Orpheum, Colonial, Strand, Palace, and Loew's Theater for a quarter. The Loew's Theater was our favorite. While we sat in the balcony waiting for the movie to start, I imagined I was close to heaven, for there were stars twinkling in the ceiling, and elaborate balconies and statues. We were enchanted by Oscar Wilde (nicknamed "Wild Oscar") playing the organ as it rose on a platform left of the stage before and after the movies. Hearing the soothing organ melodies enticed me to want to play the piano again, and I asked if I could take lessons.

It so happened that there was a music teacher who lived around the corner on Howard Street named Mrs. Winters. Dad was making enough money to pay the dollar a lesson, so my parents agreed. I had a piano lesson every Saturday afternoon, and practiced every day. Mrs. Winters was very demanding and I wanted to please her by knowing all the pieces she gave me.

A few days after settling in our new home, we discovered we were in a mysterious house. Every night we heard heavy footsteps in the attic, and called Dad to check. Mom and Dad heard them, too, but Dad never found anything when he investigated. Sometimes the curtains blew without any windows open or heat on, and candles extinguished themselves. We were puzzled, apprehensive, and frightened. Juney had outgrown most of his shyness and fearfulness, but now were all fearful and uncomfortable in this house. Francis decided to look for another home.

I had made a friend at Jennings who invited me to her home after school. We walked about two miles up Tallmadge Avenue to a trailer park. When we entered the trailer, I realized how fortunate I was to live in a house, even though it seemed to be haunted. The trailer was crowded with clothing strewn all over the couch, and there was an offensive odor. I could hardly wait to leave. It was almost dark when I arrived home.

Francis found a white frame house on Vincent Street in Cuyahoga Falls, a beautiful suburb of Akron. The down payment to purchase the house was reasonable, so we would finally have a permanent home. We bought the house at 2873 Vincent Street for $2,000.

It was a relief to leave the mysterious house I'll never forget on Penfield Avenue. I hesitated to check with any new renters of the house.

Many years later, I intended to show the house to a friend as we passed by that way because I had told her about the mysterious happenings at that house. Unfortunately, it had been torn down and there was nothing but a vacant lot where the house once stood. It was then we noticed that there was a grave stone company on Howard Street right in front of the empty plot. It gave us the shivers.

CHAPTER 14—Cuyahoga Falls, Ohio— Pearl Harbor Day

We moved on December 7, 1941 to our new home on Vincent Street in Cuyahoga Falls. It was the last house in the Falls, and the next street that it intersected was in Silver Lake. Cuyahoga Falls impressed me as a lovely clean city with good schools and churches, and a boulevard that is decorated for every holiday.

December 7, 1941, was also the day that the Japanese attacked Pearl Harbor, which was the start of World War ll. Adolph Hitler, the disturbed ruler of Germany, had been bombing England, and his rampage became the Japanese rampage. Of course, the fighting was not in America, but the rationing of food, gasoline, and paper products began shortly afterwards. Our young men were drafted to serve their country.

The news was very disturbing, but the daily living must go on. We scrubbed the house on Vincent Street from top to bottom. The boys moved furniture and boxes while Mom and I started arranging the kitchen cupboards.

There were two bedrooms upstairs, one large one for Robbie and Juney, and a smaller one for me. The house was old but adequate, except once again the dining room was used as our parents' bedroom. There was a commode in the basement. Dad said he would build a bathroom soon.

Robbie and Juney attended St. Joseph's School. They felt ill at ease there, since the nuns continually asked for money for various church and school expenses. They made many friends at St. Joseph's and our whole family attended St. Joseph's Church every Sunday. It was located approximately two miles from our home, and in the winter we took the bus if it was too cold and snowy to walk.

The bus stop was on Hudson Drive, so we had to walk about a block to cross the railroad tracks, a shortcut to get there, instead of going down Vincent to Front Street. The buses ran every twenty minutes and the fare was a dime, or three tokens for a quarter.

After we had the house in order, it began to feel like home. It was gratifying to feel that, for the first time, we really owned a home of our own, even though it wasn't paid for, but at least buying it was a start. There were so many things we wanted to do to improve the house, but it takes money to accomplish any remodeling. We hung curtains immediately, for rooms do not look dressed up without window curtains or drapes, and Mom and I had a yearning for pretty surroundings even though we rarely had them. However, we always did the best we could under the circumstances.

Years later, I wrote a poem expressing my thoughts about living in this home, the last time that we moved as a family:

THE LAST HOUSE IN THE FALLS

North to south, east to west,
The last house in the Falls was the best
Because we lived there.
Uptown, downtown, all around town,
Even when walls came tumbling down
Our spirit lived there.
Scrubbing, cleaning, washed with tears,
We lived our early formative years,
Building up, tearing apart,
Nails striking deep within our hearts,
Working, smiling, caring,
Feats that resembled daring,
Walking floors, closing, opening doors,

New additions of wood and cement,
Added structures to build and lament
But a fortress in the storms,
The last house in the Falls to store
Fond memories of love, togetherness, more
Because we LIVED there.

CHAPTER 15—Cuyahoga Falls High School and Friends

I was a freshman at Cuyahoga Falls High School located on Fourth Street,

which was a mile and a half walk from our home. I liked the looks of the school and didn't think it would be much different from all the other schools I had attended. I was wrong because there were one hundred sixty-seven students in the class and they seemed to gather in groups. Some of them had known each other since first grade. What I didn't realize then was that there were other new students besides me who came from other states. They probably felt exactly like I did, a little apprehensive. After checking out each group, I decided just to be myself and tried to be friends with everybody. And that happened. There were several classmates who sought me out and invited me to their homes, and I was content with my new school and surroundings.

Some people teased me about my Pittsburgh accent, and I noticed that Ohio residents had a different accent with some words, especially 'O's. I quickly adapted to the Ohio intonation. At the butcher shop on Hudson Drive, which was across the nearby railroad tracks, a shortcut we always used, the butcher thought it was funny that I asked for a pound of 'jumbo'. That's what we called bologna in Pennsylvania. He laughed every time I asked for it, so I asked for 'bologna' eventually.

A short time after we moved, I met a new friend, Cathy O'Brien, who lived around the corner on Vincent Street. Cathy was a half-year behind me in school. Cuyahoga Falls High had two graduating classes each year, one in January, and one in June. Cathy and I became fast friends and walked to school together some days. We visited each other after school and laughed a lot. I became rather silly at the age of fourteen, like most girls, and loved to talk to my friends.

During the winter I met another good friend, Dorothy Swanson, who also lived on Vincent Street, two doors from Cathy. I had seen her walking to school in front of me occasionally, but hesitated to make a connection. She seemed to walk so straight, never looking around. I happened to be in a hurry the day we met, so caught up with her. We introduced ourselves and became acquainted easily. Just as we were crossing the tracks, I slipped and fell on the ice, tore my only pair of hose, and let my books go sprawling as I tried to break my fall. I felt like a klutz that this happened the first time I met Dorothy. She didn't say anything but "Are you all right?" She helped me up, and I wasn't hurt except for a scrape on my knee. We continued walking across the field to Third Street, where she slipped on the ice, too. Her books scattered, and we laughed the rest of the way to school. Now we had something in common and became good friends. Cathy, Dorothy and I have been friends all of our life.

Dad was coming home most every day, and we had adequate food. It seemed only he could bring meat home despite the rationing. When Mom shopped at the butcher's, the only item he said he had was hotdogs, so we were lucky to eat one hotdog a month. Dad liked his job at Firestone, Mom made friends with several neighbors, and we all adjusted to living in Ohio.

Cuyahoga Falls, known as the Flower City, was beautiful, clean and practically crime free. Broad Boulevard was decorated for every holiday. As a matter of fact, it still is—flags for the Fourth of July, spring daffodils and tulips, Christmas decorations of all kinds. Some of the residents decorated their home elaborately for the holidays, especially Halloween and Christmas. People came from all over the area to enjoy the displays. In the past few years, not as many people are decorating like they did when we first moved there.

I began baby-sitting for a couple on Landon Avenue, the street behind us. They had a new baby who cried a lot. One evening when

I was taking care of him, he went on a crying jag, and I really didn't know what to do. I carried him into the bedroom to change his diaper, and he squirmed so much I almost dropped him on the bed. All for a quarter an hour! Not only that, but for the same pay, I babysat two children a couple of blocks away. These two pre-school children would not stay in their beds upstairs and kept coming down asking for water and cookies, etc. They flew into bed when they heard their parents coming in the front door. I always was expected to wash the accumulation of a week's dirty dishes. I knew I'd better find a job making more money.

Mom let me keep some of the money to buy material at Federman's for ten cents a yard, so I sewed most of my clothes. Cathy and Dorothy did, too. I really enjoyed making different dresses on Grandma's old treadle sewing machine.

In the dead of winter, when I was returning home from a grocery store farther up on Hudson Drive, I did a foolish thing. I had bought two gallons of milk and as I approached the shortcut across the tracks to home, I was mortified to see a hundred-car freight train sitting there. I waited and waited for the train to move, meanwhile practically freezing my hands and face. I wasn't wearing a hat or gloves, because I didn't have any. I knew it was dangerous to climb under a train, but couldn't bear the cold any longer. I decided to take a chance and, just as I was scooting under the car, there was a lurch and clanging of wheels. I never moved so fast in my life as I pulled the second gallon of milk out of harm's way just in time. I didn't tell Mom because I didn't want to worry her, and I never tried to argue with a train again.

My brothers and I still took the bus to downtown Akron on some Saturdays. I also took a bus to Howard Street once a week because I took piano lessons for another year. In the spring, I was in a piano recital and played Mendelsohn's "Spring Song." Mom insisted I buy a new dress and so there I was in my new gold, two-piece dress with a pleated skirt playing in front of an audience. I was told I played quite well. A recording was made of each student's recital song.

I took the train to Pittsburgh one Friday and stayed at Aunt Betty's for the week-end. She decided to can peaches, so we peeled peaches on Saturday. I didn't know at the time that Aunt Betty had just had another miscarriage, and that was why she stayed close to home. In the evening, Aunt Meryl took me to a carnival off Lowrie Street and we played Bingo. Aunt Meryl always liked to play Bingo one night a week at the fire station nearby.

As I looked around, I noticed Bobby Best and a few other boys I knew sitting on the steps across the way. I was hoping Bobby would come over to say hello to me—I was busy playing Bingo—but when we finished, he had left. He probably felt as awkward as I did at the age of fourteen. I didn't feel comfortable approaching him.

I did know that he and a couple of other boys from my eighth grade class came to visit me when we lived in Carnegie, but my brothers and I had gone to a movie. They tried to find me in the theatre, but evidently, couldn't because it was crowded. I thought that I heard a familiar voice in the dark theater, but didn't investigate. I presumed it was my imagination

. Dad told Mom that Pearl was in Akron working at Federman's, and that she was pursuing him. Of course he knew she was going to follow him since he urged her to so he could see her more often. Mom wasn't happy about the situation, and she absolutely forbade Dad to bring Pearl into the household again. She couldn't take it anymore, nor could we children. Nevertheless, my brothers and I stopped to see her once in Federman's because she was selling the yard goods and it was cheaper in Federman's. She seemed as pleasant as ever.

Several months later, she went back to Pittsburgh, and we were glad. We didn't know that she felt she had to leave since she was pregnant with her first child. Francis told her she had better leave, because to have two families in one city was not a good idea. Her parents were unhappy with the situation, but allowed her to live with them.

Pearl had a little girl whom she named Karen. Francis was there for the delivery and promised to take care of her. Like most men, he was proud of having sired another child, and a girl, too, since he already had two boys. He also was a little anxious about having another mouth to feed. He didn't tell Mom about the birth until much later.

Mom became good friends with several of the neighbors, especially Mrs. Wagner who lived two doors down. On the left side of our home, an old man named Mr. Coleman lived in a shack. Dad talked about buying his land when he passed away, which he did. He tore down the shack and built a driveway and two-car garage, with space upstairs for an apartment. He never finished the apartment.

Mom and I enjoyed the lilac bushes and made cherry pies from the cherry tree that was on Mr. Coleman's property, now ours. She cooked spaghetti, lentils with prunes, and baked beans most of the time, so cherry pies were a luxury. When Dad was home, she made pork, sauerkraut, and potato dumplings occasionally. Of course, he started leaving again on the weekends, on the pretense of looking for better jobs, although he was making sufficient money at Firestone. We all figured he was seeing Pearl. Mom didn't argue with him too much about his leaving, since she was afraid of his temper - at least Pearl wasn't living with us.

The last day of school, which was half a day, Cathy, Dorothy and I packed lunches and headed for the Gorge Metropolitan Park. The gorge was the dividing line between Akron and Cuyahoga Falls, and a photographer's dream. We each bought a Brownie Kodak camera for $2.00. After eating lunch at the picnic area, we explored the gorge, walking up and down the steps, walking the pipes, and sometimes walking across the breakers beneath the waterfall, the largest I had ever seen. We took pictures, explored the caves, and climbed the rocks through narrow passages.

We liked Mary Campbell's cave. Mary was twelve years old when she was kidnapped from her home in western Pennsylvania by Delaware Indians in 1759. They migrated to Big Falls of the Cuyahoga River, where they lived temporarily in the cave until their village was erected. Mary was the first white child on the Western Reserve and, in 1764, was returned to her home.

In the summer of 1942, I found a job doing housework for a nice couple in Silver Lake five mornings a week. The Davis family lived about a mile from us. I did laundry, ironing, dishes, baby sat their three children, and so forth, for fifty cents an hour. They were very good to me and I rather enjoyed working there. One day their five year old daughter, Sally, swallowed a penny when I was working there and I worried about that. When I told Mr. and Mrs. Davis about it, they assured me that the penny would pass in a day or two. Sally was fine. Every Monday, they invited me to eat lunch with them. It was leftovers from Sunday's dinner, but tasted divine. Creamed ham and peas on toast seemed like a feast.

In the afternoons, when the weather was sunny and warm, Dorothy, Cathy and I went swimming at Waterworks Park. We took a shortcut through River Estates, crossed over the railroad tracks down a slope, and swam and basked in the sun for hours. Robbie and Juney went there just about every day with their friends, which included Dorothy's brothers. Robbie and Juney could swim and dive better than I could but I could swim across the pool and back.

On Saturdays, I slept late and in the afternoon I helped Mom with the laundry, ironing, cleaning, etc. I really didn't like ironing, but some days did ironing for other families in Silver Lake. I sprinkled the clothes, rolled them up, and filled the basket. It took hours to finish because sheets, pillow cases, and underwear were ironed, and most clothing was cotton and had to be starched. Mom and I hung curtains on large wooden stretchers and pricked our fingers on the sharp holders. We hung rugs on the clothesline to beat the dust out of them with a broom.

One day Juney came home shouting "Look at the cute puppy I bought for five dollars!" He had earned the money by setting up pins at the bowling alley for ten cents an hour. Robbie and Juney both worked diligently at the bowling alley. Dad examined the pup and remarked "This dog is sickly, so return him and get your money back. If you give me the five dollars, I'll get you a healthy puppy."

A week later, Dad brought home a small black dog that someone gave him, and Juney named the dog 'Petie'. Dad never returned Juney's hard-earned money, even though he asked for it many times. One day Petie disappeared, and Dad said he would bring home another dog soon. Actually, Petie really didn't disappear, we found out later. Petie had followed the paper boy home and was fed by him much better than he was at our home, so he stayed at the paper boy's home. Robbie had seen Petie with the paper boy sometime afterwards, and told him to keep our dog. I don't remember him ever telling the rest of the family, though, about the meeting.

In my sophomore year at Cuyahoga Falls High School, I continued making top grades and made many more friends. Robbie and Juney had average grades and also made many friends. They had some trouble keeping up with the money the nuns kept asking for, which, no doubt, was intended for worthwhile purposes. Mother got so frustrated when the boys asked for money because most of the time she didn't have any. The boys felt pressured by the nuns.

On one occasion, Mom was at her wit's end and did a foolish thing. Juney kept asking for a dime to contribute for the poor people. No one realized we were the poor people. We still never told anyone our circumstances. Perhaps if the nuns had known, they wouldn't have been so irate.

Instead of a dime in the envelope, Mom put in a button the size of a dime. The nun opened the envelope in front of the whole class, and Juney was so embarrassed. Our little brother was quiet and easygoing, but that time he really complained to Mom, "How could you embarrass me like that in front of the whole class?"

Juney already was in enough trouble with his teacher. He had a way of answering her questions with a somewhat flippant remark, which she did not appreciate. He frequently questioned some of the religious teachings. One day when she was talking about getting to heaven, Juney raised his hand and asked her if he could still get to heaven without believing everything the catechism said. She answered, "No." Juney then asked her, "What about doubting Thomas?" The nun had no answer for him.

After recess one afternoon, the whole class felt the sting of the ruler on their hands. The nun punished them for going out to recess when they were told not to, although none of the students remembered her telling them that they should skip recess.

Meanwhile, I was having fun in high school, and became extra talkative, a change from the rather quiet old me. I wasn't upset that

I couldn't sign up for cheerleader or majorette, even though I would have liked to try out for one of them. Instead I worked after school for the Davis family for a couple of hours. On Mondays, they still invited me to eat with them—dinner, consisting of creamed ham and peas on toast, leftovers from Sunday. It was the best meal I had all week. I did all the dishes and then walked home. I never had too much homework, and the subjects seemed so easy for me, so I had time to help my mother, too.

On Friday evenings, Cathy, Dorothy, and a group of girls from my class, Peggy, Bea, her sister Burdie, a few others and I, all took a bus to Kent to roller skate. We met groups of boys there and some of us paired off. The boys I skated with were just friends. We also went to the Falls Theater for Saturday night movies that weren't over until three o'clock in the morning. I fell asleep during some of them. Sometimes we ate at Kippy's when the movie ended early. Dorothy, Cathy and I walked home by ourselves if the boys didn't join us. No one seemed to worry about us—times were different then.

One day my boyfriend Kenny, from Kent, challenged me to smoke a cigarette. I didn't think smoking was a big deal, and suspected I wouldn't like it, but thought I'd take him up on his dare. No one knew how dangerous smoking was. I took one puff of Kenny's cigarette, started choking uncontrollably, and never wanted to try it again.

Our dad met some new girlfriends at work. He asked me if I would like another baby-sitting job and, of course, I said yes. I had no idea what he had in mind as he drove me to a well-to-do section of Akron. We entered the lovely home and he introduced me to the mother of two young girls, and then to the girls. Dad suggested I read the girls a story, which I did gladly. After I read a couple more children's books, I was ready to go home. I walked to the staircase and saw him kissing the mother of the girls. I was so disgusted with him, and thought, How dare he carry on his infidelities right in front of me? I knew a little more about the facts of life by this time, and felt so sorry for my mom. I said in a firm voice, "I'm ready to go home now." He knew I was disgusted with his behavior. I didn't say a word to him on the way home. If I had reprimanded him, I knew he would get angry, and

I was always a little fearful of his temper. I never told Mom about this incident. Why hurt her more?

Right before that happened, I had read my first adult book The Postman Always Rings Twice. Of course, I had read other adult books with wholesome themes, such as Twenty Thousand Leagues Under the Sea, Shakespeare, and various poetry books. The Postman Always Rings Twice was rather suggestive, and I almost understood the sexual act. Since I had never seen a man, I wasn't quite sure what exactly happens. I never really had any sexual feelings, even though some of my friends seemed to know that an orgasm is like a sneeze. We rarely talked about anything sexual. Of course, we talked about boys in general a lot, though.

I thought if men act like my dad, I was glad I was a female. I didn't know any other father who strayed like him.

Mom always sent me to the store to buy the groceries. Cathy went with me to help carry the bags. We were always a little silly, but this time it was ridiculous. Cathy dared me to jump over a large puddle (after a heavy rain) while carrying two bags of groceries. I said "Okay, I think I can make it"— the eternal optimist! I jumped and landed right in the middle of the puddle. We laughed uncontrollably, and by the time I worked my way up, Cathy had wet herself, and we both went home soaked.

On another shopping venture, the grocery bag I was carrying broke at the bottom and a dozen oranges rolled down the gutter, or toward the gutter. We retrieved most of them. They were thirty cents a dozen, and it was a good thing Mom didn't count them. Mom was easy with me, though, and rarely reprimanded me. She did slap my face once when she thought I sassed her. I never tried that again.

While Dad was in Pittsburgh visiting Pearl and Karen, he checked with the doctors at Allegheny General Hospital to see if they had found any new method to help Florrie's nervousness. He had stopped many times previously, but the doctors never had an answer. This time, however, they thought they had perfected a surgical method to separate our mother's main nerve from her womb. He was anxious to tell her the good news, so returned home immediately.

90

"Florrie, you won't believe it after all this time, but the doctors want you to have the surgery we've been awaiting for fifteen years. They want you to come to Pittsburgh next week." Mom replied, "I guess that could be arranged, since Flossie is old enough to take care of the household." Mom didn't know she would be gone from home for a month.

I was apprehensive about Mom leaving for Pittsburgh and I wanted to be with her throughout the surgery, but it wasn't to be. Dad tried to reassure my brothers and me that he would take us to see Mom after the surgery. Promises, promises, I just knew he wouldn't keep this one! The weeks slowly went by, and I was extremely busy, but never too busy to worry about my mother. I didn't realize at that age that worrying is a waste of time.

I still went to work after school, and then came home to cook, clean, wash, and pack lunches for the next day. I didn't mind all the work, but I wanted to see my mom and hear from her. All we ever heard from Dad was that the operation was successful and Mom would be coming home soon.

One evening for dinner, I fried breaded veal chops in a pan that had a swiveled broken handle, made mashed potatoes, gravy, and green beans. Just as I was going to serve the veal chops, the pan turned over and deposited them on the floor. I hurriedly picked them up and put them on a plate. The floor was clean, and I took it for granted that no one would care as long as they could enjoy the succulent chops which we rarely had.

Cathy came over most evenings to help me pack the lunches, consisting of five sandwiches for Dad, three each for the boys, and one for me, plus an orange and a couple of cookies. Dad managed to get lunch meat—ham, bologna, goose liver, salami, and Dutch loaf for the week's sandwiches. When Mom was home, she usually made egg sandwiches because there was no lunch meat.

Mom was in the hospital for a month because the doctors wanted her to be strong after the surgery. Since we didn't hear from her personally all that time, I kept thinking maybe something went wrong. No one seemed to care about children's feelings, and I wondered why

Mom didn't write to us. We were so relieved when Dad left to bring her home, but I wasn't sure if I believed him. Nevertheless, this time he told the truth. When a person consistently breaks promises, it's hard to believe anything he says.

Mom felt rather well when she arrived home, and, of course, we were ecstatic to see her. It took her a few weeks to get back to normal, and she was happy the nervousness disappeared. What wonders doctors can perform! I thanked God that He gave the doctors brains to perform the delicate surgery, and guided their hands.

The last day of school, Cathy, Dorothy and I again went to the gorge for a picnic and fun explorations. While we were walking, we noticed that there was a snake crawling along on the pipe, and since we were afraid of them, we quickly turned around.

All three of us made a lot of clothes that summer, particularly skirts that were gathered at the waist, called dirndle skirts, with white gathered necklines on the blouse decorated with matching skirt material. We continued doing most fun events together, but it never upset any of us if one of us was left out or declined. We called ourselves "The Three Musketeers" after the movie of the same name.

Right before the junior year started, Mom and I witnessed an event we would remember all our lives. I was sitting on the couch in the living room about four o'clock in the afternoon when I heard an eerie sound. I knew it was storming but decided to get up and look out the door. It became very dark, and suddenly I saw a funnel midst the darkness. I called Mom to see it. Mom said, "I think that's a tornado," just as it passed by our home and swirled up Vincent Street toward Silver Lake. Luckily, it traveled up the middle of the street most of the way and only knocked down some telephone poles in Silver Lake. No one was injured. I figured our guardian angels were watching over us once again. I never believed that God caused any disasters, only that nature did. God created nature, and it was fickle.

CHAPTER 16—Francis' Second Infidelity

Dad was disillusioned about working at Firestone, at least that's what he said. He wanted to make more money and always liked driving, so he obtained a new job driving a truck long distance. He was gone two or three weeks at a time, and the food pantry was scarce again. Some days Cathy or Dorothy would invite me to their homes for dinner. Cathy's mother made stuffed noodles which I had never before tasted, and Dorothy's mom made scrumptious apple pies. I looked forward to their invitations.

After school started, I started thinking about my sixteenth birthday. Not that I ever had a party, but Mom baked a cake, though, when she had the ingredients. My favorite cake has always been chocolate, but banana cake is a close second. Mom had the best recipe for banana cake and baked it for special occasions. I planned to get a job other than baby sitting or housework so we could have more food and cake.

I took Latin again in my junior year because I became rather fluent in reading and understanding it. Behind me in Latin class sat one of the kindest boys in our whole class, David Sanders, who became the future mayor of Cuyahoga Falls. Somehow I felt that he would amount to something in later years. I enjoyed conversing with him and several other boys in our class. There were a few who were very easy to talk to as friends. I had fun talking and giggling with Peggy Jackson, and many others.

The week of October after I turned sixteen, I took a bus downtown to apply for a job in several department stores. I inquired at Byron's, the first store I approached after stepping off the bus, and they said, "When can you start—we need a clerk for the purse department?"

"Right away," I replied.

When Saturday arrived, I was ready and willing to start the new job selling purses. Perhaps I thought I would like selling because my dad was so good at it. Right away, I discovered that I did not like selling purses. I really didn't like their stock of purses, and wished I could be the buyer. It was hard selling purses I didn't like to customers in good faith. But sell I did, and worked not only on Saturdays, but two days a week after school. The extra money helped a little. I always gave Mom most of my earnings, and kept just enough for transportation and essentials.

Before Christmas, I was transferred to the sportswear department at Byron's and to my astonishment, won $100 commission for selling the most clothing in the department. Meanwhile, Robert (Robbie decided he wanted to be called Robert) and Juney were still working hard at the bowling alley, jumping two alleys at a time, saving money for boots. For lunch on Saturdays, they sometimes bought a Pepsi for and two doughnuts for a nickel each.

The walk to and from the bowling alley was about two and a half miles, and walking that winter was hazardous for people who had the proper clothing and accessories, let alone for the boys who didn't even have boots. They could hardly get their feet through the high drifts of snow and the blizzards nearly froze their bodies. One blustery day with snow up to Juney's knees, he felt that his feet were frozen after walking home. He reclined on Mom's bed and fell asleep. When he awakened, his feet were itching, bleeding, and sticking to the sheets. The next day he bought the badly needed boots. However, he didn't own them for long. Dad borrowed Juney's boots and never returned them or the money Juney paid for them. Juney started comparing his Dad to a cobra - he never knew when he was going to strike!

One day, Dad found out that Robert and some of his friends were climbing on boxcars parked on the railroad tracks. Juney was not involved. Dad took them both down the basement, beat Robert and whacked Juney. Juney hated him, and, at that moment would have liked to kill him.

Two hours later, Dad took Juney to Levinson's for some new school clothes. He chose the clothing for Juney, much to his son's protest. Juney knew that the kids at school would make fun of the salt and pepper colored railroad worker's pants, and they did.

Florrie wondered where Francis was when he didn't come home for over a month. She usually heard from him every two or three weeks. Food was getting scarce again, the bills were due, and there wasn't enough money to pay for much of anything. The kids' money didn't cover the necessities of life. She was thinking of going to the police because she had a dream that Francis was in an accident. Sometimes her dreams came true.

A policeman came to our front door the next day and informed Mom that her husband was in a hospital in Buffalo, New York, after having been in a trucking accident. He had skidded on the highway and the truck overturned. The policeman's report said Francis had amnesia, but somehow they traced him to Vincent Street.

Mom deliberated how to retrieve him. She decided that taking a bus to Buffalo might make her nervous and felt that she really needed to stay with the boys. She asked me if I would mind going to fetch my dad. I really wasn't thrilled at the prospect of going to a strange city by myself, but wasn't afraid because I felt my guardian angel would protect me. That evening I boarded the Greyhound bus bound for Buffalo. I took a book to read on the way. The bus made several stops until arriving in Buffalo at three o'clock in the morning.

I was not able to sleep on the bus and felt tired after getting off. It was startling to see that the bus station was filled with transients. Some of them stared at me, but I kept my nose in the book I was reading until dawn broke. I asked for directions to the hospital and boarded a trolley that passed by the bus terminal at six o'clock in the morning. When arrived at the hospital and I entered my dad's room, he recognized me immediately. He said he didn't remember anyone else. I found that hard to believe.

We checked out of the hospital, took a trolley to the train depot, and were en route to Akron via Steubenville, Ohio. He was unusually quiet until we approached Steubenville. Then he told me emphatically that he intended to get off in Steubenville because he had to attend to some business in that city. I pleaded, "Please, Dad, don't do that— Mom will be so upset if you don't return home with me. If you insist on getting off, I'll go with you."

He shouted, "No, absolutely not, it's too dangerous in Steubenville for a young girl like you!" I begged him again not to depart, but to no avail. He exited the train, and I continued home by myself. I took the bus home, and noticed the look of anguish and disappointment on Mom's face when she saw I was alone. All I could tell her was that he exited the train in Steubenville.

A week or so passed when we heard another knock on the front door. It wasn't the police this time, but a woman carrying a two-month-old baby with a young girl standing by her side. I happened to open the door and she informed me that she was looking for her husband, Francis Hanocek. Her name was Ellen, and the girl's name was Carmen. I stood there in shock and called Mom. She invited them into the living room, and we discussed this bizarre situation. Mom couldn't believe what Ellen was saying because she and Francis were not divorced—how could he have done this? She tried not to display her anger in front of Ellen, although it was difficult to hide. She told her about the accident and Francis' amnesia and convinced her we didn't know exactly where he was. Perhaps in Steubenville?

Ellen told her story. She said Francis told her he was divorced, and had three children. That's how she found us. She whispered that Carmen was not Francis' child, but she told Carmen he was in order to spare her the shame of not knowing her real father. At first, Ellen and Francis lived in Cleveland, and Carmen joined them. Carmen was born in January 1937 and had been living in a foster home for several years.

Their third-floor apartment in Cleveland began getting crowded with one baby after another. Carmen managed to escape all the commotion by riding streetcars for a nickel, with a transfer, throughout the Cleveland area.

When Francis was gone for weeks at a time, Ellen had to drag all three babies to the grocery store in a wagon. It must have been difficult to get three babies and groceries up and down the stairs.

The occupants of the apartment complex were all friendly and enjoyed visiting each other until they heard the thump, thump, thump of Francis' feet coming up the stairs. Everyone became quiet. They had heard the shouting arguments of Francis and Ellen, and were afraid of his temper. After Francis and Ellen left Cleveland, they moved into a basement home in the Medina area that Francis had built. Francis assured them he would eventually build the rest of the house. They also were in need of food and money.

Francis had met Ellen in 1936 when he was working for the WPA in Ohio. He had lunch at the Garden Grille on Main Street in Akron where she worked. After he ate, he walked back into the kitchen and talked to all the waitresses, including Ellen. He thought she was pretty, and asked her out. He dated her for a short while but she didn't see him again until 1941, after our family moved to Akron. All along, we thought we moved here because of his job at Firestone, but should have guessed there was yet another woman.

After Ellen, Carmen and the baby left, Mom and I were feeling anger, hurt, resentment and disappointment. We both cried and tried to comfort each other. Even though we were accustomed to his abandonment, we hadn't expected this, the ultimate deception. We kept it all within our immediate family.

My mind kept swirling like confetti dropped from a building going in every direction. Why did this happen? What compelled dad to think he needed another woman in his life? Does he have a tumor on his brain or does he know exactly what he is doing? Does he realize how he has hurt our mother, our rock in the storm?

Our dad arrived home a week or two afterwards without any explanation as to where he had been and what he'd been doing. He blamed it all on a tumor on his brain, which he suspected triggered his unwarranted behavior, and his amnesia. Mom confronted him with the fact that Ellen visited us, and Dad admitted he married her some time before the accident and that Carmen was not his daughter. He said he told Ellen he was divorced. When Mom said that was a lie, he found a paper he had stashed away that he thought exonerated him, a Mexican divorce certificate which he had obtained without Mom's permission. We always questioned the validity of the certificate. I know Mom never thought of herself as divorced.

Dad built a two-car garage behind our house. He decided to use that space for a car repair business. He had found a partner who knew how to paint and repair automobiles. He borrowed money from me which he never repaid. Some of the $1,000 he borrowed was used to support the other two families.

During that summer when I was sixteen, he built an additional room on the side of our home and an enclosed porch and the start of a bathroom in back which he never completely finished. Sometimes it amazed me how he knew how to do all these things, although he was like a jack of all trades and master of none. He harassed the boys into digging the foundation for the addition.

We had a little dog named "Tiny" that Dad had brought home a year after Petie's supposed disappearance, who delighted in running up and down the excavation. We found out later that Petie actually may have been Ellen and Francis' family dog, because their dog named Petie disappeared about the same time Francis brought us the dog he called Petie.

Robert and Juney carried many heavy wheelbarrows of cement while Tiny followed them. Tiny also followed me down the street when I visited Cathy and Dorothy's homes. Of all the dogs we had, Tiny was our favorite.

The garage was a busy place for a while with painting and repairing other people's vehicles. As usual, though, the business failed. Francis's partner had left his old car in the garage, and Robert and Juney had fun taking it out for a spin. One day Robert and Eddie, one of his friends, drove the car around the loop, turned the corner too fast, and hit a tree. The partner came back to get his car, and found it in rather bad shape, but he was able to drive it away and did not make a scene about it.

One of Juney's friends, Paul Swanson, Dorothy's brother, made some offensive remarks about Francis and the garage, so Juney and Paul had a fist fight. Juney told Paul never to come down our part of street or cross over it again. Paul avoided our section of Vincent Street like the plague after that episode.

A bill collector (there were many) came to collect the money owed to Levinson's for Juney's pants, and threatened Juney, since his name was Francis Hanocek. Prior to that, a nasty letter had been sent in his name. The bill collector tried to take Juney's bicycle for payment and Juney fought him, trying to pull the bicycle out of his grasp, but since the collector was much bigger than him, the collector won. He took the bike to somewhere on Front Street. Juney followed him and retrieved his bike, after finally convincing the collector he was the wrong Francis Hanocek.

Mom always tried to hide from the bill collectors. She got a little panicky when the house payment was due and she didn't have the money. The bank was rather lenient, though, saying if she paid at least a couple dollars each month, they would not foreclose. That's what saved us from losing our home because Mom always paid a small amount of the mortgage each month.

Mom was always kind, and people perceived her kindness and dependability. She gave food to hobos who knocked on our back door even if it was just a hard crust of bread. She believed in sharing with those poorer than us. She never let the hobos inside our home, though. They were always grateful for the little she could give them. As I recall, there were not that many transients in Cuyahoga Falls.

It was junior prom time. My friend, Donna Prescott, had asked a young man to go with her to the prom. Donna and I had become good friends the past year and she wanted me to find a date to accompany her and her date, a senior who had his own car. I was uncertain about asking anyone, and thought it would be proper only if someone asked me. Heather begged me until I said, "Yes, but right now I just like the boys as friends. I guess I could ask Aaron who sits behind me in

English class. He's very friendly and a gentleman." Donna begged, "Oh, please ask him."

The next day, with all the nerve I could muster, I asked Aaron and he said yes. I wanted to buy a new dress for this special occasion, and had fun shopping that weekend. I found a light blue dress made of lace that fit me just right and wasn't too expensive at Polsky's downtown.

The next Monday while in English class, I overheard my English teacher talking to another teacher about the fact that I had asked Aaron to the prom. She said, "It's too bad that Flossie asked Aaron, because he has been nominated for king of the junior prom." I really didn't understand exactly what she meant by that remark, but thought it inappropriate. I was a little miffed at what she said because I never gave her any trouble, and was one of the top students in her class. Surely she didn't think that I wasn't good enough for the king! I knew better, and I had great self-esteem. I found out that sometimes it doesn't matter how good a person you are, or how kind or smart you are, there will always be someone who doesn't like you. The secret to life is not to take it personally. That has always been the motto I live by.

The night of the prom, my hair turned out beautiful, and I thought I looked gorgeous in my lovely blue dress. I had naturally curly, dishwater blonde hair and it was down to my shoulders. I actually felt beautiful with make-up on and new shoes and an evening purse. You know, I didn't always feel beautiful, and I didn't think I was the most adorable girl in the world, but I thought I was attractive and different looking. I have always liked and loved myself - and that is the basis for liking and loving others. It follows that I have always thought different looking women were beautiful, women who had features that were not always perfect but attractive along with their smile. I tend to notice their smiles the most or like the tone of their voices. My favorite movie star was Ann Sheridan who was attractive and had a dulcet tone in her voice. I thought Rock Hudson and Tyrone Power were very handsome but I liked their voices the most.

On prom night, Donna's date picked her up and then Aaron and me. Aaron looked handsome in his suit. Both young men brought us carnation corsages. Aaron was chosen king at the dance, and I felt happy about that. As we danced, I knew we made a good-looking couple. I rather wished I liked him more than a friend, but that's all there was to the relationship. We had a good time. I wish, in retrospect, I had told Aaron what a nice person he was—perhaps the teacher's remark did have a tad to do with my reticence that evening.

Donna invited me to stay overnight at her home. She had wonderful parents, and I especially liked her father. He seemed gentle and kind, and was slow-spoken with a deep voice. Her mother was a good cook and sometimes I ate dinner with them. Donna had dark wavy hair, was slim, bright, and in my opinion, one of the best looking girls in our class. Most of all, I enjoyed her sense of humor, and we giggled and laughed half the night when I stayed over. Her parents put up with all that nonsense.

Their next door neighbors had a nine-year-old girl named Sally. They needed someone to help get her ready for school temporarily until the end of the school year. For a few weeks, I slept on the cot in their sun room, and struggled to get Sally ready for school on time. She was having a problem with bed wetting, so she needed a bath every morning. I ran the water for her, and let her bathe herself while I packed lunches and got ready for school myself. She ultimately fell asleep in the tub every day, so we were always rushing. I made sure she was never late for school. There was some dysfunction in the family with two women living there and one husband. But it was none of my business. We had enough dysfunction in our immediate family.

When Dad finished our new living room, the plaster looked rather crude and he had painted it pink. I liked the color pink and have always liked it. However, in this 2010 day and age, most people do not choose pink as a living room color – earth tones are most popular. At least the new room gave us more space but Mom still slept in the old living room. Mom and I always imagined and talked about having the dining room become a real dining room with a mahogany table and chairs and a matching hatch with shelves for matching china, and pretty decorative plates. Our dishes were mismatched but we did not dwell on any of that. It is fun to dream about better things as long as one does not feel disappointed at the way things really are, and it is best to pursue the dreams if possible. Mom used the dining room for sewing and ironing. We ate in the breakfast nook that Dad built which was cozy and adequate and never complained.

Donna stayed overnight once with me. I knew my room was shabby compared to hers but I was not ashamed of my surroundings. I just thought it was more fun at her house because they had a lot of food, and her brother was away at college. Cathy and Dorothy stayed overnight with me a few times but I felt more at ease with them since their homes were similar to mine.

Donna had a baby grand piano and could play with all kinds of music. She had taken piano lessons for seven years. At lunch time at school, she played Boogie-Woogie while everyone danced, and she became quite popular.

We also started going roller-skating at East Market Gardens once a week. Donna was an excellent skater, and could do the "Flea Hop" like a pro. On the other hand, I was just an average roller-skater. I was never jealous of Donna, but enjoyed going roller-skating with the old crowd a little more because they also were average skaters. We could pair off with one another and skate together. Donna was always asked to skate more often than I was since she could do all the dances.

I continued working at Byron's that summer. Dad was gone part of the time with Pearl and part of the time with Ellen. Ellen was pregnant again, although Mom and I were unaware of it. He apparently convinced himself that he was divorced from Mom, but still came crying asking for forgiveness. What a hypocrite!

Francis legally adopted Carmen, and until she was about forty, she believed she was Francis' biological daughter. He repeatedly told Ellen and their family about his experiences in an orphanage, along with his brothers and sisters. To my knowledge and the rest of the Hanocek cousins, that was a lie. He also told Juney once or twice that he had been in an orphanage. Anything is possible, and perhaps he was in the orphanage on Troy Hill for a few days, or weeks. It seems unlikely, though, since none of his siblings ever talked about that. He also told Ellen and family that when his father, John, passed away, the sons dismantled his furniture because John hid money in various couches and furniture—he didn't trust banks. That also was a lie, according to my Hanocek cousins who lived close by on Goettman St. and were there when Grandpa John passed away.

Francis made up so many stories, no one ever knew what to believe. He did do one good thing for Carmen. He insisted she attend a Catholic school because she was having trouble reading. Francis couldn't bear the thought of that. He was secretly comparing her and his other children with Ellen, to our family. I was always the head of the class, and he liked perfection, although so imperfect himself. The nun at the Catholic school discovered that Carmen was dyslexic and solved the problem. Carmen loved that nun and thanked Francis for helping her. However, there were times when she became so angry with him that she hit him or threw things at him. He tolerated her spunkiness. Carmen was a very pretty young girl, and Francis derived pleasure in showing her off, especially after her reading problem was corrected.

Ellen kept having more babies as the years went by and perhaps she didn't really want any more, but Francis wouldn't use protection because it diminished his pleasure. Always thinking of himself, that was my dad!

My closet and room needed papering or painting, and Dad said he would help me. I tried to paper the closet myself and that turned out to be a disaster. My room was always the hottest in the summer, facing the sun all afternoon. Besides the intense heat, the paste on the wallpaper would not stick in the closet and kept falling on top of my head. I gave up and admitted I could not hang wallpaper. Dad never redecorated my room, but I still enjoyed reading, writing and relaxing there when the weather was tolerable.

CHAPTER 17—Fending for Ourselves

I had worked at Byron's all summer. After my senior year started, I changed jobs because I wanted more experience in secretarial work. After all, I was the top typing and shorthand student in my class. I could type 100 words a minute, and take dictation at 120 words a minute. I obtained a typing job at Catholic Service League on Portage Trail typing up case histories. I found out there were many families more dysfunctional than mine. Working there saved bus money, since I could walk there after school, and walk home from there three days a week.

The other two days, Donna and I usually stopped at the pharmacy on the corner to get a cherry coke. Sometimes Peggy Jackson walked home with us. She and I always enjoyed each other's company. After walking Donna home, we continued on together to Norwalk Ave. where Peggy lived and from Norwalk, I walked to Hudson Drive and crossed the tracks to Vincent Street.

Other days, Shirley Selby, who lived on Bailey Rd., joined us. We all chatted on the way home. We still went in groups on the weekends to skate in Kent or Ravenna. The group usually consisted of Cathy, Dorothy, Peggy, her sister Pud, Burdie Cardwell and her sister, Bea, and me. Shirley accompanied us occasionally. We skated with boys we knew and sometimes they brought us home. There was one boy who seemed to like me, Vincent Orlando, and he was nice, but I thought of him as just a friend. On the other hand, Burdie and Norman were a pair.

Peggy's grandfather, who owned a lumberyard, was also an inventor. He designed the roller coasters that were built in Ohio. The one he built at Silver Lake Park had been torn down long before we moved to Cuyahoga Falls. People from the area formerly took streetcars to get to Silver Lake Amusement Park.

Dorothy and I bought some green jodphurs which were popular for horseback riding and general wear. We went to one of the riding farms, and thought it was easy to ride a horse. The horses we rode were rather old and not cantankerous.

Donna and I went riding the next week, but had an entirely different experience. We were trotting along and thought we'd try galloping. Everything was fine until my horse tripped in a hole in the dirt road, sending me over his head in a somersault. I landed on my backside, stunned that this could happen. My horse side-stepped me, or I could have gotten hurt. This was another time my angel was watching over me. Donna and I could hardly stop laughing. Life certainly was a new adventure every day.

Tom Schaefer, a classmate, asked me out on a double date along with his friend, Foozie Tides and his date. We went to the movies in Foozie's car. Tom was a very congenial person and I liked him as a friend. He asked me to his home for dinner, which I enjoyed thoroughly. His parents were friendly and seemed to like me. We dated for a while, until Tom decided to join the army. I wrote to him and to a few other soldiers, some I knew and some I didn't know. Most of us girls understood how lonely it must be for the young men to be so far from home, and wanted to cheer them. They all wrote that they had good food, and I was happy about that, even though I didn't always have what I would have liked to eat, especially since we only had meat when Dad was home, which wasn't often. I continued praying for the soldiers and for the war to end.

Dad was doing odd jobs, and took Robert and Juney to New Philadelphia with him one cold winter day. They weren't dressed appropriately for the frigid weather and had nothing to eat that whole day. They shivered in the house where they were repairing a furnace. Instead of bringing them home, he put them on a bus to Akron, and they waited a long time in the freezing cold for the Cuyahoga Falls bus. Francis drove back to Medina and his family there.

The rationing of sugar, gasoline, meat, paper and nylons, among other things, was still in effect. Girls wore leg make-up that tended to streak, or socks, and unpolished saddle shoes, or penny loafers. We buttoned our cardigan sweaters and turned them backwards. Pleated skirts were the rage. Boys wore argyle socks. Tangee and Taboo lipstick, pancake make-up, and Evening in Paris perfume were popular. Some of the girls were sporting home permanents but I still had naturally curly hair. My hair sometimes looked a little straggly when the weather was damp and rainy. We put our hair up in bobbie pins, a nightly ritual. The pins dug into my scalp, but the results were remarkable.

Robert was a freshman when I was a senior. I was so proud of him. He was six feet tall, very handsome, and an excellent football player. He played both defensive and offensive tackle. We became good friends, and walked together to some youth group dances at St. Joseph's. We actually appreciated each other.

Juney requested that everyone call him "Frank" now and that was understandable. That way people might not connect him to Francis. It took a while to get used to and occasionally I would still call him "Juney." He also was growing into a very handsome young man. Both boys still jumped two alleys at the bowling alley to make extra money.

I started writing the gossip column for the school newspaper, The Commercialite, besides other columns. I tried not to offend anyone, and mostly asked questions. Some of the kids loved to see their name in print, and passed notes to me. I never included anything about myself, although I was mentioned in columns written by others. One column referred to my "little brown outfit" which I wore a lot. I didn't have that many clothes but enough for some variety since I made some of them myself. I especially liked to wear my brown pleated skirt and matching brown sweater. After school, I also worked at soliciting advertising.

Our literature class included a course on poetry. I always enjoyed writing and poetry and put together scrapbooks of my favorite poems and poets, some as class assignments. My favorite poem was "Trees" by Joyce Kilmer, and I also delighted in "Abou Ben Adhem" by Leigh Hunt. The third year of Latin helped me to understand the Latin used in Catholic churches, and I could speak Latin fluently that year. Of course, most people didn't fully understand what was being said and chanted in church, especially non-Catholics. The Gregorian chant overwhelmed my heart and soul, and I felt closer to God. When the church eventually changed its liturgy to English, most people thought it was a good idea, but there were some diehard Catholics who objected. I have to admit that at first I questioned the change. As with everything else, I became accustomed to the English masses.

Donna asked me to attend her Baptist church with her. I was always curious to see other denominational services, so I accepted. What a shock it was, for although we worship the same God, the Baptists were very vocal and jumped up and down throughout the service shouting "Praise the Lord." Donna accompanied me to Mass at St. Joseph's a week later. She thought it was much different, too. I went to confession once a month, but I never confessed that I went to a Baptist church, because I didn't see anything wrong with that. Common sense told me it was a proper thing to do, and years later, churches were encouraged to unify. Some church rules change as time goes by.

A rather sparse Christmas came and went that year. However, we always looked forward to gifts that Aunt Betty and Uncle Pat sent us. That was always the brightest spot at Christmas. Sometimes Mom peeked at them ahead of time. Aunt Betty, bless her heart, remembered all the nieces and nephews each year, no matter what tragedies she had. She continued having miscarriages.

Dorothy, Cathy and I went ice skating frequently at Silver Lake when it was frozen over. I could ice skate with more ease as compared to roller-skating. Although I was no expert, I could do a figure eight. One day while I was skating near the island away from the shore, someone yelled, "The ice is too thin out here." I immediately skated back and just as I skated safely out of harm's way, a skater fell in the water. I watched him being rescued immediately. My angel's watching again, I thought and said a prayer of thanks.

Because of the paper shortage, our class voted not to have a yearbook. To this day, I wish we had voted otherwise. I would have liked to work on it. We had senior pictures taken and exchanged them. I put them in a scrapbook, and it's interesting to read what some classmates wrote. A comment by one of the boys is one I have always cherished. He wrote "To the most cheerful girl in our class." Little did he know what was going on behind the scene. No matter what, I was happy and cheerful—it was my nature. If I had trauma going on at home, I never talked about it except once. And I regretted that I did. I confided to Donna that my dad had another family—I begged her not to tell anyone and she agreed. I should have guessed that she would tell her mother. The word spread all over the factory where she worked. I was disappointed, to say the least, that Donna betrayed my confidence. I forgave her the indiscretion, and we remained good friends, although I never confided in her again.

Shortly before graduation, my friend and classmate, Burdie Cardwell, contracted chicken pox and three weeks later passed away from Bright's disease, an inflammatory kidney disease. It seemed unbelievable, and our group and all our classmates were saddened. Burdie's family took a long time to recover from this tragedy. Her mother became a Jehovah's Witness and went door to door promoting that religion. We all felt sorry for Bea, her sister, and for her whole family.

Senior prom time was approaching. Luck had it that Tom was home on leave from the army, and asked me to the prom. I said yes and went shopping for a fancy dress. I found a black formal with a large white collar trimmed in lace. Donna was voted prom queen, and I was delighted for her. She was the prettiest girl in the class, in my opinion, and evidently others.

The night of the prom, Tom and Foozie picked me up. Tom brought a corsage of white carnations. I felt pretty, and knew Tom thought so, too. He was very attentive, and we danced the whole evening. Afterwards, we went out to eat, and after that, Foozie parked his car in an out-of-the-way parking lot. Tom repeatedly kissed me. I had thought I liked him somewhat, but felt smothered. At the end of the evening, I mentioned that I really didn't want to date him again. Maybe that sounds cruel, but I have always believed in being honest. I didn't want to lead anyone on where I didn't want to go. I wondered if I ever would feel at ease with men.

A scout from the General Tire & Rubber Company visited our commercial classes, and asked for the top student. They asked me a few questions, and told me I was hired for a job that would be available in a few weeks, a private secretary for the Comptroller. That was fortunate for me since I knew I had to help support our family. They told me that I could start after graduation. I would have preferred to go to college, but even if I had received a scholarship, wouldn't have been able to accept it.

I graduated eleventh in my class (the first ten received scholarships) with an average of 3.492 out of 4 points only because I received a 'G' for good in gym. Every other grade was an 'E' for excellent. Miss Fryman didn't like me that much because I couldn't hit the ball when we played baseball for gym credit. Other than that, I excelled in all other aspects of gym class. I looked at the whole picture, and knew what happened was for the best in the long run.

The last day of school, Dorothy, Cathy and I packed our lunches and took our usual trek through the gorge. It was a warm, sunny day and we took pictures of the waterfall, the pipes, the steps, and all the surrounding beauty that satisfied our senses. Being in the primitive natural setting was almost surreal. When walking in the gorge, the world seems at its best. To this day, I get that same perception.

Graduation day, Donna and I donned our white caps and gowns and felt we had fulfilled part of our dreams, and were looking forward to the future. We stood with pride as we sang our Alma Mater:

As we stand with heads uncovered
On this hallowed ground
Let there be in all our voices
Gratitude profound —

Alma Mater, Alma Mater
Echo far and near
Sturdy sons and loyal daughters
Hold your memory dear.

Of course, no one knows what the future will bring, but we lived our lives one day at a time, making the most of what we had. We took pictures that, when I look at them, seem like only yesterday.

Flossie's Graduation Picture - June 1945 from
Cuyahoga Falls High School.

CHAPTER 18—Supporting the Family

The next Monday, I started working at the General Tire & Rubber Company. I took two buses to get to the office off East Market Street. At first, I worked for two weeks in Mrs. Turner's training pool, because Mr. McTavish's (the Comptroller) present secretary, Anita, wasn't leaving for a month. Two weeks later, I transferred to the Comptroller's office. Mr. McTavish had a thick Scottish accent, and I had a hard time understanding the brogue. Somehow, I managed to get the letters right most of the time. If I misunderstood him, he just asked me to type the letter over. That was the easy part of the job.

Anita taught me how to type up financial statements, and that was time-consuming. I used a large typewriter to type all the numbers. If I made an error, it took a lot of erasing and correcting. Immediately I thought there must be a better way to do this. I didn't excel in typing numbers, only words, so it took extra long to type the financial statements.

After Anita left to get married, I was on my own. At last, the first month's statements were finished, but I had fear overtaking me when I thought about typing up the next month's statement. However, when I saw my paycheck, I was encouraged to forge ahead no matter what - it was for fifty dollars. That would help our family so much. I gave Mom forty dollars and kept ten dollars for expenses. It was surprising how much the $10 would buy at that time. I paid for my transportation, bought material for dresses or put needed clothing in lay away and paid for entertainment.

Mr. McTavish had three assistants, two in one office, and Mr. Knapp, who sat behind my desk which was right outside Mr. McTavish's office. Lyle Knapp and I conversed a lot that summer when the work was lighter. The yearly statements had been typed and sent, and he told me about his daughter, Kathy Sue. He was devoted to her and to his wife, and I admired that. He listened to my adventures, although I never confided in him about my Dad.

Ian and Jasper were in a separate office behind Mr. McTavish's. I sometimes took dictation from them, but mostly typed up financial statements. Ian took pity on me, since I complained about the lengthy statements the first couple of months. He devised new financial statements on regular 8 ½ by 11 inch paper which I typed, and ran off on the ditto machine. I thanked God for that each month, and it was a lifesaver as far as I was concerned. Ian was unique, and I couldn't help notice that he wore the same suit every day, month after month, and year after year. Jasper was very friendly and easy to get along with, also. I became friends with everyone in the accounting department, especially Mary Marsala. Even though she was older than I was, we enjoyed each other's company, and ate lunch together in the cafeteria once a week.

Dorothy started working for Mr. Becker in the accounting department, and we both sought transportation to work. Mr. Corey from Silver Lake worked at General, too, and, since he passed our homes on the way to work, we asked him if we could ride with him for a minimal fee. He agreed, and thus began the saga of rushing around to be ready on time. For some reason or other, when I knew I could sleep in later, I overdid it, and was always scurrying around to be ready when Mr. Corey arrived.

One snowy, icy, winter day, as we were driving down Brittain Road, we hit a patch of ice at the top of the hill and Mr. Corey banged into the curb all the way down to keep control. I believe that encounter started my fear of driving in bad weather in anyone's car. Mr. Corey didn't seem too shaken up when we slid.

Dorothy and I joined a company bowling league, and we took the bus home every Tuesday afterwards. My average was only 120, but once in a while I bowled a high game. I never improved on the 120 average, though, but it was fun trying.

General Tire was a good company to work for, and had employee Christmas parties every year. One of the messenger boys, named Bob, started conversing with me every day as he delivered mail. Bob was tall, dark, and rather handsome. He asked me out on a date and we went to a movie and stopped at Swenson's for a burger. We also went to a dance, but he was just a friend, and the relationship went nowhere. I liked the fact that he was very much a gentleman.

In the spring, the company decided to hold an employee beauty contest. Since I was the only young girl in my department, Lyle, and all the other men, Ian, Jasper, and Ron Logan more or less begged me to be a contestant. I said at first, "No way, I don't want to do that!" All the other departments had several entrants, especially Mr. Becker's. So Lyle and the others kept talking about it and repeatedly asked me to participate. I finally gave in, mostly because Dorothy cooperated. I knew I'd feel uncomfortable in my two-piece white bathing suit parading in front of the judges and all the older men since I was very modest. Our family never walked around unclothed.

I weighed 117 pounds and was very thin, except top-heavy. Boys had been ogling me since the eighth grade. That was another reason I didn't want to be in the contest. I was self-conscious of my endowment. As the contestants walked around in a circle in an upstairs room in front of the judges, I could tell they were ogling all twenty of us.

After the voting took place, I was awarded a Third Place ribbon. A picture was taken of all of the contestants while I deliberately hid behind Dorothy. I was very uncomfortable with all the hooting and whistling.

It was fine when Dorothy, Cathy and I took pictures of each other posing in our bathing suits but another story when stared at by men. But we got through it, and they never had another beauty contest there. One interesting thing about the contest was that Evelyn Lane was awarded second place and later on she became my cousin by marriage.

The age of eighteen became a soiree for me, date after date with so many different young men, coincidentally most of them named Bob. Some of them I dated only twice, and just thought of them as friends. A redhead from Mantua intrigued me, but I had a feeling he already had a girlfriend. I didn't see him after three dates. Then there was Gary, the Gary of the caramel episode. I just went out with him to have a fun time dancing, or movie, or out to eat. He, like all the others, had been gentlemanly until the night of the caramels. We were going to a fancy dress-up ball, and he brought me a corsage which I pinned on my black and white formal. Frank was sitting in the living room and offered Gary some caramels, which were a luxury for us. Gary snickered, and replied "Who would stoop so low to eat caramels?" Frank thought, Well, hoity-toity to you, too, or words to that effect and immediately disliked Gary.

I just passed off the remark, and enjoyed the evening dancing at the ball. When we arrived home, Gary parked his car in the driveway and kissed me a couple of times. I had been dating him for about a month, but there was no romantic feeling. He asked me an unprecedented question, "How about it?"

I said, "How about what?"

He replied, "You know, what you do with others!"

Irate, I replied, "I don't do anything with anybody. I won't be going out with you again." I stormed out of the car, slammed the door, and ran into the house. That was the last of Gary.

Eighteen was also a discovery time for me. At puberty, I never went through personality changes like most girls seem to, and I didn't do that at eighteen, either, but I started thinking seriously about what direction I was heading, and what I was going to do with my life. I knew I'd keep working until our family situation improved. Dad was hardly ever around, and I really didn't miss him although I sensed that Mom did.

The last time Dad had shown any affection for me was the year when I had a bladder and kidney infection and could have died. I had fever and chills and my stomach was swollen up like a balloon. He climbed beside me in bed, and put his arm around me and said he loved me. He had never touched me sexually but since he brushed my breasts as his arm encircled me, as sick as I was, I exclaimed, "Don't ever do that again!" In retrospect, I don't really think he meant to touch me. He was very worried about me, because the doctor whom they finally called mentioned that I had to drink a gallon of water that night or I might not live. Mom filled a gallon jug with water and both Mom and Dad kept checking on me to make sure I drank it all, for my kidneys were locked. Somehow I forced myself to keep drinking. I broke out in a cold sweat, and by morning the fever was down, and I finally was able to urinate. In a few days I felt like my old self, and never had any similar problem again.

Frank was fourteen and had been asking for a bow and arrow. Dad promised he would buy one. Frank was hoping he might get it after Francis returned home from one of his trips.

World War II was still in progress, so one day when Frank looked up, he saw a P-40 flying overhead, with smoke enveloping the tail; next a parachute landed on the east side across Bailey Road. As Frank was running up Front Street to check it out, he saw Francis's truck approaching. He ran back home in anticipation of receiving the long awaited bow and arrow. Not this time! He knew it was time to realize that his dad rarely kept any promises.

When Frank played baseball for St. Joseph's school in the eighth grade, he was an excellent pitcher that he won all of his games. Immediately before pitching the championship game, the priest approached him and asked, "Are you pitching tonight, Hanocek?"

Frank answered, "Yes."

The priest replied, sarcastically, "I bet they knock you out of the box."

That remark didn't ruffle Frank, since he knew the priest didn't like him. He was determined to do even better than his best after that. He struck out most of the batters on the other team, hit a home run, and St. Joseph's went undefeated. The Akron Beacon Journal wrote an article praising Frank's pitching.

Robert, at sixteen, was very athletic and strong. He started boxing at the Akron Armory downtown on the weekends. I watched all his boxing matches with trepidation—I didn't want him to get hurt. Mom never attended any of the matches, although she went with me to two of his football games. Fortunately, he won all of his matches by a knockout, until months later when he was knocked out. He wisely decided to quit boxing since he didn't want to lose any of his senses.

Francis never went to any of his children's activities. He thought football was a baby sport when it actually builds character. The boys learned to appreciate anything that built character because their father was a poor example, and they never wanted to be like him.

When Francis still worked on our home, he always forced the boys to shovel the dirt for the two storm cellars. They had to throw it out the windows. He applied metal lathe he had picked up at a junkyard for the bathroom, and used bricks and ugly used mortar from a bridge for the front steps and walkway. At the same time, he was also building the first story of his home in Medina. The family there kept growing. It was damp in the basement home causing the children to catch colds.

CHAPTER 19—Meeting My Husband

The young men I dated at the age of 18 and 19 were very respectful. We went to dances, movies, and/or out to eat. Evenings ended with a kiss or two, and no more was expected. Dating was filled with merriment.

The Catholic churches in our area held ecumenical dances every Friday or Saturday. My friend, Mary, who lived near the corner of Vincent Street, asked me to accompany her to some dances. We danced with each other and with different young men the first week. The second week I met Barry, who I thought might be the love of my life. I had a strange, yet familiar, nervous feeling when he asked me to dance. It was more explosive than I felt with Bobby Good in the eighth grade.

Barry asked me out that very night. He wrote down my name, address, and telephone number and said he'd call me, which he did. Some of the men I met said they would call me but did not. That is still the case in any era.

We had a movie date the next Friday evening and he met Mom, went to the movie, and to Swenson's. I had suggested Swenson's because I had enjoyed the food before at this popular drive-through restaurant.

Barry was tall, had dark wavy hair, and was very handsome. Some might say he had a baby face, but I thought he was the ultimate date. I knew immediately that I cared for him, this was not a "just a friend" feeling. He opened the car doors for me, helped me with my jacket when I wore one, and was a perfect gentleman. I could tell he cared about me, also. His kisses were tender, he was kind, but I should have known he was too good to be true.

We dated for a month when he told me he had kept something from me intentionally because he knew I was a devout Catholic. He quietly said,

"Flossie, I need to tell you something which I should have told you in the beginning of our relationship. I'm divorced and have a two year old little girl named Sandra. I'm sorry, but I had to tell you this, because I'm falling in love with you. You are so beautiful, and a beautiful person. I can't deceive you any longer."

I was numb for a moment or two. I told him I appreciated his honesty, but I wasn't sure if we should date again. He said he'd call me in a few days. He also revealed that the reason we went out only on Friday nights was that he had another girlfriend he dated on Saturdays. He would drop her, though, if I would continue seeing him.

What did I feel? Betrayal in a sense, although we had no commitment. Fear, because I was afraid to tell my mother. She would never approve of me dating a divorced man. But I was deeply in love. When Barry called me a few days later, asking whether I had made a decision, I knew I wanted to see him again.

We saw each other once or twice a week after that for several months, and when he asked me to marry him. I said, "No, I can't." After I told Mom Barry was divorced, she constantly preached her disapproval. That was the only time in my life she was a little irritating. I thought that I could never marry him, but didn't realize that there was a chance of him getting an annulment. He asked me once more a week later,

"Please, will you marry me? I love you very much."

I tried to explain how I felt, and perhaps if we waited for two years, I would be older and more mature to make that decision. He indicated he didn't want to wait. I also felt obligated to keep working to support my family until they were able to do that on their own.

Barry and I were very compatible in our dispositions, and we enjoyed the same fun activities. One evening he took me to a nightclub. I wore my dressy gray suit and fancy white blouse, we had a delicious dinner, and laughed at the comedian's jokes. We danced till the wee hours of the morning when the nightclub closed. He paid for a picture of the two of us as a remembrance. I kept praying for a solution to our dilemma.

There was another factor involved which I don't believe I ever mentioned to Barry. He had taken me to visit his mother and father in West Virginia. They were taking care of little Sandra, a darling and bright child. Barry had left her with them since he had obtained custody. He said the reason he wanted custody of Sandra was because he caught his first wife with another man. I loved Sandra right away, played with her and slept in the same room with her that weekend.

I wasn't feeling well, though, because I had been having frequent nosebleeds. While we were at a movie one night, my nose bled for two hours. The entire visit was pleasant except for Barry's dad making remarks about my abundant figure. I liked his Mom; she was very nice and a good cook.

However, the idea of becoming an instant mother at eighteen didn't thrill me. I just wasn't ready for that responsibility. If Barry had waited, perhaps it would have worked out. We dated twice a week for six months. I repeatedly said no to his marriage proposals.

He met another girl at a church dance, and told me he was dating her and me at the same time. I would not stand for that and we broke up. They were married a few months later. One has to question the good sense of ecumenical dances, for it caused some people unexpected problems when they fell in love with members of other faiths.

While I had been dating Barry, Cathy fell in love with a handsome young man named Todd, and Dorothy fell in love with David who was also good looking. We triple dated sometimes and had so much fun together. In the summer, the three of us, along with Peggy, Connie (our friend from North High School), and a few other friends rented a cottage at Portage Lakes for a week, and the guys, Barry, Todd, and David, came out to visit us in the evening. During the day we swam, went canoeing and basked in the sunshine. Shirley and some of our other girl friends visited us. What a glorious summer it was! However, all three of us, Cathy, Dorothy and I failed to marry our first true love.

Although I was devastated at first by the breakup with Barry, being resilient, I bounced back quickly. Mary and I started going to various dance halls again. One Wednesday evening in August, she literally coerced me to go to the last dance at Summit Beach. I was tired that day after work and the intense heat only added to the indecision, but I finally agreed. That was the very same night I met my future husband, Robert (Bob).

Everyone was dancing when Mary and I entered the ballroom at Summit Beach. We stood along the sidelines watching the dancers. I wore a blue satin blouse that Peggy had made for me as a gift (she was an excellent seamstress). I looked around at the young people dancing and noticed Bob who stood out in the crowd. He was tall, had brown wavy hair and was handsome. I whispered to Mary, "Do you see that guy dancing over there, the one in the gray suit? I wish he would ask me to dance."

Bob kept glancing at me. As soon as the music stopped, he walked over, introduced himself, and asked me to dance. We danced the night away to such tunes as 'Melancholy Baby' which was his favorite song. The orchestra played 'Sentimental Journey', 'I'll Get By,' 'Always' and 'Sundown'.

I became nostalgic when I heard the latter song, as it had been Barry's and my favorite song. It seems that couples usually have a favorite song that they feel is theirs alone. I felt secure, though, in Bob's arms, even though I had just met him. He seemed friendly and down to earth. He asked if he could take Mary and me home, and we agreed. Mary had danced with Bob's friend who owned a car. They dropped each of us off at our respective homes and Bob mentioned that he would be calling me.

Two weeks went by and I didn't hear from him. Oh, well, I thought. Some males say they will call but they never do. It didn't bother me. Then I saw Bob one night as I was coming home from work on the bus. He was standing on the sidewalk, recognized me and waved.

He had been waiting for a bus to West Hill where he lived on Valdes Avenue. He intended to call me, but didn't know how to spell my last name. Three weeks later, Mary and I saw him at another dance. He immediately asked me to dance and asked me for a date. The next Saturday, he took a taxi to my home and brought me flowers. A week later, Bob bought a used Plymouth car from his cousin. The car broke down constantly, but we managed to get to some dances, movies, and out to eat before it completely conked out.

Mom didn't really like Bob at first, mostly because he wasn't Catholic, but also because he liked to tease. I did notice the teasing a little, but it was all in fun, and he didn't seem to tease me as much as others. For obvious reasons, I thought that Mom would disapprove of anyone I brought home to meet her. Some, perhaps most, mothers are unwittingly like that. No one would be good enough for their offspring.

Bob took me to meet his family. I immediately felt at ease, for their home wasn't quite as nice as ours. He introduced me to his mother and father, Opie and Myrtle. Bob was the eldest of eight children, two boys and six girls. I thought his two youngest sisters were so cute. Helen had blonde curls, and Donna, the baby of the family, had red hair. Bob loved to tease them but I could tell he really loved his family.

After Bob arrived home from the service, he had no choice but to sleep on a cot that was held up by buckets in the dining room. The house was too small for so many people. Bob's family had had a hard time during the Depression, although they always had food to eat. His Grandmother and Grandfather had a garden and gave them vegetables and apples from the orchard. Donna was raised on applesauce.

Bob's dad was laid off from the Goodyear Tire & Rubber Company in 1935 and signed up for the WPA (Works Progress Administration) established by President Franklin Delano Roosevelt to work on humanitarian projects. He was rehired by Goodyear in 1939.

At the age of 18, Bob was ready to graduate from Buchtel High School but instead decided to join the three C's (Civilian Conservation Corps) to help his family survive during the Depression. He traveled by train to Black Rock, Utah, where he and other recruits built water reservoirs for sheep. After serving the-six month enlistment period, he refused reassignment, and was honorably discharged. After a year at home, he was hired in June 1941 by The B.F. Goodrich Company. He worked in the tire room as a ply boy.

He joined the Army in November 1942 and was assigned to Fort Campbell, Kentucky, for training then sent to North Africa. He was a private in the Twelfth Armored Division, but when they were ready to be shipped out for combat, he developed an infection in his big toe which required surgery. Thus he stayed behind, while most of his division was shipped out. He was then assigned to First Replacement Depot and sent to Marina de Pisa, Italy, where he worked in the post office as a mail clerk. Bob was promoted to corporal. He loved serving in Italy and the children there. He learned to speak some Italian, and handed out chocolates to them. They called out to him, "Roberto, Roberto" when he left for home after three years service: thirty- one months overseas, nineteen in North Africa, and twelve in Italy.

Corporal Robert E. Hall, U. S. Army

Bob had saved about $2,000 while in Italy, so when he arrived home he bought himself a used car, and bought his mother an expensive watch and a new washing machine. He more or less squandered the rest of the money. When I met him, he was twenty-five years old, and had had his fill of dating. He had been engaged to one girl but she broke off the engagement two months before we met. So you might say both of us were on the rebound.

There was something intangible in our feelings for one another, an affinity that kept us together. I liked Bob's family and especially little Donna, who at nine years old was the sweetest little girl. I took her to General Tire's Christmas program where she received a free toy and candy. I felt comfortable with Bob even while he flirted with most other women. It didn't really bother me because he kept telling me that he loved me. He even asked me to marry him on the second date. I didn't take him seriously and thought perhaps he was just joking.

The business course I was taking at Akron University in the evening became tiresome and did not help me with my job. One had to be cautious about walking home alone in the dark after exiting the bus. There had been stories I had heard for years about a white-haired witch that walked the railroad tracks late at night. I always ignored it until one November evening as I was approaching the tracks, I looked up, and there she was. Her white hair stuck out like a porcupine, and in the moonlight, I could see she was unkempt with a wild look in her glossy eyes. I ran home as fast as lightning and never crossed the tracks late at night again. The walk home along Front Street seemed safer.

When my dad met Bob, they were compatible. Bob actually thought he was a nice person. There was no reason to tell Bob about the other families. He wouldn't have cared about that, anyhow, just as long as we could be together.

Tonsillitis gripped me in November that year causing me to miss a few days of work. The doctor told me I needed to have a tonsillectomy. Never having had any surgery before, there was no reason to be nervous about it. After taking the bus to City Hospital, my doctor performed a local tonsillectomy. It was rather unpleasant afterwards, especially throwing up blood for hours after drinking tomato juice which stung my throat. They kept me overnight and in the morning I felt fine and packed my little suitcase and took the bus home.

The tantalizing aroma of hamburgers frying greeted me upon entering the front door. Mom discouraged me from eating something other than soft foods but I ate the hamburger regardless. That was a decision which caused regret because my throat took longer to heal, and there was much bleeding. Live and learn!

On Christmas Eve, Bob and I had fun picking out a pine tree. Our whole family had fun decorating the tree. Bob asked me to marry him again, but I just laughed at him and said it was too soon. He kept singing the song "How Soon" to me after that. He had a very good singing voice, and I loved to hear him sing.

Bob always asked Frank if he would like to borrow his car when we stayed home for the evening. He slipped him some money to go to a movie—Frank was always obliging. That way we could be alone. Mom visited with Bob for a few minutes, and then she stayed in the kitchen or went to her bedroom and read a book. I wasn't sure whether I wanted to marry Bob because I didn't know if I could trust him. Flirting with my friends was fine with me up to a point. To be married to someone who paid so much attention to other women could be a problem. Could I even trust any man? My dad was unfaithful, and I began to wonder how anyone could tell when they are dating if their intended spouse would always be faithful. Trust is an important factor when it comes to marriage.

Bob kept repeating the marriage proposal and we became engaged on Valentines Day. He gave the ring he had bought for his former fiancée. It was beautiful, but Mom thought that I shouldn't accept a secondhand ring. It really did not matter to me. There was no hurry to be married. Trust is important, and time would tell.

Mary had met Dave, her future husband, a few weeks after I started dating Bob. We double dated on weekends and went on picnics in the summer and dances in the fall. Mary and Dave were married on May 20, 1949, and moved to Florida in 1952.

During the war, I had kept in touch with Charles (Chuck), my friend from the eighth grade who had enlisted in the navy. He wrote a letter to me asking permission to visit us. It was evident from his letter that he still cared for me and also wanted to see my brothers. Bob agreed that I should see Chuck and make sure that I had no feelings for him. Chuck had always treated me with respect and there was no harm in seeing him again.

Chuck looked quite handsome in his navy uniform, and asked if he could take me to a movie and out to eat. It was pleasant conversing with him, but the mutual romantic feeling just wasn't there. When he kissed me goodnight, I told him that I felt like a traitor kissing him when I was engaged to Bob. He accepted this, and left the next day.

Bob wasn't upset that I went out with Chuck. He gave me a chance to decide who I wanted to marry. Neither of us was prepared for what was about to happen.

We had planned to visit his Grandma Zona and Grandpa Preston. He said he would pick me up at two o'clock and we would drive to Loyal Oak where they lived. They had a large home and an orchard filled mostly with apple trees.

I was ready at one o'clock when I saw a familiar car drive up in front of our home. It was Barry. I became flustered since I couldn't imagine why he would be coming to see me. He asked me to go for a ride with him. At first I declined since Bob was coming in an hour. He begged me to get in his car, saying he needed to talk to me and he would have me home in time. We drove around for about forty-five minutes. He told me he had made a mistake not waiting for me, and that he was unhappy with his marriage. He asked, "If I got a divorce, would you consider marrying me?"

My heart fluttered as I answered, "I am engaged to Bob."

Barry answered, knowingly, "I know, I've been keeping track of you. I was worried when I heard you had problems bleeding after you had your tonsils removed and lost so much weight."

I answered, "I'm feeling fine now, Barry, thank you for caring."

Barry replied, as we drove up to my home, "I'll give you some time to think it over, and call you in a week."

126

"All right, good-bye," was my only reply.

When Bob arrived a few minutes after Barry left, I told him about the encounter, and assured him I would stay with him. I knew in my heart it was the right thing to do. In the end, it all worked out the way it was predestined. Barry didn't call me the next week, but had his friend, whom I knew well, call for him. He said Barry was sorry but could not leave his wife now because he found out that she was pregnant and he would never leave his child. I was so relieved because I felt that the less complications in life, the better! I never heard from Barry again, although I saw him once after Bob and I were married. We were looking for a new car. Barry was a car salesman at a dealership in Akron and Bob insisted that we go talk to him to try to get a good deal. The meeting was uneventful, and we found a better offer elsewhere.

I was pleased with Bob's acceptance of the men in my life, but knew he was secretly jealous of Barry because he kept asking me questions about my feelings. I reassured him many times that I wouldn't change anything.

Mom started to accept Bob even though he wasn't Catholic. He complimented her when he ate with us, "That was the best spaghetti I ever ate."

"Thanks, Bob, I simmered the sauce all day."

Bob loved to eat, and we enjoyed our meals with my family. He really liked Mom and she in turn laughed at his joking.

Dad was very seldom around during this period. He and Ellen kept adding to their brood, and the strange and interesting thing is that they named some of their children with variations of some of our family names.

On one of his rare visits, he insisted on taking me to see his home, which was close to finished, with not only a basement but a first and second floor. Not wanting to argue with him and perhaps out of curiosity, I accompanied him. He actually did a better job building that home than he did on the additions to our home. Three little boys resembling him were running around. We stayed only a few minutes.

Peggy was the first of our group of girls to get married. She and Duke Wellingham were married in the fall of 1947 and moved first to Elyria and later on to Illinois.

Donna was the second of our group to tie the knot. She was going to college in Florida, and met Jared Olson there. They married and had a little girl named Kimberly. She had invited me to visit her in Miami many times. I really didn't want to travel alone, so I asked my friend, Sarah, from work if she'd like to accompany me. Bob took us to the bus depot.

The bus trip took three days and three nights without much sleep. We finally arrived in Miami, and Donna drove us to her home. Donna and Sarah got along famously, and we had a wonderful time in the sun and fun of Miami. We stayed at Donna's home and played with Kimberly. We called Dorothy and Cathy who happened to be vacationing in Miami at the same time. All five or us met at their hotel beach. Donna took us to visit her mother. That was the last time I saw Donna but her mother wrote to me until she passed away some years later. Donna had four children, two boys and two girls and soon after she and Jared divorced. Donna attended the university there and became a nurse.

Bob was waiting for Sarah and me when we arrived home. He said he had gone to a couple of dances alone while we were gone and I believed him. He also said he missed me and asked me to set a date for our marriage, but every date I mentioned didn't seem to suit him. The ultimatum was that I would break up with him if we did not decide on a date immediately. Our relationship was getting too intense – there was no intention on my part to have sex before marriage and he knew it. We agreed to marry on New Year's Eve, December 31, 1948.

In the meantime, we had an exciting time going to see the Cleveland Indians win their 1948 pennant and become Major League Champions. We went to dances, movies and wrestling matches. We were happy when we won a whole ham at one of the wrestling matches. We had a lot in common, except for liking to swim and that did not matter. Planning the marriage on New Year's Eve kept me busy looking for a gown, etc. I found the dress of my dreams with a sweetheart neckline that fit perfectly. It cost fifty dollars.

I arranged for a reception at the YWCA in downtown Akron. Aunt Betty agreed to be my matron of honor, and Bob asked my brother Robert to be best man. We found an apartment on East Avenue in Akron.

Two weeks before Christmas, Bob told me he would bring a Christmas tree for us to decorate. Saturday came but Bob never showed up. That did it! He called the next day to say he went to a dance by himself instead of bringing a tree, so I told him the wedding was off. We had already received gifts from relatives and friends, but it did not matter. Gifts can be returned. Once again, my trust in a man was broken. Love and trust have to go hand in hand. I would never want to go through what my mom did.

The week before Christmas, Bob's brother Bill called me to ask me to forgive Bob. His mother also implored me to forgive Bob and promised me that he would never deceive me again. Bob admitted he met a girl at the dance, but did nothing more than dance with her. Bill asked if he could come to pick me up and take me to their home to discuss this matter. Bob's remorse was driving them all crazy, and they believed I was the right girl for him.

I finally agreed to see Bob, mainly to please Opie, Myrtle and Bill. I prayed, Please, God, help me to make the right decision.

After Bob's apology, I forgave him. He said, "I'm so sorry. I love you, I want you, I need you and want to marry you." He had hardly slept for a week.

I lost eleven pounds and had to have my wedding dress altered. I weighed about 117 pounds again. Wedding jitters, ceremony off and on again!

Aunt Betty arrived the day before our wedding. She had bought a turquoise satin dress and hat. I had always wanted to get married in church and walk down the aisle, but that was not meant to be since Bob was not Catholic. Marriages to non-Catholics were performed in the parish house. That was another church rule which was changed a few years later.

I have to say my life with Bob has never been dull. The eve of our wedding found me running behind schedule. I didn't plan to be late, but it was the fashionable thing to do. What with Dad and Mom, Aunt Betty, Robert, Frank and me trying to occupy the bathroom the same time, no wonder we were late. Bob was even later.

We waited for an hour for him to show up. I wasn't really worried because I knew he needed to buy new shoes, a shirt and tie and had put that off until the last moment. I didn't believe after all we'd been through the past two weeks he would stand me up again. His mom and dad were waiting with us, and assured me he'd be there. He arrived smiling that sheepish smile of his when he was embarrassed.

The wedding took place as planned. Afterwards, we all went to the reception downtown. My afternoon was spent decorating and picking up the cake and making punch. Many of my relatives from Pittsburgh were there, and most of Bob's family, Uncle Lonnie, Aunt Ruth, Bill, Eleanor and most of his sisters. Our friends also enjoyed the tasty cake from Budd's Bakery, the nuts and mints and the punch. I opened all the gifts, and was amazed to see sixteen tablecloths, two irons, a toaster, a mixer and many other gifts.

Bob and Flossie Cutting Their Wedding Cake, December 31, 1948

About ten o'clock we headed home. Uncle Phil, Dad, Bob and most everyone was drinking beer. It was a little disgusting that all of the men were trying to get Bob to drink more beer. Driving after drinking is not a good idea.

Although Bob had tried to teach me how to drive, it was not my cup of tea. We arrived safely in Cleveland on a starlit evening.

131

CHAPTER 20—The First Years of Marriage

We stayed at a hotel in Cleveland for the weekend, went to a play and ate all of our meals at upscale restaurants, except for breakfast. Since we both had to return to work on Monday, we postponed the honeymoon until spring.

Our apartment on East Avenue was already furnished. It had a living room, a kitchen with a dining area, one bedroom and a bathroom. It was comfortable and we enjoyed living there. Our landlord was named Florian. He and his wife were hospitable and we visited them occasionally. Their apartment adjoined ours.

Every Friday evening I cleaned the apartment, and on Saturdays we bought groceries, and I baked a cake and/or a pie. I was the perfect little housewife and was employed, also. Bob worked from noon to six in the hose room at B.F. Goodrich where he had worked before he joined the army.

I was up every morning at six A.M. because I had to take two buses to work. I never thought of disturbing Bob's sleep, except once when I was late. He would have taken me to work every day if I had asked, but I was so used to doing everything on my own, and I was maybe too kind. After arriving home each day, I took the time to make nourishing, wholesome meals. I had always heard 'The way to a man's heart is through his stomach.' I might add that it was gratifying to be able to buy any foods we desired.

Three weeks after we settled into our apartment, Bob told me he joined a Friday bowling league. He got dressed up to go bowling and immediately I was suspicious. Of course, I stayed home and scrubbed and cleaned our apartment. He arrived home at eleven P.M., so I dismissed my questions and thought I should trust him.

However, when he put on a suit for the third bowling session, I decided to check up on him. I called the bowling alley, and they confirmed that they did not have a league on Friday night. When Bob walked in the door at eleven, I confronted him. He once again grinned sheepishly and said he went dancing every Friday because I was so involved in cleaning.

"How could you do that? You know that I would be hurt and not trust you again," I shouted. "I don't care about the cleaning. Why didn't you ask me to go dancing with you?"

He had no explanation, but became angry with me for shouting at him, and shoved me into the open kitchen closet. I sobbed, and told him flat blank that he'd better never do that again or I would leave him, and he knew I meant it.

That was the end of the lying and deceit. We went dancing on Fridays together for a while, and then to movies or just stayed home together. We visited my family and his family on Sundays after I went to church. Bob especially enjoyed visiting his sister Elaine, her husband, Harry, and their two sons, Jimmy and Ronnie, who lived down and across Valdes Avenue not far from his parents. I could tell how much he loved his nephews, and thought he would make a good father. We also visited his grandparents every other week.

I had asked Bob if he'd like to go to church with me, but he said he wasn't interested in the Catholic religion. He had, as a young boy, attended the Wesleyan Methodist church with his grandparents, Zona and Preston. I encouraged him to go to his own church once again, but he also wasn't interested in that. His grandma Zona talked a lot about her church and I was under the impression that she wasn't in favor of the Catholic religion. His grandpa never said a word against anything or anybody. In my heart of hearts, I knew I could win them over to at least understanding and respecting my religion. I could tell they really liked me as a person and so did his Uncle Lonnie and Aunt Ruth who lived with them temporarily.

During that summer, Frank was working as an usher at the Falls Theater. One Saturday, upon his arrival home, he heard Francis and Florrie arguing as he walked in the front door. Francis slapped Florrie, and Frank told him to get out. He made up his mind that his dad would never hit his mother again. Francis realized his son was getting stronger than him, for Frank had beaten him at arm wrestling a few weeks before, so he left and didn't return for several months.

All the while we lived on East Ave., Francis never came to visit Bob and me, and we never saw him when we visited Mom every other Sunday. He rarely came to see Mom or the boys or to give her money. If he did stop, it was during the week, or on Saturday.

Before the summer was over, Aunt Kathryn, who lived in Wisconsin, wrote to her sister Florrie and asked for help. She was having trouble with her marriage, and needed somewhere for her son Buddy to stay during his senior year in high school. Evidently, Uncle Don had found a new woman and had been gambling away all their money. Their eldest son, Bob, was on the road playing his trumpet which he had been doing since he was fifteen, to help the family's finances. Aunt Kathryn could only take care of baby Janice.

Without telling her sister of the meager existence our family was experiencing, Mom wrote, "Yes, of course, I will help you out. Send Buddy here and I will take good care of him." Buddy took the bus to Akron and then another bus to Cuyahoga Falls.

Our cousin was a wonderful, kind young man, who really was no trouble for our family. He accepted what food Mom was able to make, and never complained. He and Frank went to school together, and since they were both seniors, became good friends. They played checkers every chance they could. Buddy went to see Frank play football. Frank played several offensive and defensive positions, most notably end. On weekends, he still worked as an usher at the Falls Theater.

Mom was working at McCrory's five-and-ten-cent store on Front Street selling notions. She enjoyed her job working five days a week. Robert had worked at Swenson's for a while, then a machine shop, and was now working at Brown & Graves Lumber Company as a mechanic. He was also going to Kent State University studying toward a degree in aeronautical engineering.

One Saturday, on the way home from a supply store, he and Francis were almost hit by a bus. Francis lost his temper, a bad case of road rage, and cut off the bus. The bus stopped and Francis pulled the bus driver out and punched him, knocking him down. They never went to court.

Our dad was trouble with a capital T. Why did he keep coming around to torture Mom and my brothers? In one respect, our family was at the point of independence. Looking at the situation realistically, of course, the extra money he occasionally doled out helped. Francis had an inflated ego and he thought he was needed by all his families. He really thought that all of his children loved him. The truth is we were all fed up with his antics. I had stopped thinking of him as my dad and he was a non factor in my life.

Bob and I were getting along well. We invited his brother Bill and wife Eleanor for dinner and I made pork chops. We visited Bill and Eleanor many times. For quite a few years, Dorothy and her husband, Joe, and Cathy and her husband, Ted, joined us for dinner. We played cards afterwards but sometimes we just sat, talked and laughed at Bob's and Joe's jokes.

It was Frank's last football game of the season. It had been snowing hard while the team bus traveled six hours to Middletown, Ohio. During the first half of the game, the opposing center had warned Frank not to hit the quarterback. Of course, Frank paid no attention to him. Both the other end and the quarterback and center fell on top of Frank's knee and it started to swell immediately. He was in terrible pain all the way home on the bus and fell asleep immediately upon his arrival home. The next morning, Saturday, Francis insisted that Frank help him carry the 100-pound bags of concrete mix and they worked all day on the sidewalk. When Frank said, "I can't keep working, my knee hurts so much,"

Dad said, "It doesn't matter, don't act like a wimp, just keep working."

Bob and I were invited to a New Year's Eve party at our friend Connie's house on Dayton Street. Bob drank beer occasionally in hot weather and at parties. Connie was serving all kinds of food, beer, wine, and mixed drinks. I had a small glass of wine, and

Bob kept on eating and drinking every drink they had. He became inebriated, and started crawling under the living room rug. Everyone thought he was funny, of course, except me. How disgusting, and even more so was finding him upstairs kissing Connie. I knew it was time to go home. I helped him to the car where he leaned out the door and threw up all the food and drinks he had consumed. Bob learned a lesson, for he was very ill for three days after that, and he never drank too much again.

During that winter, while I was checking the time, I saw bugs crawling out from under the bedroom clock on top of the dresser. Being petrified by any bugs except spiders, I hurried out to buy some roach spray since I thought the bugs were roaches. We had never had roaches in my whole life, so I was shaking. We asked our landlords if they had seen any and since they hadn't, I assumed we had brought the roaches home with the groceries. I sprayed everything and in a week or so the disgusting roaches were gone.

Bob and I had been talking a lot about going to California. He wanted to be a movie star and since anything is possible, I thought it might be a good idea. Bob was handsome and tall and looked a lot like Fred MacMurray, except his face was rounder than Fred's. Bob had a pleasant speaking and singing voice. We talked it over with his parents and my mom, and they felt we should try it and see what might happen.

Bob turned in his notice at Goodrich, and I told Mr. McTavish that I would be leaving. Bob decided to take a three-week vacation upon the wise advice of his boss, just in case it didn't work out. That way he would be able to come back to work at Goodrich if necessary.

I had some misgivings about leaving, as I really wanted to live near my mother and family. Something told me we would be back, though, and it's okay to try new surroundings for a while. Anyhow, we needed a vacation. The only trip we had taken was to Niagara Falls for a belated honeymoon.

We packed up most of our belongings, said goodbye to family and friends, and started on the long trip. It was another adventure passing through states that Bob and I had never seen before. We drove all day, stopped for breakfast, lunch and dinner, and then stayed all night at a motel. We had no reservations, but still managed to find decent lodging.

When we were driving through Arizona, it was 105 degrees in the shade. I knew I wouldn't want to live there. In Phoenix, Bob had some friends whom we stopped to see, and I couldn't believe my eyes as I viewed hordes of large cockroaches, some of them bright red, crawling through the front yard. Inside the home were more of the same. It was like a nightmare for me. We only stayed an hour and were on our way.

We carried extra water with us passing through the desert. Our radiator needed it once, and after that we had a flat tire. I stepped out of the car along the side of the road while Bob jacked up the car and changed the tire. That evening I noticed a rash all over my body and started itching uncontrollably. We stopped at a pharmacy where they diagnosed the rash as poison oak. I covered myself with calamine lotion and tried to sleep. I was miserable for a few days, and thought I should never get out of a car in the desert again.

We arrived in Los Angeles during a downpour. Bob had a cousin, Emma, who lived there, so we stopped to visit her and her husband. They offered us their trailer in the back yard to live in temporarily. It was still raining and it continued to rain every day while we were there. Evidently, April was the wrong month to visit California.

Nevertheless, Bob and I looked for jobs. First we went to Paramount Studios where we both read a part. They liked his voice, and also said that they might like to try me out for storytelling on the radio. They told him to come in to try out for a cowboy movie in two days.

The next day, Bob wasn't feeling well but drove me to interview for a secretarial job I had seen in the newspaper. I was hired immediately and started to work the next day. It is always a challenge starting a new job, and I felt a little pressure at first but the day after I was up to it.

Bob still wasn't feeling any better the next few days. He wasn't eating much, and I knew that was not a good sign. He felt too ill to try out for the cowboy part.

We had stayed in the trailer in Los Angeles for two and a half weeks when Bob wanted to return home to Akron. It had rained cats and dogs the whole time, and Bob had lost thirteen pounds in two and a half weeks. He never admitted it but I speculated that he was homesick. I missed my mother, too, and did not object to starting over in Akron. The one regret I had was that I never saw the beach and the ocean because of the inclement weather.

We called our parents, told them we were on our way home, and asked my mom if we could live with her for a short while. Of course, she said we were welcome. We intended to build or buy our own home as soon as possible.

. The trip home was uneventful except for enjoying the beauty of Albuquerque, New Mexico, and the various states we traveled through on the route home, which was entirely different from the route we took to California.

Since Mom had told us we were welcome to stay with her, and Frank had left for Florida while working on the Goodyear blimp, there was plenty of room. Robert was still working and studying at Kent State. The trip home made me recall that when Robert had received a football scholarship to the University of Oregon, he had hitch hiked there. It seemed like such a long way from home that he opted not to go there. We were all homebodies at heart, it seemed, and home is where the heart is.

CHAPTER 21—The Hall Family

We moved some of our belongings into Mom's house, and stored the rest. Bob was able to start working at Goodrich after his three-week vacation, and I looked for another job. The truth is, I was a little reluctant to return to General Tire since they had a going-away party complete with gifts for me before we left. I also like variety in life, and didn't mind starting a different job.

I was hired at the United Chemical Worker's Union as a secretary to Mr. Kurt Schmidt. Wouldn't you know he had a German accent that was hard to understand! Of course, I got used to it, and enjoyed the job. Bob and I looked for a home to buy, and after investigating the best possibilities with our limited funds, we decided to use the Veteran's Administration loan with only $100 down which I had saved. We bought a

Friedhaven allotment home. We had a choice of location to build, either in Cuyahoga Falls or West Hill. I could not convince Bob to buy the home in Cuyahoga Falls, even though I tried desperately. I loved Cuyahoga Falls and wanted to live near my mother.

Since Bob had grown up on West Hill, and wanted to be near work and his family, we settled for a Friedhaven home on Crestview Avenue, about eight blocks from Valdes Avenue where his family was living. The house was supposed to be ready in three months, but it took a little longer.

In the meantime, I kept feeling nauseous and realized I was pregnant. The baby was due the first of March. What a surprise it was, after just starting a new job, but we were immensely pleased. Bob and I had discussed having children before we were married, and we both wanted at least four children. If it was a girl, I wanted to name her Cynthia or Joyce. If it was a boy, I liked the name Steven. After just starting my new job, I thought I'd better keep my pregnancy a secret until I started to show.

Mom, bless her heart, made chicken noodle soup for me constantly, for that seemed to be the only food I could digest without becoming more nauseous. At least I never really threw up, but always felt like I'd like to. I didn't start to show until my seventh month, which was when I told my boss and co-workers. Everyone was surprised and happy for me.

Francis hadn't come visiting all the while we were living at Mom's. Bob and I had not seen him since our wedding. We also rarely mentioned him. Mom, Bob and I liked to keep life peaceful. However, one day he stormed in after I arrived home from work demanding that I borrow $1,000 for him for his Medina family. He wanted me to say I was single, but there I was filling out with child, and I refused to do it. Bob said, "Absolutely not." He told my dad to forget it, and be on his way. Instead, Dad ran upstairs and dragged my roll-top desk that I was saving for my children to the top of the stairs and threw it down. It broke into many pieces, and the papers, including stories and poems that I had saved in it, were scattered and torn. He screamed at Bob and me, "Get out of this house or I'll throw you out!" Bob didn't want to hit an old man, and I was frightened. Being pregnant, I didn't want anything to happen to our baby.

Upon his exit, Francis said, "You'd better not be here when I come back." Bob and I were too upset to stay, anyhow, and we didn't want him to take it out on Mom. Francis was very intimidating in his rage, and after this incident, throughout the years, I had occasional nightmares that he was coming to hurt me and my family.

Bob and I gathered our clothing and left Mom's house immediately. We found a room in a home on West Hill where we lived temporarily.

It was inconvenient living in one room, not having washer privileges, etc. I read several books while waiting for Bob to arrive home after work. Our new home was in the finishing stage.

Francis felt remorseful after telling Bob and me to leave Mom's house. He realized that he should stay away and that everyone was better off without him. Being desperate for money because his tallow company was failing, he had no one to turn to for help. So many children depended on him for support. After a few weeks, he was able to obtain a job driving a truck long distance. While on his route, he stopped in Pittsburgh to see Pearl and their daughter. Pearl was not happy with him and that was depressing. Ellen and their kids were demanding more and more of his time and money and he felt like he was in a vicious chasm of no return to a normal existence. He wished he could turn back the clock and start over.

He confessed his sins to the priest and sought forgiveness. In the meantime, more babies were born and Ellen started to nag him. Francis did not seek help for his depression and ultimately thought of a plan to escape all of his many troubles.

He drove his truck to Lake Erie and left a change of clothing on the shore to indicate that he had jumped in the lake and drowned. The newspapers carried the story that Francis Hanocek had committed suicide. This article was so embarrassing to his families and especially to Frank who had the same name.

Frank's boss, who was well known in politics, read the article in the Beacon Journal that Francis Hanocek had committed suicide and asked Frank if he knew him. Frank denied knowing him at first but the next day told his boss the truth because he did not want to be like his dad who lived a life based on lies.

None of our family believed that our dad had drowned. Another lie! Ellen did not believe it, either. Francis disappeared for a while, but like a rolling stone reappeared a few months after the staged suicide.

Three weeks after we were forced to leave mother's house, we were able to move into our home on Crestview Ave. There was so much work left to do to make our new home comfortable.

Whenever I have any project to do, whether sewing, decorating, cleaning, or writing I can't seem to rest until it's finished. Thus it was with cleaning and decorating our home. It was so rewarding to have a place of our own. I didn't realize that cleaning the scum out of the bathtub and scraping the caulking off the windows was going to send me into premature labor. I started bleeding one evening after work and while working on the house. The doctor sent me to the hospital, where I had to lie flat on my back for three days until the bleeding stopped, and it did. God was taking care of my child, because the doctor's prediction was that the baby would not live if born so early—he estimated the baby only weighed about three pounds. I was so thankful that the labor stopped. Evidently, I was losing placenta.

The doctor said I could return to work as long as I rested when I was home. I followed his orders, but two weeks after returning to work, I started bleeding again. This time I stayed home in bed for three days. Bob placed a pitcher of water beside our bed, along with a few snacks until he arrived home at 6:15 P.M. to try to cook dinner. The word "try" is significant, because Bob knew nothing about cooking. I instructed him how to prepare simple dishes. I was craving mashed potatoes. He burned the potatoes, mashed them, and when he brought them to me, I nearly gagged. However, I ate them anyway.

The bleeding stopped once again in three days. I was told to quit work, and reluctantly called my boss to convey the news. Thus I began taking it easy the last two months of my pregnancy. I read books and watched television which we had just purchased, crocheted and made dinner. Other than that, I rested, but the inactivity was difficult for me. I've never been one to sit around and do nothing.

My due date arrived along with spring-like weather. I sat on the front steps in the afternoon for almost two weeks waiting patiently. The neighbors kept asking me, "When are you going to have that baby?" Finally, on March 12, I started having true labor pains at one o'clock in the afternoon. I had wash hanging on the clothesline in the back yard. After calling Bob, I took down the clothes, folded them and put them away.

Thoughts of what my baby would look like rambled though my mind. I prayed that my doctor wouldn't get my baby mixed up with the other woman who was expecting at the same time as I was. He kept getting the two of us mixed up at every appointment.

Bob drove me to the hospital, where I labored for two hours. When I first saw Cynthia upon awakening from the anesthetic, the nurse was holding her above me. She looked at me with eyes wide open, as if to say, "Hi, Mom, here I am." She weighed 8 pounds, 8 ¼ ounces, had a wisp of dark hair on top of her head, a round face, and the biggest bright blue eyes. I thought she was the answer to my prayers, and she has always proven to be just that. I tried to nurse her in the hospital where I stayed for a week. The doctor wouldn't let me get out of bed, and I had to use a catheter, which was really a nuisance. I couldn't sit without pain, so had to use an inflated pillow when the nurse escorted me in a wheelchair to the hospital exit.

I knew that I never slept more than five minutes at a time the first year of my life, but I never expected that my beautiful little daughter would copy me in that respect. She was so wide awake all day and all night for the first three months that her dad and I had to take turns taking care of her. Bob's answer always was to give her a bottle after I found out I didn't have any milk. We tried putting cereal in a bottle, and that still didn't do the trick.

The first three weeks were full of joy, pain, and sleeplessness. My many stitches became infected, and I had to sit in a hot water bath for twenty minutes three times a day. My mother was a big help, but she was working doing other people's housework, and couldn't be with me for more than a week.

After three months of walking around in a daze most of the time from lack of sleep, I insisted that the pediatrician do something to get Cindy on a schedule. He said he would do this for our sake, and not Cindy's, since she was perfectly healthy. He put her on a small amount of paregoric at bedtime and in a week's time, she was sleeping all night. She only took one catnap during the day, but that was fine with us. We never gave her paregoric again. She was a delightful, happy, smiling baby, and very bright.

Cindy was truly an amazing baby, and we were so proud of her. She started sitting up alone at four months, and crawled at five. She walked around furniture at seven months, started walking alone at nine months, and put words together at eleven months. Because she could talk, she told me when she had to go potty, and therefore was trained before she turned one year old. When her pediatrician examined her at her one-year-old checkup, she said to him when he was about to give her a shot, "No, no, do, do." She also said a few other words and he proclaimed her a "Quiz Kid."

Frank came to visit us when he was in the neighborhood delivering rental chairs, one of his temporary jobs. He loved his little niece.

Frank married his girlfriend from high school. They had a baby girl named Christie. When they lived on Brown Street, Francis came driving up the street one day in a tallow truck. He knocked on Frank's door. Francis was with a young girl he introduced as his daughter. They entered the apartment and sat down. After a few amenities, he told Frank, "You can do anything you want with her" as she saddled up to Frank. Frank was appalled and told his dad, "No, you'll have to leave right now." The girl looked like she was in a dream world and Frank suspected she was on drugs. Francis left but as he was leaving, offered his son his hand which Frank refused to shake. He said, "Just leave."

Frank and his wife also had a son, Jeff, but later divorced.

We kept in touch with friends from high school, some who had married.

Bob and I had two more children while living on Crestview Ave. David was born when Cindy was seventeen months old and Bobby was born when David was nineteen months old. They were good babies.

When David was two months old, I was watching Cindy outside while she played with neighbor girls, all of them older than she. I had planned to go to the shopping center at Wooster-Hawkins Avenue when David awakened. I told Cindy about the excursion, fed Davie as we called him, and put him in the carriage outside the door. Just then the milkman approached to collect his money. I picked up Davie, and went inside to get the money. When I returned, Cindy was nowhere in sight. I nearly panicked, and the whole neighborhood helped me search for her. Regina, my neighbor, watched Davie in his playpen, and April, another neighbor, offered to drive me around the area.

I questioned the four-year-old girl, Kellie, who had been playing with Cindy. She explained that she told Cindy I had already left for the shopping center. I figured that's where she went since we had walked that way many times. I silently prayed as we drove the eight blocks toward Wooster-Hawkins. April and I entered the parking lot by Penney's and, with a sigh of relief, we saw my precious little girl with her blonde curls fluttering in the breeze nonchalantly swinging around the pole in front of Penney's. I gathered her in my arms, all the while thanking God for answering my prayers to find her safe. I asked her why she left without me, and she confirmed that Kellie had told her I left.

Mother had stayed with me for a week when Davie was born, and because he slept a lot, I was feeling back to normal after a few weeks. Shortly after the scare with Cindy, my next door neighbor, Inge, a good friend of mine from Germany, asked me if I could help her out. She had been having kidney problems since the birth of her twenty-one-month-old son, Scott, and had to have surgery. She had been in such pain from kidney stones, and one day while visiting me, she rolled on the floor in anguish. I felt so sorry for her. When she asked if I could watch Scott while she was in the hospital, I said, "Yes, I'll be able to watch him for two weeks." I liked to help people and knew she only had one other friend in Akron, an elderly lady.

What a challenge Scott was as he continually jumped in the crib, in the living room, and anywhere he happened to be. I tried not to let it bother me, but when my carpet bulged about three inches in the center, became a little upset. It wasn't easy taking care of three little ones, and Davie was only two and a half months old. I thought I could make it to two weeks, which I did. Then Inge called from the hospital to say she had some complications and would have to stay another week. I loved her and Scott, but my strength was waning. I was totally exhausted, and told her I just wasn't able to watch him another week.

I suggested calling her other friend, who did watch Scott the third week. Inge arrived home in good health, and thanked me for helping her. She moved shortly after that, and I missed her.

The new neighbor, Kitty Marshall, and I became good friends. She had three little girls with whom our children played. Those were happy times.

Bobby was a rather mischievous baby who climbed on top or the refrigerator and was very busy getting into other things. He had a friendly personality. We moved to Winton Ave. when Bobby was 18 months old. Marlene, our fourth child, was born two years later. We were ecstatic to have another girl. She slept all night and most of the day in the first three months. She loved to sing and dance to the tune of 'Poor Little Robin'. She could twirl the hula hoop at two years old and performed on TV one day. I enjoyed taking care of the little ones.

CHAPTER 22—Our Present Home

Our home

Five years later, we moved to our present home on October 2, 1960. We scrubbed the walls of all the rooms and each child except Marlene washed down a room. Mother helped us move and was always there for us. She was still working at McCrory's five and dime store and did housework for people to make ends meet.

Brother Robert graduated from Kent State University with a degree in Aeronautical Engineering, married Pauline and they moved to San

Diego, California. They never had any children and the marriage broke up later on.

Frank married Gayle on Valentine's Day which was Gayle's birthday. They had one child, Lori, and were later divorced. Frank is spending some time now watching Lori's two children, Leo and Ayla while Lori works at a photography studio. Gayle passed away from Alzheimer's on November 11, 2010. She had spent her life as a nurse and mother.

When Marlene was four years old, I decided it was time for me to learn to drive a car. Bob had been taking me to church and various stores without complaining, but it seemed feasible to me that if I took a driver's course, I might be able to drive myself to wherever I needed to go. It was a chore for the instructors because I kept knocking down the cone every time I tried to back up. After the third time, the instructor passed me probably because I had received 100% on the written test.

Our car was a DeSoto stick shift and that seemed difficult for me to drive especially up hills behind trucks. However, driving became a habit and we bought a Dodge with automatic shift the next time. It has always been a blessing to be able to drive even with anxiety about traffic. When I was 54 years old, I quit driving on the expressway because I felt like I was a hazard when merging.

Joyce, our fifth child, was born when I was 35 years old. The two weeks prior to her birth were memorable. David suddenly had pus pouring out of his neck while eating. At first I thought it was spilled food or drink. I took him to the doctor who immediately diagnosed it as a branchial clift cyst. I questioned the doctor because I had never heard of that. He said that a branchial clift cyst is a fish gill and it would have to be removed at once or David would have many infections in all parts of his body. The significance of the diagnosis did not strike me immediately but it made me wonder how that could be possible. I always believed that God created Adam and Eve and still do. Perhaps the passage of time, what was presumed to be a day of creation was in reality many years. I am no expert on evolution but believe that God and evolution go hand in hand.

The surgery was successful and the fish gill is preserved in a jar for all time. I spent the day at the hospital with David who recovered in time for his Confirmation at St. Martha's Church.

Mother had helped me for a week when each of our children was born. This fifth time, she asked me not to have any more children because she felt six children would be more than she could handle.

Cindy was twelve years old at the time and helped me take care of our little baby. To this day, Joyce sometimes thinks of Cindy as her second mother. The boys were so proud of their little sister that Bobby brought his whole Boy Scout troop to see her when she was three weeks old. David took care of her when he lived at home during his college years at Kent State while I was working at Summit County Courthouse for three and a half years. Bobby received a full paid scholarship from Cornell University for his high school grades and his football prowess. He was six feet five and weighed 220 pounds. Going to all his games at Cornell was such fun for Bob and me but I am sure Joyce did not quite understand what football was all about. She did enjoy the parties afterwards and staying all night in an Ithaca, New York hotel.

Our mother, Floriana Schmitt Hanocek—June 1964

On August 16, 1965, when Joyce was two years old, our wonderful mother passed away from a coronary occlusion. Frank called me in the middle of the night and I was shocked and so very sad. Robert and I gave Frank permission to take care of the funeral arrangements and he paid us each $500 for the privilege of living in her house. He had been living with mother for several years after his divorce from Carol, his high school sweetheart. Frank updated the house and lived there until he married Gayle. The house with the brown shingles still stands on Vincent Street and has had a couple of different owners.

CHAPTER 23—The Years Go By

Christmas was always exciting at our home. Early on, I had taught the children to help others. Each year we chose a family to help, sometimes someone we knew, sometimes anonymously. All of the children donated one of their new toys to an unfortunate needy child. As the children grew and were married, I continued to donate to our church's giving tree at Christmas.

All five children are married. Cindy and Russ, her childhood sweetheart, had two boys after they moved to Texas Three years later, they moved to Kansas. Cindy and Russ divorced and now Cindy is married to Larry and they live in a beautiful large home in Overland Park, Kansas. Larry owns his own insurance company and Cindy works for Larry part-time. Cindy retired from teaching last year after twenty-three years as an elementary school teacher.

Cindy's sons both graduated from Kansas University. Phil is a wonderful person who never makes waves. He owns his own home in Kansas, and is currently working as a medical bill analyst. Shaun is a doctor in Radiology and Shaun and Samantha have two babies, Ava, two years old, and Shaun, six months old. Bob and I were excited to become great-grandparents.

David is married to Jean and they have two children, Thomas and Heidi. David is still working in Forestry. He obtained two degrees, one from Kent State and one from the University of Michigan. Tom, their son, is to graduate from Computer College and Heidi is in high school. They live not too far from us.

Bobby married Jan and they have two sons, Ryan and Eric who are both college graduates. At the present time, Ryan and Eric both have good paying jobs in the food and beverage industry. They all live in Texas. Bobby owns his own Food Sales and Purchasing Consulting Business. He comes to visit us, as does Cindy, at least twice every year.

Marlene is married to Don and they live in Cuyahoga Falls, Ohio. Don is a foreman and Marlene works in the office of a delivery company. They have a daughter, Shelley, who is graduating from Mt. Union University in Alliance with a summa cum laude degree in Music. She will be a music teacher soon. Shelley is very sweet and compatible with everyone.

Music has always been a part of our family life. All of our children played an instrument starting in grade school and Cindy and Marlene were majorettes in high school. Cindy and David were in the North High School band at the same time.

Joyce is married to Edward and they have a daughter, Nichole, and a son, Michael. Ed is an electrician and Joyce works for works for a delivery company. Michael is a graduate of Kent State and is working as a sales representative. Nikki is married to Andrew and they have a beautiful daughter, Kaleigh, who is almost two years old. Nikki is expecting another child in 2011. Andrew has a good job. Andrew and Nikki both graduated from Bowling Green University.

CHAPTER 24—Headlines and Lies

When we lived on Winton Ave, it had been ten years since I had heard from Francis, my dad. I never really cared one way or the other. When I thought about him once in a while, it was with a feeling of relief that he did not care to keep in touch. However, one day there was an article in the Akron Beacon Journal along with his picture and the gist of it was that he was having a property dispute with his neighbor. The writer of this article was Dorothy Fuldheim, a very popular reporter. Little did she know of his many escapades which would have been shocking.

Shortly after the article was published, Francis appeared at our side door as if from out of nowhere. He was carrying a bag of mints and a bag of candy. It was bewildering to see him but I invited him into the kitchen. He tried to hug me but I shied away. He acted like it was yesterday that he had seen me, and started making over his four grandchildren sitting at the table. They wondered who this old man was who was trying to hug them. I explained that he was their grandfather. Of course, they liked the candy he brought. After half an hour, he said he had to go back to work. I had a gut feeling that it would be a long time before he would make an appearance again.

Francis left Ellen and all their children a few years later. He may have been depressed because he was overwhelmed with the responsibility of taking care of so many families and so many children. He envisioned starting a new life. That was our dad, always putting himself first. He should have thought about the consequences of marrying three women, only one legally.

Ellen had so many mouths to feed, she applied for welfare. It was a dire situation.

One of the worst things that Francis did was sexually abuse a couple of his daughters. He lured them by telling them a horrendous lie - that I would let him fondle me. The girls were afraid to say no to him. This lie about me was the most difficult to forgive. How dare he say such an untruth? How dare he manufacture a lie about me to get them to cooperate? How could he do such a horrible thing to his own flesh and blood? Was our dad really mental, or did he have a sexual phobia?

Francis confessed his sins to the priest and was forgiven many times. What made him think he was still a practicing Catholic when, in fact, he was a bigamist and a child molester?

My life has always been far removed from dwelling on him because I never dwell on anything, especially negatives. Taking care of my own family consumed most of my time. I nursed them through their illnesses and worked for three and a half years at Summit County Court House when Bob had three hernia surgeries. Bob also was diagnosed with rheumatoid arthritis in his back and feet and could scarcely walk because his feet were so swollen. If I ever admired my husband, it was during this trauma. He was so brave and strong with all the pain and went back to work two jobs soon after against the advice of his doctor. He rarely complained when he was young. Cortisone seemed to help him and he had only one attack of rheumatoid arthritis five years later. After taking cortisone for a while again, the rheumatoid arthritis has never returned. Faith, prayer and determination! His recovery seemed like some kind of miracle and I thanked God for His help.

As far as my own health was concerned, I kept going no matter how many times I had pneumonia. At one point, I went on a hike with friends when I had walking pneumonia. God has always been there for me and I believe He has never given me more than I can handle.

CHAPTER 25—
Francis' Remorseful Letters

Although I hadn't heard from my dad for years, in 1970 a letter arrived which was to be the first of many he wrote me during the next two years. What to make of them, I'm not sure except I perceived a man crying out for help, for forgiveness, and for validation. Was he sincere, or was he all mixed-up? I'll let you draw your own conclusions.

The letters came from Francis M. Hanocek, Rear 2616 1/2 Parade St., Room 2, Erie, Pennsylvania, 16504. The first one, dated 5-5-70, verbatim, which I assumed was meant for my mother:

> *There is no words I can say to make and change the situation I made of my life. I sure made a mess of it. My Father always said the way make your bed that's etc. I am atoneing and doing penance and praying like I never prayed before in my life, I mean a real praying. I had a dream I was holding your hand and we were walking up on the Troy Hill road and I walked into a hole filled with water. I left go of your hand and was going down and down and down and I saw a real bright light as I was looking up and you were standing looking down at me. I started to say the act of contrition and was praying out loud and crying when I woke up. Will pray for your happiness and the children and grandchildren. I do hope and pray that you found happiness, you our children deserve it. May my*

Lord and my God be with you and yours always. Settling down in Pitts.

Just going to church is not enough and confessing our sins to a priest. We have to confess only to our Father in heaven. We have to live Jesus Christ, believe in Jesus Christ, talk about Jesus Christ, pray to Jesus Christ and do all things for Jesus Christ and know the scriptures in the bible and the commandments which I did not keep. Now I live them, I am atoning for my many sins.

Just as I am thou wilt receive
Wilt welcome, pardon, cleanse, relieve
Because Thy promise I believe.
O Lamb of God I come I come

Just as I am Thy love unknown
Has broken every barrier down
Now to be Thine, yea, Thine alone
O Lamb of God, I come I come
This is my faith in My Lord and Saviour
I am saved by His Blood
Jesus Christ, believe me, I mean it
And praise Him.

The next letter I received from Francis was dated 5-13-70, as follows:

To my children in Christ:
I am writing this letter to let you all know that I am going to settle down it is about time, I was possessed by this lust of this world long enough but I am just living for Jesus Christ my Lord and my God. I went to the sheriff's office in Akron, Ohio, and gave myself up, told them who I was and what I did, they kept me in jail overnight and

they checked and double checked on my record, but they have nothing against me so they let me go. I write to them and tell them where I am in case they get anything against me. But they say it is so long ago that nobody cares about what I did anymore, but I sure care about it. How a person could do the things I did I cannot tell you because I sure was with the devil and he sure had me in his power. I could write a book about myself and you would be amazed. I hope you and yours and Robert and Frank and your mother, are in the best of health. Praying like I never prayed before but it is praying with my mind, heart and soul and repenting for all my sins. Oh sure I get tempted but I say to my Lord and my God help me I really need help dear Lord. Will pray for you all every day in my prayers and never cease.

Yours in Christ Jesus,
From your no good old man
OVER

Tell your mother that I never forgot the prayer she taught me when I first met her. I know this prayer helped me. It is a beautiful prayer. "Hail and blessed be the hour and moment in which the Son of God was born of the most pure Virgin Mary at midnight in Bethlehem in piercing cold. Oh my God hear this prayer through the merits of our Lord and Saviour Jesus Christ and His blessed Mother, Amen." Here is a beautiful prayer I say since I was saved by grace. I know these prayers by heart I say them every day and night on retiring. Just as I am without one plea, etc. The 23 Psalms, 51 Psalm, John 3-16 and other prayers I know by heart and I pray them and I learned to pray on the Rosary. I go to a Baptist church beside the Catholic, but the Catholic church does not have the spirit any more to me. I still pray all my Catholic prayers, too. I will never forget them and the good old songs I used to sing. The will be the last I will

write to you. I want to atone for my sins and for all the
hurt I caused all of you Goodby and God bless.

When I realized that Francis wasn't aware of the fact that mother
had passed on, I sent him a short letter acknowledging that fact. He
must not have received it, because another letter followed on 7-17-70
written to our dear departed mother:

> *Dear Florrie::*
> *I have not long to live. Have to get right with God and*
> *you. I am very very sorry what I did to the children and*
> *you. But God punished me with cancer of the spine for*
> *all my sins and they are many I mean many. I wish God*
> *would of did it sooner but I guess it is never too late for*
> *God. My Father had the right idea he used to say Francis*
> *the way you make your bed that's the way you will sleep*
> *in it. I do wish you all the happiness in this world you sure*
> *do deserve it. By the grace of God, please please forgive*
> *me what things I did to you and the children.*
> *180*
> *Until God takes me from this earth I have been saved by*
> *the Blood of the Lamb of God and atoning and repenting*
> *for my sins.*
> *Yours in Christ Jesus*
> *My Lord and our God,*
> *Francis M. Hanocek*

On the very same day, I received another letter from him:

> *Dearest Children of God:*
> *Will you please forgive me for all the talk I did to hurt*
> *you Dearie? I am so sorry for my sins and paying very*
> *dear for them now. Have not long to live have cancer of*
> *the spine. Was in the hospital for a week and they sent*
> *me home they cannot do anything for me. Dearie by*

*the Grace of God please forgive me for hurting you as
I talked, very very sorry now for my sinning and sinful
ways. I am so glad I found my Lord and our Saviour Jesus
Christ by being saved by the blood of the Lamb of God.
Will pray for you all and God be with you and yours.*
    Francis M. Hanocek

I wrote to my dad to tell him that I forgave him and his tortured soul, and once again explained the death of our mother. I received a letter from Francis on 7-31-70.

*Dearie: Greeting in Jesus Christ Our Saviour
She was only a mother some folks lightly say
But to those who more wisely can see
She was really in manner, and in every way
As God had intended she'd be every day.*

*For the days of her life were selflessly spent
In helping her children to grow
In knowledge and love of Him who had sent
Until now His own likeness they show.*

*Only a mother, God grant us that we
May never count lightly that call
For a woman who's willing a mother to be
In giving herself her all to God and her children.*

*Dearie, I know and I can feel she is in heaven and I
know she had prayed for me every day in her prayers and
you children. There was never a mother like her. How I
hurt her and you children. God knew all that I done and
how I hurt you all Psalm 6-6 - O Lord I am weary with
my groaning all the night make I my bed to swim I water
my couch with tears.*
    Yours in Jesus Christ My Lord and our God OVER

I will not write or bother you any more, just had to write this to let you know that my love for her had never changed. But its too late now. My Father always said Francis, the way you make your bed that's the way you will sleep. Truer words were never spoken. God love you and yours and your brothers and theirs. Goodby. Tell Frank and Robert to read John 8-2-12. I am a sinner saved. There is one more thing I want you all to know she never never taught you children to hate me. I know this down deep in my heart. Do you know this song I sing it and pray it by heart.

> *" Just as I am without one plea*
> *But that Thy blood was shed for me*
> *And that Thou biddest me to come to Thee*
> *O Lamb of God I come I come. Just as I am poor wretched blind*
> *Just as I am and waiting not Sight riches healing of my mind*
> *To rid my soul of done dark blot. Yea all I need was Thee to find*
> *To Thee whose blood can cleanse each spot O Lamb of God, I come I come, etc."*
> *O Lamb of God I come I come.*
> *Just as I am though tossed about*
> *With many a conflict and many a doubt*
> *Fighting within and fears without*
> *O Lamb of God, I come I come*

I again wrote to Francis to say that I forgave him, but I couldn't speak for my brothers. I did suggest that if it made him feel better, he could pay off his debts a little at a time. About a month later, I received this letter from him:

161

Dearest Son, Daughter and Grandchildren in Jesus Christ My Lord and My God:

Dearie: I do not know just how to thank you for forgiving me my trespasses and all the wrong I did to you children. I had so many dreams about Mother last Tuesday, I dreamed we were sitting in a room I could feel her hands holding mine it was so real she told me to pray and I said do you really know how I pray and I woke up. Why does Our Father in heaven take all the ones he loves and lets a RAT like me live? But my day will be real soon do not know. So glad that I found Jesus Christ and am saved by the Blood of the Lamb of God. Have sugar very bad and cancer of the spine. Was in the hospital for six days for a real check up but they told me its no use. I gave them permission to cut me open but they refused and told me to go home and rest as much as I can it will help me to prolong my life. But I do not care to live anymore. Since I found grace in God's sight and yours. What was wrong with Bob, was he real sick tell me please and God gave you five children. God love you and yours. Where is mother buried? Let me know please.

Yours in JesusChrist, my Lord and my God.
Francis
P.S Now I can die in peace.

I sent him a note telling him that mother was buried in Oakwood Cemetery and that Bob had had three hernia operations in two years but was recuperating nicely. I also said I would pray for him.

I didn't hear from him again until January 5, 1971. He wrote:

HAPPY NEW YEAR to all of you, Bob, Dearie and Children:
That might of been a little note to you but it was ten million billion words to me. Feel like a new man since I

was born again in Christ and saved by the grace of God - what a wonderful feeling it is to live and be cured of all my ills. But it was by the grace of God. No more cancer no more sugar, no more low blood pressure, etc. I had it but God tried me with all of those ills. So when the doctor said they could not do anything for me just go home and take it easy. I got down on my knees and begged God to help me that I will live my life for Him only. How are the children coming along and does Bob feel better? Praying for you all and our Robert and Frank and their families.

Yours in Christ Jesus our Lord and God. Much happiness.

Shortly after, I received a note from him, indicating some sort of will:

Dearie—Have my saving account in your name and mine. Mrs. Robert E. Hall,, Security Peoples Trust Company, 18th Parade St. Erie, 16503 Penna. You will not have any trouble on this. When I die, all my personal belongings, they are your and yours, you do what you want with them. Singer Sewing Mach., Television, over $110 in groceries and five suits and five topcoats, tools and everything that I have written down on my Sewing Machine. It is all yours and your brothers.

God love you and yours

On January 17, 1971, I received this letter:

Dearly Beloved Children:

Just a line or so to let you know I am thinking and praying for you all. Children, pray Jesus is coming. Watch, wait and pray. Behold He is coming quickly Rev 22-7.

Will be in Akron around 25th to see Mom's grave.

Dearie, believe with the help of God, I am going to live a long time yet, maybe 20 or more years only God knows. But I am ready when He calls me home my vessel and lamp is full of oil when the bridegroom cometh.
    Yours in Christ Jesus My Lord and Our
God Bless you all

P.S. Is Bob's mother and father still living?

Francis never mentioned anything about cancer for a while, and I wondered if he really had had cancer. It would be a miracle if he had been cured of all his ills. He said he might live a long time yet, and perhaps he never had cancer. With him, it was always difficult to tell truth from lies.

Another letter arrived in January, dated 1-29-71:

Dearly beloved in Christ Jesus:
Just a few lines to let you know I am thinking about becoming a missionary. I am also praying for you all the grace of God to watch over you all. I never realized that it was so wonderful to live for Christ and wake up in the morning with a song and a prayer in my heart. Praise the Lord. Sending you a box of candy. I have no one to buy gifts for but you children. Jesus said better to give than to receive. God bless all of you. Never felt so good in all of my life. No aches or pains. I am living because Jesus Christ liveth in me. Born again in His Spirit. God love you all. Pray Jesus is coming again soon.

Francis did not send the candy. I don't know if he came to Akron on the twenty-fifth or not. However, his next letter was dated 2-10-71: (There was no salutation).

Do not write to me till you hear from me. Where I will be I do not know yet, praying to God to guide me in the work I want to do for Christ Jesus. Praying for you all every day and praying to our Lord and Saviour Jesus Christ and to the Blessed Virgin Mary to convert Russia, to the Immaculate Heart of Mary. Especially for God to bless and spare America. Our country is doomed if we do not pray for God to save it.

Yours in Christ Jesus My Lord and Our Great big God—God be with you all my children and bless your every breath you take in life.

In April I received a letter dated 4-4-71 that had a new return address - Room 9, 1206 East 6th St., Erie 16507, Penna.:

Dearest Children in Christ Jesus Our Saviour

Was in Pittsburgh and visiting friends and sister Anna, my brother's wife in Mayview mental hospital. She is confined to that hospital for 37 years she did not know me this time but she did the first time I was there in 41. If you ever saw a beautiful old lady not too old 67 years, not a wrinkle in her face and I gave her a big kiss and told her who I was. She was overjoyed but her mind wanders. I asked her if her husband ever comes to see her and her children and she said no that I am the only one that ever came. Children, she is as beautiful as any beauty I ever saw. Going to see her again next week. If I do not hear from Lincoln, Neb. She asked me to come, I told her I would. I sure come from a good father and a good second mother and my mother was also good to my knowledge from what I heard about her. But their children aint worth a darn including me. Not one of my brothers or sister Anna ever went to see her especially her husband. He could not wait till he got a divorce from her. I know I was a rat and no good. But his children do not know where he is. Went up to his daughter Charlotte's home to talk to her but she does not get home from work till late.

Dearie, will never lose the faith for what God has done for me. Could get into lots of mischief and sin like I used to not no more. Just living for Jesus and making a good showing in the eyes of God that is all I care for now. Praise the Lord, and will be good like you wrote to me. Be good. Thank God everything is fine and everybody is well, praying for you all and your brothers and their families. Working makes life a little harder on you but offer it all up to God and He will take care of you. Starting back to work for myself and setting up housekeeping and cooking. What I like to eat, love to cook and make my sweet potato meat loaf it is out of this world, you should make one sometime for the family they will love it. Tell Bob I said hello and to pray it is so easy when we make up our mind, love to pray and sing religious songs. Praying for you all and asking God to bless you abundantly. Pray for me I can use all the prayers people can say for me because Jesus loves, loves me so. Praise the Lord. God be with you all till I write again and meet in heaven some day ready to die for Jesus Christ my Lord and our great big God. Praise the Lord.

Another letter dated 4-5-71 came the next day:

Dearie and family my children in God's eyes. Would you believe I cannot get that smile and looks out of my mind since I saw sister Anna in Mayview Hospital. Believe she is a saint, only a saint could have that smile and a beautiful face like that not a wrinkle at her age it is hard to believe but only God knows. Dearie, she used to be in church every possible chance she had and she prayed to the Blessed Virgin every chance she had just like your Mom and they really believed in the Virgin Mother.

They were good women like you of God. And only God can perform miracles. Went up to see My Father, Mother, and my second mother and relatives graves, Mother's Father and Mother Schmitt. Do you ever hear from Aunt Betty or any of the family Uncle Joe, Jim, Phil and Aunt Kathryn in Waukesha Wis. Have a very nice Easter and take good care of that wonderful family I am praying for you all. Pray for me like mother used to pray for me believe she still is praying for me in heaven and you children. Dearie send that card to brother Robert for me please. God Bless and keep you all in his grace's that he bestows upon us when we do His will and obey with Patience, Obedience and self understanding, Amen Amen."

I answered his letter and all his questions, but was confused by him saying his sister Anna was in the mental hospital. I evidently read the letter in haste and stashed it in a drawer, where I kept all his letters. After receiving the following letter dated 4-14-71, I reread the previous two letters, and realized he had made it quite clear.

Dearest Children in Christ Jesus:
Received your letter. God bless all of you and was so glad to get all that information. Dearie my sister Anna is not in Mayview she is still living and 75 years young and her husband is 79 years young and he is still going strong. My sister Anna can not get around like she used to but she does very well. Her legs are so fat bigger than a one gallon jug. When I said sister Anna I meant my brother's wife she is my sister in Christ Jesus she is a gem in God's great big eyes. Dream of Mother so much and had the most unusual visions and dreams. She must be praying for me from heaven because I am so happy that God lets me dream of Her the way I do. I cry but it is too late for that. Repenting and atoning for my many sins many — sins I mean many. Praying for you and your's in all my

prayers. Did not know Aunt Betty had any children sure was glad to hear that. Uncle Albert lives in Bloomfield, Ptts. The last time I saw him he was walking down Liberty avenue in Bloomfield I talked to him but he kept on going so I let well enough alone. Got an answer from Lincoln Neb but have to write to these other missions. I sure did like the line on Mrs. Rankin that you wrote. Dearie you can never believe How many women I can pick up if I would want them. I never believed any man could do it. But believe me it is something to fight that old slew foot the devil. Quit going to church and dropped out of the legion of Mary society I go to the cathedral here in Erie in the morning I do not bother with any one, try to keep away from men and women all they got in their minds is filthy thoughts. It is something to keep from those kind of people. You know how some women dress today it is a shame to insult the Most Blessed Virgin Mary the way women do today and they have no shame. Was in the First Baptist church about two months ago and a woman sat down beside me about 35 or 40 years old she had a dress on or would you call them dresses, that came up to her thighs and she crossed her legs the man beside me started to nudge me in the ribs, to look at the woman. I got up and went to another seat. How can men keep from looking at some of these women. So I just quit going to church for any kind of service in Protestant or Catholic. Will send you a picture of me Dearie looks like I am about 50 years old and you know how I like to dress when I am dressed up the way I like it is something.

People do not believe me when I tell them I am 65 years old. When I send the picture look at it and tear it up. Have to get a new photograph when I go to the mission field. Cannot wait till I go to work for the Lord and God. God bless you all. I am praying for you and yours.

Did Robert ever write and tell you if he cashed those money orders in. I hate to lose that money and have the bank go all the way back to the dates of these copies almost 5 months. If not, tell him to send them back to you and you can have the money I know you can use it. I know you checked with Frank so that is taken care of. Dearie I have a gallon of relish. I usually take it out of the gallon and put it in quarts and seal it good and it will keep for some time. Do not hear like I used to getting old and do not want to get heavy. I have a nice built and going to keep it that way. Still want to be a spry old man at 65. God bless you all and praying for you all. Pray for me do need prayer for a good life."

Francis included his picture in the last letter, so I wrote and thanked him and told him he looked good for his age. The next letter was dated 4-16-71:

Dearest Children in Christ Jesus:
Made my visit to the cathedral and talked with the Bishop he was kneeling at the high altar, and told him about myself and that Mother was dead five years and some months, that I would like to receive the Holy Eucharist. He asked me if I was living with a woman now and told him no. He told me I can receive Holy Eucharist but to talk to a priest and explain what I told him and tell the priest I talked with the Bishop and he gave me his permission. It will be so wonderful to receive holy communion again. Have not received holy communion in a Catholic church since 1928 I believe I do not want to die unless I am in the state of grace. Dearie so you can see that Mother is praying for me abundantly. Still going to the mission field if Christ willing and God spares me since I want to do his will With the help of God trying not to sin anymore. Placing myself in Gods hands and my

169

guardian angel. This is a battle I have to fight with the help of God. Praise the Lord. Do you ever hear from Aunt Kathryn is she still living or Uncle Don Take good care of those children keep them in God's eyes do not let them go astray, am praying for them and you and your wonderful husband he is a gem and you take good care of him. In God's eyes he is priceless.

Have about $200.00 or more dollars in groceries. Will pay for the truck for you, sewing machine, TV, lumber, etc. Know he can use all of this. Drapes and drapery material, toaster, new, and tools I will not need, bolts, nuts, nails and thread, etc., whatever you want, about fourteen pounds of candy."

At this point, I believe Francis thought he was going to be a missionary when he kept listing all the items he would leave to us. I really didn't want or need any of them, but rather than offend him, I didn't mention that in my letters.

I didn't hear from him until a letter dated June 23, 1971, arrived, thus:

Dearest Children and grandchildren in Jesus:

Thanks for the compliment Dearie, sure glad you like the picture. Dearie, you believe in miracles because God sure is taking care of me after how sick I was and hurt so bad from cancer, the sugar was bad enough let alone the cancer with low blood pressure. Was down for checkup and my sugar is normal and no cancer how about this thing what God can do, nothing is impossible for God, believe this. You know what kind of a rat I was and possessed by the devil. Can not let God out of my mind for one moment. Praise the Lord for His good he does for us, I sure appreciate what He done for me. Why is God so mindful of many a sinner that I was and given the grace to atone for my sins and live like a man should live. Sure

170

temptation is great but we can overcome anything with the help of our Father in heaven. Our mother had a lot to do with me being given this grace. She must have prayed and prayed unceasingly. She is in heaven and looking down at me now saying to God the Father in heaven, Well done, one more soul trying to get to heaven. Praise the Lord, Praise God.

I talked with her aunt who lives in back of my brother John. She owns her own property. You know how close homes are on Troy hill. Was in the yard where you were born but Harriet Gammel was not home. So I went next door to Madeline Seisel and her husband is dead he died June 12, 1965. She used to be my school days sweetheart and I sure got a big kiss from her she wants me to write and stop next week and visit her she is all alone. Do not want to go back to see her or write. Only interested in Christ Jesus and not to sin anymore. Old slew foot that dirty devil won't get me in his clutches anymore if I can help it. Madeline Seisel is a very good woman but not for me.

I told you about the other Battle Axe she was here in Erie to see me. She found out where I was through Social Security. Should have had my head examined when I met that woman. But there is no fool like an old fool. Done all the sinning I want to do in my life. It is so good to live for God and His Blessed Mother. Do you remember the prayer Mother taught us - Hail and Blessed be the hour, etc. I really like that prayer. Sorry to bore you but I just had to tell you about the place where you were born. Never for one minute will I forget that night and day. What Mother suffered. God Bless you all and I am praying for you all and brother Robert and Frank and all.

The last letter I received from our dad from Erie, Pa., was dated July 5, 1971, as follows:

Dearest Children in Christ Jesus:

Mr. Watson and I are not going to Ecuador, they came up with a new policy for retired people that we have to pay our own way and furnish all our own tools. I receive $127.85 allowance for a month and the cost to live in Ouito, Ecuador or any place in South America costs around $185.00 a month or more. Mr. Miller from the missionary alliance was here tonight and talked with Mr. Watson and I. Watson told Mr. Miller that is not what they wrote to us at first. Watson and I told Miller that somebody must think we are Crist Kringle or Santa Claus. I asked where in the world they get the idea that we have money to donate everything. Work 10 to 12 hours a day six days a week and our tools and work clothes they cost money to replace at the prices today of tools and clothes. Somebody is stealing that money that is donated to Missions, does not make sense. What is religion coming to, and Christianity. It just is not good the way people donate to the missions. Going back to work for myself."

There was no communication for some time after that, except in person. One September day in 1974, just as I was preparing dinner, and Marlene was getting ready for her first date, Francis knocked on the back door, and walked right into the kitchen as if it was an everyday occurrence.

Needless to say, I was surprised to see him - he hugged me and kissed me on the cheek, went right over to Marlene and hugged her and kissed her on the cheek. Marlene wasn't sure what to think as she hadn't seen her grandfather since she was four years old and didn't really remember him. What a shock! Joyce had never seen him.

Francis sat down at the table and ate heartily of liver and onions, mashed potatoes and gravy, peas, and chocolate pudding. Marlene and Joyce hardly said a word. Francis did most of the talking, telling us that he intended to move to California soon, but wasn't sure what city.

He looked older and thinner than I remembered him and had less hair, but still had the same gift of gab. We talked about things in general while eating, and as soon as we were finished, he said he had to leave but would get in touch with me from California.

The children were astonished that he appeared out of the blue and acted like he had always kept in touch. I had told them some of the past, but they were into their own busy lives, and I wasn't sure what they absorbed. It was all in the past, so I had rarely even mentioned my dad and his infidelities.

At first I wondered if he went to California, but since I didn't hear from him, put him completely out of my mind.

CHAPTER 26—Vacations

We didn't take many vacations with all the children, but now we could just take Joyce since everyone was going to college or working. The only other vacation we took with the children besides Wildwood by the sea, New Jersey, New York City, and Florida was to Washington, D. C. when I was three months pregnant with Joyce. Marlene stayed with my mother at that time because she always seemed to get carsick, and she really didn't want to go. Mom made her popsicles and they enjoyed being with one another for a week.

The rest of us had so much fun in Washington. We stayed in a lovely efficiency hotel and Bob and I took the three children to see all the historical sights, including the White House. We noticed how elaborately the rooms were decorated. Bob thought the best part of the trip was the pancake breakfasts (made with real cream) at a restaurant a near our hotel. Even though I was pregnant, I was able to walk everywhere, but we stayed in the hotel at night so I could rest and for safety's sake.

When Joyce was seven years old, Bob drove all seven of us to Fort Lauderdale, Florida to visit his mother and sisters. As crowded as the car was, the kids all behaved well. Bob, Dave and Bobby sat in front. At six feet two, six feet three and six feet five, it was very crowded. All four of us girls occupied the back seat while Joyce reclined on our lap part of the time. Everything worked out to our expectations except that we had a difficult time finding his mother's home. After three tries, Bob was ready to start driving back home when we finally found the right 24th Street. We stayed at a hotel on the beach and had a cookout there. Bob's sister, Helen, prepared a picnic on the beach with all the family in Ft. Lauderdale the day before we left for home.

We later took a trip to Boston with Joyce to walk along Paul Revere's riding trail. I was intrigued by the Bostonian accent. We always had a good time on all of our vacations and learned something new about each city we visited.

When we went to restaurants for dinner, Bob ordered spaghetti whenever he could. Spaghetti was usually the least expensive dinner on the menu and he wanted the rest of the family to order whatever they wanted. Of course, he also loved the Italian feast.

Even when Bob and I took a bus tour of Europe with Trafalgar Tours in 1984, Bob still ordered spaghetti, especially in Italy.

Bob had promised me that he would take me to Italy someday, and thanks to Bobby who was purchasing agent for Sky Chefs at American Airlines, that dream came true. I thought it would be fascinating to see how other people lived. We booked a tour with Trafalgar Tours, and Dave (who was living at home temporarily at that time) drove us to the Cleveland airport on August 25, 1984. The flight stopped at DFW airport where we planned to board the plane to Gatwick Airport in London, England.

There was time to visit Bobby, Jan, and Ryan who lived in Texas. Cindy, Russ, Philip and Shaun had already moved from Texas to Kansas. We listed standby first for the flight, and then spent some time with the family. Jan had made Sloppy Joe's for lunch and Bobby took some video pictures of all of us. We enjoyed Ryan running around and playing happily. Bobby drove us back to DFW where we ran a marathon from gate to gate after an agent gave us the wrong information. Bobby saved the day, and we boarded the plane just in time, and flew first class. That was luxurious.

Europe was more than I expected, without a doubt the most exciting trip we ever took outside of visiting family. In London we saw Buckingham Palace, Green Park, Trafalgar Square, Westminster Abbey, and Big Ben as we walked along the River Themes. We took the underground to St. Paul's Cathedral where services were being conducted, and I lit a candle for Joyce. Then we took the underground to the Tower of London.

I worried, although I know it is a waste of time to worry, about Joyce. She and her husband, Edward, were living in North Carolina in a trailer at that time, and she was pregnant with her first child. They had married in Virginia in December 1983. Ed was an electrician and was earning only six dollars an hour. Joyce had been working at a department store selling shoes trying to make ends meet. Her baby was due in March 1985. Right before we left for Europe, Joyce called to say she was in the hospital and had lost one baby. She found out she was pregnant with twins.

I wanted to be with her, but she insisted that we go to Europe since we had already paid for the trip. I lit candles in every city we visited. When I called her from London, she told me that the doctors might have to take the other twin, as she kept hemorrhaging and it might cost her her life. I asked her if she had slept at all in the hospital, and she hadn't. I suggested that she ask for a sleeping pill since I believe that sleep is a healer. She did take a sleeping pill and when I called her the next day she had quit bleeding. I prayed ardently that she would carry the child to full term.

The fifty people on the tour were very congenial. They were from Australia, South Africa, England, and the United States. Our tour guide, Isabelle, was originally from Portugal, and the bus driver, Oscar, lived in Belgium.

We drove to Paris after crossing the English Channel and passed through Calais, France, where we saw ruins from World War II. In Paris, we stopped at Montmarte, where the artists display their paintings, then drove to Sacred Heart Church where we had a panoramic view of the city.

The next day we saw the Arc de Triumph, drove down Champs Elysses, stopped at the Eiffel Tower and the Square where Ann Bolyn and others were beheaded, toured and lit candles at Notre Dame Cathedral, and ate at fabulous restaurants. We decided not to go to the Palace the next day, so explored Paris on our own. The rate of exchange was confusing in every country, but somehow we managed to buy food and souvenirs. The room at the Hotel Brochant La Tour was very small, but the bathroom was large. I couldn't figure out how to turn on the water in the bathtub. After turning every faucet on the sink, water finally flowed from beneath the soap dish into the tub. In the morning, Bob and I awakened with our mattresses halfway on the floor. The beds in Europe were not made for tall people, and Bob fell asleep in a fetal position in some of them.

I wrote and mailed about ten post cards, some of which were never received. Part of our group were stuck on the elevator while Bob and I sat in the lobby and watched the TV show "Dallas" in French. JR's deep voice was dubbed in, and the commercials were funny, but not as 'cutesy' as in London.

The hotel clerks at the desk were not friendly, but I smiled at them each time I asked for or returned the key. I was determined to get a response in kind. I knew a few words in French and was able to converse with a waiter at an outdoor cafe up to a point, and he was very friendly until I had exhausted my French vocabulary. He immediately changed his attitude. As we checked out of the hotel, one of the clerks finally smiled in return. Leaving France, we passed through Alsace-Lorraine, from whence my ancestors came, the Schmitts and the Becks. It was beautiful, plush, grassy farmland.

In Switzerland, we saw a folklore show which featured yodeling, and since Bob loved to yodel, he entertained the group on the bus back to the Hotel Central—everyone clapped for his rendition of yodeling. When we arrived at our lodgings at 11:15 PM, the seventy year old woman on the tour still wanted to go to a discotheque. Everyone chuckled.

The next day we took a cable car to the top of Stansehorn with its spectacular view of the Alps. I took pictures with my new Minolta camera which happened turned out to be a lemon. That particular roll jammed in the camera, I found out later.

In Lucerne, I had a rather frustrating experience. Throughout Europe, everyone knows the word "toilet" or "toilette." It's a good thing, especially when you have a stomach ache. I was directed to the elevator in a department store, and when I stepped out, there was a maze of mannequins and other items stored on the same floor as the restroom. Finally, relief! I tried to find the flusher, but it wasn't up, down, on the side, or on the floor. No one was around to ask, so I left without flushing after hesitating for about ten minutes. Bob was waiting for me and I did not want him to worry.

There were attendants at most of the restrooms in Europe, and that was the one time I needed one. Some of the attendants were very clean and cordial, but others went berserk if a tourist didn't tip them. One of the attendants banged on all the doors while I was in the toilet because a user didn't tip her. Others wiped off the toilet seat for everyone, and some sprayed air freshener. I never knew what to expect.

The scenery was breathtaking passing the lakes and mountains on the way to Arona, Italy. Isabelle played tapes, enchanting French and Italian love songs as we traveled, and sometimes we sang along. The houses near Bologna were unusual, stucco or brick houses with barns directly attached. We passed grape vineyards, palm trees, lovely azaleas, geraniums and various flowers and trees. The Highway of the Sun, in the Appinines mountains, had forty-seven bridges, forty-seven tunnels, and thirty viaducts to cross until we entered Tuscany, the most beautiful part of Italy with its cypress and olive trees, and vineyards.

We stayed at the Globus Hotel in Rome, which had larger rooms with two commodes in the bathroom. Dinner was amusing at Magnani's, for we sat with our favorite friends on the tour, Casey and Olivia, from Sidney, Australia. As we entered the restaurant, the waiters pinched some the ladies on the buttocks. It made us jump and when we turned around, the culprit was no where in sight. Roses of all different colored roses were presented to us while we were seated at the tables.

I called Joyce from the hotel. Alas, it took a while to get through since I had trouble understanding the operator and vice versa. I was relieved to hear that Joyce and the baby were fine.

Oscar drove the bus past the Forum, the Coliseum which was being renovated. We stopped at Trivi fountain and then St. Peter's where I could have spent several days but there was no time on this trip for an extended stay. I went to Mass and confession. The priest suggested that I try to influence Americans to go to confession more often. I bought a sparkling blue rosary for Marlene and had it blessed.

Before dinner that day, we went to Tivoli gardens. Tivoli had many fountains, trees, and statues. The statue of Diana, the goddess of fertility, had fifteen breasts. All the men remarked about that and even the women could not help notice the ridiculous abundance.

The next morning we saw the Vatican and the Sistine Chapel. Majesty such as we had never imagined greeted us. Michelangelo, master painter, depicted all the beauty of the Bible with Jesus and the Angels so elaborately portrayed and we were almost breathless in awe of the ceiling and tapestries.

Bob and I were always on time returning to the bus, in fact, we were the first ones to board (and the last getting off). We had occasionally waited for the two teenage boys from California. When they didn't show up on time, Oscar decided to teach them a lesson. The bus left without them but Oscar went around in a circle and finally caught up with them. In the meantime, their mother was very upset because she said they had no money with them to take a taxi to the hotel.

Two other incidents occurred in Rome. Oscar drove the wrong way up a one way street while Bob and I were occupying the front seat. Passengers all took turns rotating seats. Luckily, there was no accident, but in general, the driving in Rome was atrocious. An Italian driver cut in front of our bus and it was a close call. Isabelle exited the bus to check to see if everyone was all right. That turned into a war of Italian words, with the driver calling Isabelle names. Since Bob knew some Italian, he stepped off the bus to defend Isabelle, and called the driver some unmentionable names. The driver calmed down and left after he saw Bob's stature.

Leaving Rome, we drove to Florence. On the way, we stopped at a small city with artists and fountains. Bob asked Isabelle if there were any restrooms there. She replied that he could relieve himself under a tarpaulin if he couldn't find a toilet. Bob did not choose to do that, so he walked about a mile until he found a bar with a toilet. That was the only exception to being the first ones back on the bus.

In Florence, we had a group picture taken and afterwards walked to Holy Cross and Annunciation churches, where I lit candles for Joyce. As we walked around the city, we encountered young women begging for money. Some of them had small babies in their arms. I felt sorry for them, but had been warned that their plight was not always legitimate. However, being sympathetic for the poor just in case it was legitimate, I gave a few coins to one of them. It made me feel better to give than to deny.

Venice was very romantic. We cruised around the islands, stopped at Ruono island which was unique with its different colored stucco homes—blue, green, red, etc. The inhabitants hang their wash outside their windows, which is common in Europe. We also stopped at Lido Island where film festivals were held each year. Lunch was at an outdoor cafe. I ordered a fish dish, and to my surprise, learned that I had eaten squid, mussels, shrimp, and other delicacies I had never tasted. Unfortunately, that did not change my preference for most seafood except for shrimp.

We ate lunch and dinner with various couples. At one of the lunches, we were all discussing our families. When Bob and I remarked that none of our children had ever been in serious trouble, one couple did not believe us. Their sons had been in jail for minor offenses. Bob and I both insisted our statement was true, and then dropped the subject. The couple had laughed and asked us if we were the Brady bunch. Perhaps we were a little like them, but there are probably no families exactly like the Bradys.

St. Mark's square was unique. The shops sold lovely lace baby clothes, and gorgeous glass objects. After touring the glass factory, Bob and I toured the canals of Venice in a gondola. The accordion music and Italian songs were so enchanting, it seemed almost like a second honeymoon.

Passing Verona, Italy, the next day, we took pictures of the statue of Juliet, and the Roman Arena. Although the pictures in Venice turned out, these didn't. We stayed at Innsbruck, Austria and saw a folklore show.

Before crossing the border to Germany, we passed snow-covered mountains. Some South Africans and Australians had never seen snow before, and were amazed. We also passed areas where there had been concentration camps, and Bonn, the temporary capitol of Germany. We were told that Berlin would once again be the capitol in the future. Germany after the war was one of the most successful industrial countries in the world. We drove past the Black Forest. One of the passengers was having intestinal problems and the bus driver had to stop several times on the way to Munich. I offered him some Kaopectate and that helped. In Munich, we stood in the rain to watch the Glockenspiel clock on the square, and bought some beer steins at a modern department store.

The next day we drove by the Danube heading north to St. Goar, where we boarded a boat to cruise down the Rhine river. We passed a few cities and castles and then stopped at Koln (Cologne) where Oscar was waiting for us to drive to the Netherlands. Amsterdam was next on the agenda, and one the most fascinating cities on the tour. It is thirteen feet below sea level and only the dykes keep it from being flooded. They have a special Ministry of Water for that purpose. Dutchmen say, "God made the rest of the world, but Dutchmen made Netherlands."

It was raining and chilly while on the canal cruise, but that didn't take away the excitement of seeing Holland. The gothic architecture was interesting, with narrow buildings and houses along the locks. Furniture has to be hoisted up through windows because the stairways aren't wide enough. After exiting the boat, Bob and I took a walk and looked for a restroom. We entered a bar where the bartender motioned me to a small room where there was no toilet, just a hole in the floor. There was no toilet paper, either, and now the "Softie" toilet paper used in other parts of Europe that I thought felt like sandpaper would have been welcomed. The next day, though, we found a rather modern restroom in another bar. One thing that made it easy in Amsterdam was that the people spoke English.

We were on the final leg of our journey as we passed Rotterdam, canals, windmills, and tulips on our way to Belgium. As we drove through Antwerp, Oscar pointed out his home.

When we departed the bus in Brugge, we tipped Oscar generously. He was not only a careful driver, but a very courteous person. Some of us had tears in our eyes. In Brugge, we boarded the ship to Dover, and afterwards climbed into the bus to London. We had a new driver, an amusing Englishman.

The driver had dropped off some of the passengers when we found ourselves trapped in an alley behind the hotel because there was a parked car blocking the exit. Bob, along with Roy, who was also a big, strong man, lifted and moved the car over close to the other side in order to make room for the bus. We blew kisses to our friends on the tour, especially to Teddy and Beth Anne, such well-behaved children. Isabelle told all of us that we were one of the most congenial tours she had ever guided.

We arrived at Kensington Close Hotel to find our room had been given to someone else. They paid our taxi to Royal Kensington Hotel. It was one o'clock in the morning before we were settled. The mattresses were as hard as rocks, and we didn't sleep well. The next morning, Sunday, Bob and I walked to Westminster Cathedral for the 10:45 A.M. Mass, then on to Piccadilly Circus and Green Park where an artist's show was on display. After eating at Kentucky Fried Chicken, we took the double-decker bus back to our hotel where we slept soundly regardless of the beds.

The last morning of our trip, we took a taxi to Victoria Station where we boarded the express train to the airport. I still marveled at the remarkable architecture of the roofs and chimneys in London as we passed the heart of the city. We obtained carts at the airport and waited in the standby section for our names to be called. It was a full plane, and at first they were going to sit us in different seats, but somehow changed us to First Class, where we received royal treatment. From DFW, we flew to Chicago O'Hare, and ultimately Cleveland, arriving at 8:10 P.M. Dave picked up us, and, although we had the time of our lives, it was also good to be home. It really is true—there's no place like home!

CHAPTER 27—Devastating Lies

I didn't hear from Francis again until he called me from Long Beach, California, the last part of October, and gave me his address. I sent him a short note with the current news. On November 9, 1976, I received a typed letter from him. It read as follows:

GOD Greetings in the most Holy Name of Jesus, and HIS Most Blessed Mother, Mary:-
To my children, the BLESSINGS, from above, and my blessings. Received your letter, and all the wonderful news. Was so pleased to hear the news. I have moved, the place where I was living was too noisy. I made a BO BO, I sent my change of address, into the Post Office too soon, and it was a BO BO, believe me. My State of California check was sent back to Sacramento, and probably will not get one this month. I am in the best of health, the weather is super here. Its up in the 90's, and it is beautiful. Go to Saint Vibeanos Church every Thursday and make a sacrifice for my many sins I had committed in my life, they expose the BLESSED SACRAMENT, from 12/30 till 5 P.M. and they have Mass. MAY GOD BLESS YOU ALL ABUNDANTLY, IS MY PRAYERS FOR YOU ALL. Excuse my many mistakes in typeing cannot remember like I used to, that is the real sign of old age.(SO L).

Yours in Christ Jesus, and His
Blessed Mother Mary.
1255 East 10 Street,
Long Beach, California 90813
LMH Francis M. Hanocek
P.S. Was in San Diego, and do not care for it, and do
not care for Los Angeles.

The only time I heard from him after that was, I believe, in 1980. I received a telephone call from California. Francis talked to me for a few minutes, and then asked if he could put his lady friend on the phone. I said, "All right."

Her name was Gwen and she sounded very nice, so when she commented, "Your dad is such a wonderful person," I reacted in a negative way, by answering, "Well, you don't really know him."

I said that because I was afraid he didn't tell her his past. He had also promised to stay away from any other women. I wanted Gwen to find out about him so he wouldn't commit bigamy again, as he did with Pearl and Ellen.

On his last visit to our home, he told me that Pearl had cancer of the throat. I thought that would be a terrible way to go, and never found out what happened to Pearl and their daughter.

I didn't hear from him after that. I assumed that he married Gwen in California.

Gayle and Lori went to visit Ellen without mentioning it to anyone else. They learned a little about what happened while Francis was living with Ellen and their children.

They said that he had sexually molested a couple of his daughters. He coerced them by telling them that I had let him make advances toward me, a total lie. That is the explanation of his letters when he begs my forgiveness for lying about me.

I have to admit I was furious when I heard this information. But it didn't surprise me too much because he lied to us all of his life, and his whole life was a lie. I did forgive him everything, because I've never thought of him as stable. Not to forgive only hurts the offended.

I have tried to live my life forgiving people, stable or unstable, and I pray for them. The most difficult thing to forgive is when someone tries to take away your dignity or questions your integrity.

Most people think of themselves as stable or normal. But what and who is really normal? Some abnormal people think they are normal. It takes a lot of courage for a person to admit they have a problem. When one acknowledges the fact that they have a problem, whatever it may be, that is the first step to recovery. In that respect, no one is perfect except God, and we all have faults.

With Francis confessing to his sins, one would think that was a start to bettering himself. Perhaps it was and when he lived in California, he may have been a solid citizen and a good husband to his new wife.

He left behind a legacy of children who live respectable and successful lives despite his abandonment. I never pity people who blame their childhood or their parents for their adult problems. One has to rise above whatever happened as children, and live in the present. The past is gone, today is here, and the future is not foretold. We must do our very best each day in everything we do and be a good example to future generations.

Grandchildren Shelley, Tom, Nikki, Shaun, Michael, Philip
Front Row—Flossie holding Heidi, Bob

CHAPTER 28—Sad Demise

Francis did marry Gwen, the sweet-sounding woman to whom I spoke on the phone, shortly after his phone call to me. He wasn't pleased that I had remarked, "You don't know him." He didn't understand that even though I had forgiven him, I still wouldn't recommend him for 'husband of the year'.

They lived in Los Angeles, California. I believe he remained faithful to her because he was, as the saying goes, 'over the hill'. His diabetes that he mentioned in one of his letters had returned causing him to be impotent. It was difficult for Francis to stick to the diabetic diet, and some of the better medicines were not on the market yet. Gwen took care of him as best she could, but had debilitating ailments herself. Her heart problems accelerated and when she passed away, he was all alone. She left him enough money to pay for the nursing home where he lived.

He had an infected lesion on his foot that wouldn't heal because of his advanced diabetes. Gangrene set in, and there was no alternative but to amputate his leg up to the knee. Shortly afterwards, the other foot was amputated likewise. He lived for a year after the amputations, but passed away from congestive heart failure on August 21, 1988, at Orange Grove Rehabilitation Hospital. He was cremated August 30, 1988, by The Neptune Society at Anaheim, California.

I had obtained his death certificate by writing to the State of California Department of Health Services, Vital Statistics Branch. I learned of his death from my cousin Edward Hanocek. Edward had received a letter from a private investigator in Modesto, California, stating that he had spent considerable time and money locating him. He asked for fifty percent commission if he could prove that he was the heir.

Edward didn't want anything to do with Francis's supposed inheritance, so his wife wrote me a letter dated September 1, 1990, stating that the investigator was looking for the heirs to Francis's estate of $23, 321.34. She wrote that in California they hold estates for five years. I assumed that, if there was an estate, it would have been money Francis had inherited from Gwen.

I told my brothers Robert and Frank about the letter, and they, like me, didn't believe there was any money, or if so, that we would never get any of it. None of us really wanted his money. However, we did send the forms to the investigator. I also contacted Dorothy, my lawyer friend. She received a reply from the public administrator of Orange County, California, confirming the fact that there were no funds left in his estate. We weren't surprised.

Francis died a pauper, all alone. It must have been painful not being able to walk and to have to rely on others for care. I would have compassion for my worst enemy in that situation, so I felt sad that he had to suffer so much no matter what he had done.

I thought of my early childhood, the happier times when he had been a real father who loved us children. Perhaps, because I was the eldest, only I can remember that he was proud of us and cared for us. The fact that he loved other women besides Mother was due to either a defect in his personality, a brain tumor, or a sexual addiction. There are men and women who can love more than one partner at a time. Some are weak when it comes to sexuality, some are alcoholic, or are abusive in many ways, verbally, physically, or sexually. At least our dad was never drunk and never abused me sexually.

I have heard it said that men weren't meant to be monogamous. I really don't believe that is true, because there are many men who are. I do think that some men struggle with their sexuality. And, as I stated before, I would never want to be a man and have to deal with constant arousal. I thank God that I am a woman who has never had that problem.

God created us with the purpose of procreation in mind. He gave us the Ten Commandments to follow to help us along life's path. Obviously, not everyone agrees with that. Some things are a mystery not meant to be solved, though.

Anything I can't solve, or really don't know the answer to, I give up to God. However, I also believe that God helps those who help themselves by praying for answers. I apply the Serenity Prayer in most situations before complete surrender: God, grant me Serenity to accept the things I cannot change, Courage to change the things I can, and Wisdom to know the difference.

My dad was a mystery to me, and I am not his judge. God even forgives sinners if they plead for forgiveness an instant before death. Perhaps he did that - his letters indicate that he may have. I believe anything is possible.

CHAPTER 29—Life Goes On

We had a cute little part Chihuahua and Toy Manchester Terrier dog, Chico, which Bobby had bought when he was sixteen. After Bobby left for Cornell University to study and play football, Chico became our dog. Bob and I each walked him twice a day.

One morning before Bob left for work at five-thirty AM, Bob lost track of Chico while walking him in the dusk of early morning. He heard him barking but did not see him at first. Chico had fallen down the sewer on the corner of the next street. Somehow Bob retrieved him and brought him home. Chico was shaking until I calmed him down with loving arms.

Chico lived for fifteen years and became near blind and could not keep food down so Bobby and I had him put to sleep. It was a difficult decision but for Chico's benefit. Bob was disheartened and still thinks of Chico every August to this day. Most of the older neighbor's remember Chico and the Man, as they called him, walking the dog while talking to everyone.

Bob worked for over 45 years at B.F. Goodrich until he retired when he was 65 years old. He spent his retirement listening to his beloved music while smoking cigars in the garage. He and I walked the parks for a while until he just did not want to walk much. We went to movies about once a month and visited our children.

The first time I noticed anything strange about him was about thirty years ago. I asked him, "Bob, would you please plant the petunias I just bought while I go to the store?" The petunias were sitting on the back porch table beside some artificial flowers. Bob replied, "Okay, I have time for that." When I returned, I noticed that the artificial flowers were missing and when I looked in the back yard beside the garage, Bob had planted both the fresh petunias and the artificial flowers. Pondering on that for a moment and amused at the sight, I did not dwell on it. Some people do plant artificial flowers in their yards.

Some years passed before Bob caused me to panic at what was happening with his mind. After returning from a trip to visit Cindy, I arrived an hour late at the Cleveland airport. I had no cell phone at that time to call him. I expected that he would have come into the airport to check my flight's arrival time. As I stood out in front of the entrance for him to pick me up, I saw our car drive by me. I waved but Bob did not acknowledge me or circle back. It was midnight and getting chilly. I went back in and found a cell phone to call Joyce to tell her what happened. She left a message for her dad to drive back to pick me up. When he did not come back in an hour, I called our number. He was furious with me for asking him to come back to pick me up again and said he thought that I would want to stay at the airport all night. The drive back home was frightening. His anger triggered his speed and I felt lucky to be alive when we arrived home. Once in a while after that incident, Bob lost his temper with me over trivial things. He also started cussing and saying the 'f' word and became prejudiced against different nationalities and races.

A year later when I went with Bob to see our family doctor for a routine checkup, an intern came into the office and questioned him, the usual questions which Bob answered. However, when the intern left the office and Bob's doctor arrived on the scene, the first thing Bob said to him was, "I don't like people of your intern's nationality." When I reprimanded him by saying, "Bob, don't say that," Bob looked at me in a hateful way and told me to mind my own business. Of course, the doctor noticed a change in Bob's attitude. Bob had always joked with his doctor and asked the doctor about his family and he still was cordial in that way but he had never before said anything negative about others nor treated me unkindly in the doctor's presence.

The doctor asked me, "How long has this been going on?"

My reply was, "For the last six months, Bob has been like a different person. He has become prejudiced against other nationalities and races, loses his temper occasionally and is cussing, something he never did when he was younger." The doctor came to the conclusion that Bob showed signs of dementia and thus prescribed Aricept to keep the problem from getting worse.

My understanding of dementia is that it can affect different cells in the brain and it usually starts with repeatedly asking the same questions. Bob did that and also started to interrupt me constantly when someone asked me a question or when I started talking about any subject. Perhaps he did not even listen when I spoke because he was so used to me after so many years of marriage. His dementia affected his common sense and his temperament. My reaction was to try to tell him how he should act and that did not work. I guess I wanted him to be his old easy going self. However, some people believe that all the elderly and perhaps some people of other ages have a little dementia. We all can forget things occasionally. I know that once in a while I go into another room to get an item and when I get there, I forget why I went into that room. So many people I know tell me the same thing, middle aged or older.

Bob still expected me to wait on him even if I did not feel well or was recovering from an illness or surgery. His former compassion was missing. Perhaps a man can be spoiled by too much attention and perhaps modern day women are wise to expect their husbands to help with the children, housework and cooking. That way the men do not get spoiled.

Bob also lost interest in me showing me no attention in any way. He did not even want to hold hands and was reluctant to help me when I wanted to take his arm for support. He shrugged and released my arm as soon as possible.

Bob seemed to stay about the same for many years, and I was grateful that his doctor prescribed medication to keep Bob at the same level, although I worried sometimes that he might get into trouble saying anything negative to people, especially racial comments. Bob always loved to talk to little children and people who walked by with dogs on a leash and was still a very friendly person. We sat on our front porch and many a neighbor or stranger visited with us and brought their dogs up on the porch for Bob to pet. The dogs always loved Bob, too.

CHAPTER 30 —My New Ventures

Bob and I celebrated our fiftieth wedding anniversary in grand style. Our children rented a hall nearby and we invited 100 people. Bob and I danced the evening away along with our relatives and friends.

Bob and Flossie with their children on their 50th wedding anniversary. Back row—Bob, Bobby, David.
Front row—Flossie, Marlene, Joyce, Cindy

We celebrated our sixtieth wedding anniversary in good health with immediate family at a Tallmadge restaurant in a special Trolley Car.

Bob and Flossie with Grandchildren on their 60th Wedding Anniversary. Back row—Shelley, Michael, Nikki, Eric, Ryan Front row—Philip, Flossie holding great-granddaughter Ava, Shaun and Bob

I started writing poetry and books when I was sixty-eight years old. The children were all grown up and most of the grandchildren were beyond baby sitting age. I was looking for a way to help make the world a better place for my having walked here. Two weeks later, the answer was given to me. I was inspired in church to write my first published poem, Love Never Dies, which won the Editor's Choice Award at the National Library of Poetry. That inspired me to keep on writing poetry. Shortly after having more poetry published, our daughter Cindy, who was teaching fifth grade, asked me if I would write a children's book about my unusual but exciting life during The Great Depression. I thought I would give it a try. As you can see, I am still writing at the age of 83 and still enjoying it.

During the following years, I had two major surgeries. In August of 2003, I discovered through a series of tests that I had four blocked arteries. I had no apparent symptoms beforehand. In September 2003, I had a quadruple heart bypass because my main artery was 100% blocked, two arteries were 90% blocked and one was 95% blocked.

When my brother Frank came into the hospital to see me after my heart surgery, I suggested that perhaps he should have his heart checked. We both had high cholesterol just like our mother.

Frank saw his doctor and also had a quadruple heart bypass a month later. Cindy, Marlene and Joyce all helped me with the recovery. Frank went to a care home for two weeks to recuperate. We have both lived without another heart incident so far. We told Robert in California to consider being checked but he opted to take his chances.

When I was seventy years old, I woke up one day with excruciating pain in both my legs, especially the right leg. I could not walk. I crawled to the bathroom for several days and did not see the doctor immediately because the pain left and I was able to walk again. Several months later when the pain which had lessened seemed to increase, I had some X-rays taken at St. Thomas Hospital. The doctor told me that I had spinal stenosis and two bad hips. He suggested that I could have three surgeries or wait and see what develops.

After about ten years, the pain increased and became unbearable during the winter of 2009 and 2010. I wondered if I could get through another winter of so much pain. During the summer of 2010, I decided to have another X-ray of my legs and hips. I found a well-known surgeon at the Crystal Clinic on Portage Trail in Cuyahoga Falls who took an X-ray of my hips. My right hip had no cartilage left but my left hip seemed to have sufficient cartilage. He told me that it was my call and that he could not guarantee that all my pain would leave because of spinal stenosis but he thought that having a complete right hip replacement might ease the pain.

God seemed to be telling me to go ahead with the surgery and I just knew that I would be all right. I wrote the following story about the incident. Some of it is a repeat of this book, but perhaps you might need a review of what transpired so far. Sometimes I wish other authors would go back and refresh the memory of the reader.

HIP, HIP, HOORAY

When I look back at my childhood, I was a 'hip' child in the sense that I was knowledgeable about many things such as school work, how to make friends, respect others and how to be happy despite any circumstances. I was also very courageous. Perhaps I was not 'hip' in today's sense of the word, but 'hip' for a child who was born in 1927.

As I was growing up during The Great Depression, I cannot say that I ever thought about my physical hip or what would happen to it as I grew older. I was mostly concerned about having enough to eat each day, church, school and my family and friends. My two brothers and I had fun each day despite not having the necessities of life. We never dwelled on the adversity for long. Robbie, seven years old and Frank, five years old, picked crabapples and that helped them to fill their empty bellies. My digestive system would not tolerate crabapples. My brothers called out to me to try them,

"Sissie, these are so good." But I learned to refuse them because it was better being hungry than having a sick stomach.

All three of us picked blackberries when we could and enjoyed their sweet satisfying flavor. The boys called out to me when they found a new berry patch in the hills across from our home in Kittanning, Pennsylvania, where we lived for almost three years.

One of the reasons that we could not always pick fruit was because we moved eleven different times to eleven different cities or towns near Pittsburgh, Pennsylvania. Our dad was constantly searching for new jobs because of The Great Depression. He had a gift of gab which helped him acquire all types of selling positions. He sold meat at different meat companies, bakery products, and tallow at his own company which was temporary because no one had money to pay him and he extended credit much too freely. After that, he worked on building the railroad from Pittsburgh to Akron, Ohio.

He was away from home more than not and left our wonderful mother and the three of us constantly. When he was absent for three weeks at a time and the stipend he gave our mother was gone, she baked home made bread every other day and we subsisted on the gift like manna from Heaven. The aroma of fresh baked bread perked us up and mother gave us a piece of bread for breakfast, lunch and dinner. Most of the time we had no oleo, jelly or lard to spread on the bread. It was an occasional treat to have lard with sugar sprinkled on top.

When mother had some spaghetti or lentils to cook, she gave us her share if there was not enough. She was a wonderful person from a practicing religious family. She taught us manners, morals, character, respect and cleanliness. No one ever suspected we were so poor and we never told anyone, not even our relatives. That was the way back then. Most people kept things to themselves and children did not tell tales. Children were more or less seen but not heard. We felt loved despite the lack of hugging and had great self esteem because we all excelled in school. No one constantly praised us for our accomplishments because it was expected that we would do our best at all times.

We played kick-the-can outdoors with our friends and used our imaginations to put on plays in the summer season. In the winter, we sledded down the steep hills and built snowmen and snow forts.

We studied every evening. Our mother helped us by asking us questions but we did most of the work ourselves. Each evening, we were permitted to listen to the radio for an hour to enjoy the programs of the times. Robbie and Juney loved JACK ARMSTRONG, THE ALL AMERICAN BOY, and I loved to laugh at FIBBER MCGEE AND MOLLY.

Occasionally, our dad would drive us to Pittsburgh to see our relatives. What a treat that was! Grandma Schmitt cooked satisfying meals. She gave us some of her tomatoes and corn in season. The yards were so small on Troy Hill where Grandma and Grandpa lived that she could only grow a few plants. She also cured sauerkraut in a crock pot on the back porch and sometimes served us pork and sauerkraut. Grandma also gave us a penny each visit and sent us to the nearby candy store to buy caramels or licorice. Uncle Joe who still lived with Grandma and Grandpa Schmitt gave us each a quarter which he supposedly snatched from behind his ear. We usually bought an ice cream cone or a banana split.

I can remember that we were in very good health in spite of the lack of food. We were all thin but not too thin. We loved to run, jump rope, play jacks and marbles. One of my favorite things to do was to try to dance like Shirley Temple, the darling child movie star of the era. I practiced flipping cartwheels, standing on my head and walking on my hands daily and became adept at those feats.

Summer days flew by because I also helped my mother, not only by doing dishes every evening, but by going to the grocery store with my brothers. We pulled a wagon as we walked down the highway to the main street where we shopped at the A & P store. Food was very inexpensive compared to today's prices. We could buy cans of soup, a pound of spaghetti, rice, beans, lentils and bread for a nickel. We did not always have the money to buy bananas which cost 25 cents for six pounds, but we bought oranges when we could afford them. Our mother seemed to know about the nutritious foods needed to keep her family healthy.

During the summer of 1936, my brother Juney and I climbed a tree on the steep hill by our apartment. That was not unusual, except that this particular time the branch snapped trapping Juney's collar bone which broke as I fell tumbling down the hill. Our dad reprimanded me and blamed me for the accident. Poor little Juney was taken to the doctor who put him in a cast that held his arm at an uncomfortable angle. He ultimately developed eczema under the cast and constantly complained about the uncontrollable itching. I did not get hurt in the tumble and felt remorse for not taking better care of Juney. That was the first time any of us children were under a doctor's care.

When I was a junior in high school, the police came to our front door to inform our mother that our dad had been in a truck accident and was in a hospital in Buffalo, New York. They told us that he had amnesia. Mother decided that it was best for me to take a bus to

Buffalo to bring our dad back home. At the age of 16, I took the bus from Akron to Buffalo arriving in the wee hours of the morning. As some transients stared at me, I kept my eyes glued to the book I was reading.

After retrieving Dad from the hospital (he knew me), we boarded a train to Akron which passed through Steubenville where he suddenly decided to get off. I begged him not to do that, but he would not listen. He told me to stay on the train because Steubenville was too dangerous a city. After I arrived home, Mother was dismayed that he left the train.

Two weeks later, a woman carrying a baby knocked on our front door. I opened it to find that she was looking for her husband with the same name as my dad. She and mother discussed this bizarre situation. My dad had married this woman with a false divorce certificate and they already had two children. Mother was very hurt.

Two weeks after that incident, our dad came home without any explanation about getting off the train in Steubenville. He begged our mother's forgiveness for starting another family and she forgave him. He kept telling her that he had a tumor on his brain caused by the truck accident.

Years earlier, he had begged and asked for forgiveness for having an affair with our so-called maid he hired after our mother was ill for a year. A daughter was born of that affair who he tried to support.

After I graduated from high school eleventh in my class of 167, I was chosen to be a private secretary for the Comptroller of The General Tire & Rubber Company in East Akron. My salary was very good and I was able to support my mother and brothers. Dad was gone most of the time.

When I was 21 years old, I met and married my husband on December 31, 1948. We met at a dance which was the popular place to meet young men and women in the forties. We have been married for almost 62 years and have five wonderful children, nine grandchildren and three great-grandchildren who never wanted for anything.

I did not see my father for years and he subsequently left all three of his families, a total of fourteen children, because he found it impossible to support all families. He was filled with remorse and years later sent me letters from California asking for forgiveness.

HIP IN THE GOLDEN YEARS

As my husband and I celebrated our fiftieth wedding anniversary, we were both in very good health. I had had pneumonia quite a few times in my thirties and forties, but other than that illness, could not complain.

When I turned seventy years old, I suddenly could not walk for about a week and had to crawl to the bathroom. After having X-rays, I found out that I had spinal stenosis and both my hips were deteriorating. The doctor said I could have three surgeries or keep going to water exercise and see what happens. At the time, I decided against the three surgeries.

For ten years, I was able to walk without even a cane for support. I did water exercise at the Natatorium at least four times a week.

At the age of 82, everything changed and I was in almost constant pain during the winter of 2010. It was the worst pain I had ever experienced in my right leg. I don't remember ever being so cold and shaky in my whole life. One could call it the winter of my discontent.

HOORAY FOR TOTAL HIP REPLACEMENT

In September 2003, I accidentally discovered that I needed a quadruple heart bypass. I had no symptoms. Everything went well, but that is a story in itself which is detailed in my book HEARTS ON THE MEND. My heart specialist moved to Indiana.

In 2010, I made a routine appointment with a new heart specialist who prescribed tests that showed my heart to be sound. One test showed that I had a partially blocked artery in my right leg.

The heart specialist sent me to a spine surgeon. I waited two months for the appointment. After an X-Ray was taken, it showed that it was my right hip that needed replaced. After seeing the hip surgeon, I opted for the first appointment I could get because I did not want to go through another winter like 2010. The other reasons I chose surgery were so that I could take care of my 88 year old husband who had recovered from a stroke and so that I could enjoy a quality life. I had heard that hip replacements were very common and successful for elderly people. So many friends at water exercise class told me that they had had hip surgery and were free from pain afterwards.

On July 26, 2010, Dr. Myers of Crystal Clinic performed the total right hip replacement. It was not a convenient time for my family but it was convenient for me. My eldest daughter, Cindy, who lives in Kansas, was expecting her second grandchild soon but planned to come to help me on August 7. She has always been a helper and took care of me for a week after my heart bypass. I called her 'Florence Nightingale'. My youngest daughter, Joyce, was on vacation in North Carolina and was on her way home July 26.

My middle daughter, Marlene, who works from 2:30 PM until 9 PM took me to St. Thomas Hospital where I was admitted. The surgery was delayed for two hours but was performed at about 1:30 PM.

The anesthesia method was discussed and it was decided that a spinal would work better for me. They were very careful and it did not hurt. As I slowly drifted off to sleep, I prayed that God would guide the doctor's hands and that the Angels would watch over me. I always believed in God and Angels and could feel them surrounding me. When I was seven years old, I almost drowned and after spiraling through a tunnel of light I saw Angels reaching out to grasp my hand. As I extended my hand to them, I woke up on the side of the creek. A sixteen year old girl had found me and saved my life.

After the hip replacement, I woke up about an hour and a half later and found out that I could wiggle my toes. Feeling gradually came back into my body like a renewal of spring.

Later on, I found out exactly what the doctors did. I had not read the brochure thoroughly beforehand because I am better off not knowing all the details. To do this hip surgery, one's body is more or less up in the air. The incision is made and the old hip is hammered out, the new one inserted and cemented in place around the ball joint. The cement *has to harden and new cartilage is formed. It all has something to do with age as to what type of hip, titanium or metal, is inserted and how.*

The day after the surgery, my daughters were surprised to see me sitting up in a chair fully clothed with make up on. One daughter called our daughter in Kansas and told her that I looked like a movie star. Oh, well, that might be far fetched but I have always believed in taking good care of myself no matter what.

The only problem I had was that I could not sleep in the hospital bed because of intense pain (a 10 on the scale of 1 to 10). The wraps on my legs to keep circulation going intensified the pain and I rang the buzzer after an hour to be moved to the chair where the pain level diminished to a 5.

Many gifts were sent and brought to me, a FEEL BETTER balloon attached to a box of candy and other treats, flowers, cards, a stuffed elephant, a Red Hat Teapot, and a Raggedy Ann and Andy ceramic set. Everyone who came into my room seemed to notice the window arrangement of gifts.

Three days later, I was moved to St. Thomas Rehab because there was a room available for me. No one told me ahead of time that I would have to share the bathroom with the next door neighbor. The lady in the next room was named Florence, so I decided to have the sign on my door read FLOSSIE to avoid any confusion.

Never share your bathroom with another person when recuperating from any surgery! It was very inconvenient for me to wait when I had a stomach ache or needed to empty my bladder. Sometimes the aides did not answer right away and I was lucky to make it to the commode in time.

A nurse came in to check my bandage and literally ripped it off my incision. It really hurt and my leg kept sticking to the sheets and clothing. I could not see the incision and thought it might be adhesive from the bandage. The next morning a doctor looked at my stitches and remarked that I had three places where my flesh was torn. I told him about the nurse ripping of the bandage. I remembered her face but not her name. The doctor assured me that I would be treated with antibacterial cream. I was lucky not to get a staph infection.

In Rehab, I still had trouble sleeping on the bed, and spent most of my time in a reclining chair. Meds were given, but I have a distinctive reaction to most pain medicine which is not favorable because I remain groggy for a long period of time. The nurses gave me a combination of Ultram and Vicodin. I kept waking up with a jerk and a feeling of flying away. After I told the kind nurses this, they allowed me to take just extra strength Tylenol which did the trick and helped me to sleep.

My family and friends continued to visit. It was enjoyable and passed the time. One friend brought me a real orchid which she said only required three ice cubes a day to continue to bloom all winter, another friend brought cookies, and a poet friend brought me roses with an angel attached, cookies and the ceramic Raggedy Ann and Andy figures. So cute! Two of my friends became confused as to where I was because the Rehab is a separate section at St. Thomas Hospital. They were told that I was not in the hospital.

Members of my family called every day. I had my cell phone and a hospital telephone. The days went by fast. The mornings were consumed with a shower or sponge bath, breakfast, grooming, and Rehab exercises down the hall.

One day when I could not seem to summon an aide, I decided I would have to go to the bathroom by myself. I used the walker but when I came out, I sat in a wheelchair in my room and inadvertently tangled the wires to my cell phone, telephone and TV monitor as I moved around. I ended up sitting in my chair not able to reach a thing. When the cleaning lady came in half an hour later, she said she never saw such a mess. A nurse asked me what happened and I told them I did not know. Of course, I did not want to get in trouble by telling them that I had gone to the bathroom by myself!

Some of the nurses were very kind. One of the aides always answered my call when I buzzed and always had a smile on his face. He left me a note on the board when I left that said "Good luck at home, Sweetie" and he drew a heart.

The hospital had a really good rehab room with wonderful instructors. Kim and Corey were my favorites, but they were all nice and knew what each person recuperating should do. I was told that

I was a full weight person and that meant that I should put all my weight on my right leg. Each day we went through a series of exercises. Because I had upper arm strength which had developed from water exercise, I was able to do the exercises with more ease than some of the other patients. The instructors called me MISS FLOSSIE and asked where I was going because I was doing the exercises too fast. I told them I was headed to the beach.

There was a ninety-one year old man who had fallen and broken his hip and was recuperating from a hip replacement. He seemed to be doing well. We played catch with a large ball for strength. Some of the patients had knee replacements and cried as they did the exercises. One of the ladies became ill and threw up. They quickly had me move to another area.

One day at Rehab I was asked to do the dishes in the sink and unload the dishwasher. It was not that hard with a grabber. I had a grabber at home and one of the ladies at water exercise had given me her equipment to use which pulled on socks and that was a big help. I had borrowed a walker without wheels from one of the local funeral homes which offers that courtesy. The hospital told me to use a walker with wheels. I had one with wheels at home which my husband had used recovering from his stroke.

Next to the Rehab room was a beautiful guest room which was decorated in deep blues and other lively colors. There were windows to look out on a patio. When some of my family and friends came to visit, I walked down or was pushed in the wheelchair to this room. In Rehab, patients are not allowed to go to another part of the hospital or outside.

The day of my dismissal from Rehab was coming and I was more than ready to go home even though my experience there was a positive one. My middle and youngest daughter came to pack up my treasures and I arrived home at about 1 PM on August 7. My daughter from Kansas arrived that evening. Her new grandson was thriving.

Needless to say, I had a lot of help from my daughters and my son Dave. He helped clean up the house that day because my husband did not do much of anything while I was gone. He came with the girls to see me a couple of times, but I think he missed me. He has some dementia but not to a great extent. It is difficult for him to realize that I have needed help since coming home. He has made me a couple of sandwiches but I have been able to get most of my meals myself. Because my leg felt like lead for a while (typical), moving around with a walker in small spaces was a little difficult. A hip patient is not supposed to bend over, twist, or cross their legs for three months.

It is now a month after my surgery and I am doing just fine. Because my doctor was called out of town for a week, my X-ray has been delayed until Tuesday, August 24. The swelling around my knee and ankle has gone down to nil and I can walk a few steps without the walker or cane.

Since I had Summa health care at home I have not been allowed to go anywhere but church, the beauty parlor and the doctor. They told me Medicare would not pay for it if I fell at any other place. So far, I have attended church twice, been to the beauty parlor and next the doctor. One day, our daughters took me to the B & W Root Beer Stand. As long as I stayed in the car, that was permitted.

HIP, HIP, HOORAY

HOORAY, the worst is over! Dr. Myer released me to drive and go back to water exercise on August 24. I am able to walk with a cane already but decided to use the walker for a couple of weeks to go back to water exercise because the floors are always slippery on the way to the pool.

On August 25, everyone I know well greeted me at the pool and the instructor announced that I was back from surgery after one month.

That afternoon, I went shopping and bought a new refrigerator since our old one was falling apart. Jars of jelly or juice kept falling off the shelf as I opened the refrigerator door. And not being able to bend, etc., I was unable to clean up the mess. My husband cleaned it up later.

The only drawback is that I will not be able to bend, twist or cross my legs for two more months. There goes the housework, but it will wait for me!

I am looking forward to a much better winter in 2010-2011. HOORAY for medical science!

AND HIP AGAIN

My husband and I flew to Kansas on September 25, 2010 to visit our new baby great-grandson. We enjoyed our visit immensely until the night before we were supposed to leave for home. He fell and broke his hip and was taken to Emergency at the Overland Park Hospital where he had surgery the next day. Right now he is in a Rehab Facility in Kansas and I am home. I was released by Dr. Myer to bend and twist but he also told me that I cannot be a caregiver for anyone at this point in time because I am still healing. We are all praying that my husband will do his exercises and be able to be driven home by our daughter and son-in-law soon. This whole experience was bizarre, to say the least!

CHAPTER 31—Flying Bob Home

Bob was so disoriented after the surgery. The anesthesiologist gave him a local anesthesia instead of the spinal which I had asked them to do because Bob has a slight dementia. I had heard that a local anesthetic aggravates dementia. That proved to be the case. Bob seemed delusional and could not do the rehab exercises. He wanted to come home.

Cindy and her family visited Bob every day but he seemed to be going downhill. After three weeks in the hospital and three hundred calls (I tend to exaggerate) I finally found a medical plane that cost $7,900. Medicare had asked for $13,500 for the flight, so $7,900 seemed like a bargain to me. I split the amount on two charge cards.

The plane was small and Cindy actually sat in the co-pilot's seat in the harrowing flight in the propeller plane. It took three hours to fly Bob and Cindy to Akron, bedside to bedside to a care home in Cuyahoga Falls where Bob is still living (or trying to live) at this moment.

Bob has not done well with physical therapy and still cannot walk, pull himself up or go to the bathroom by himself, so there is no way that I can take care of him. It takes a machine and two people to get him out of bed. Our family here visits him nearly every day.

We finally granted his wish to have a head scan which he had been asking for ever since the fall. He had the MRI, EKG, and neck and back X-Ray and the results were that he had arthritis in his neck and back. He has had two urinary tract infections, fainted from low blood pressure, lost 25 pounds and could not seem to eat, and has just recovered from pneumonia. He choked a lot, but that has been solved and he is now eating well. He likes the facility's soup and drinks tomato juice like his body is craving for it.

After all these health problems, the only good thing that has happened is that Bob is able to tolerate sitting in the wheelchair for at least six hours a day in order not to get more bed sores. He has two sores on his feet since he arrived in Cuyahoga Falls from Kansas, probably because of his diabetes.

Bob has had so many other issues since he has been in the nursing facility, it is difficult to mention all of them. One day he was taken in the medical van to an appointment he did not have. However, I have come to the conclusion that all nursing homes make mistakes. The care home is close to my home so I do not mind the drive there except some days I cannot get out of my driveway unless I have it plowed.

Bob's clothing has been lost or given to another patient even though I have marked every item. Some of his new shirts which were Christmas gifts are missing, too. Of course, the same thing happened when he had a stroke almost two years ago. He was in a different care home to recover and most of his clothing went astray.

One problem is that there is another patient by the same name and I have been billed for his haircuts but have that straightened out now. I had to find out by myself ways to pay for the continuing care of over $6,000 per month because no one told me exactly what to do. I found out that Medicaid helped with the cost after Medicare was exhausted. I also found out that there is a Homestead Act that helps with taxes. Everyone I called did not seem to know all the answers or did not think to tell me.

And to top it all, this winter has seen so much more snow and ice all over the United States that it leads one to believe in global warming. I was coming home from my heart doctor's office yesterday and from visiting Bob when my car was stuck in the driveway because of the ice buildup. The plowing costs money, too.

There is always hope that Bob will walk again but it may take a year. He actually is pushing his wheelchair by himself for me but usually will not do it for anyone else. He seems to like all the women and men who take care of him but did not like getting cut while being shaved. Perhaps he will start to shave himself. When I ask him why he has not shaved himself, he answers "They get paid for doing it."

We wanted to have Bob's 89th birthday celebration in January at Belgrade Gardens in Barberton. I arranged for a bus to take Bob and some of the family there to celebrate. The irony of that was that the bus driver was someone who went to school with our children and I also knew him. We had a grand old time even though Bob was just recovering from pneumonia.

Each day, I say the Rosary and ask God to help Bob's strength of mind and body be restored. I never give up hope. Here is a poem I wrote when Bob had pneumonia:

IT IS WHAT IT IS

Vast canyons echo
Reverberating memories
Voices from the past

Chasms of charm and wit
Slide slowly to wither away
Confusion left in the wake

Whispers of love and rapture
Intensify in the loneliness
Of one instead of two

Whistling in the light of day
Jesting in the peak of time
Composed yet complex

Whiffs of smoke encircle
'Melancholy Baby' sounds
Contented in the cave

Tenacity like a river
Flows over the cliffs
To a muddled puddle

Silence envelops the walls
Heroic symbol wanes
It is a matter of fact

Floriana Hall

CHAPTER 32—
The Recession and Unemployment

Our family has seen significant changes in the economy and has been affected by the recession in many ways. Ohio has had one of the highest levels of unemployment in the past ten years. Jobs in Ohio are difficult to find even with a college degree. Graduates of college and baby boomers who are laid off accept menial jobs, sometimes at minimum wage at fast food restaurants.

Even with the prospect of being hired, there is always the possibility of glitches in the system. For example, here is what happened to our grandson, Michael (Mike).

Michael is the epitome of what a gentleman should be. He is polite, kind and respectful of others. Michael had just graduated from Kent State Magna Cum Laude and started looking for a new job in his field of Hotel Management. He applied for three different jobs in another area and was interviewed for all three jobs. In the meantime, he started looking for an apartment in that particular area in case he obtained one of the jobs.

Michael was called back for a second interview by all three places of employment. He felt that one of them was the best opportunity for him to advance. The job was his and now he had to find an apartment within a short driving distance. He looked at about five apartments. Like most young men, he did not want to look at too many so as to make it simple. He found the perfect apartment for him, not too old with modern appliances and an interesting view.

All the papers were signed, but the apartment owner wanted our grandson to have a co-signer. I said I would be happy to help him. However, the apartment owner did a background check on Michael who had never been in any kind of trouble. He told Michael that he found out that he had a criminal record in Texas, but it happened to be another Michael with the same last name. The apartment owner rejected Michael even though it was another person. Evidently, the Social Security office had made a mistake when they typed in the criminal's Social Security number. It was the same as Michael's.

How could that happen? Now Michael did not have the apartment of his dreams. He and his mother and I tried to prove that it was a mistake. Mike had excellent credit, and the apartment owner admitted that not many criminals have excellent credit. Nevertheless, they probed my credit as co-signer and found out that I also had excellent credit but they wanted proof.

After sending all my papers, the apartment owner asked for more. No matter what Michael faxed them, they wanted more proof. The family was all getting tired of the apartment owners being so picky and not believing us. My message to them via Michael was "If they don't accept this proof, tell them to go jump in the lake." I searched once more for proof of sufficient funds, went with my daughter and Mike to Columbus to sign many papers. Michael was finally accepted for the apartment.

Talk about hassles, people even today learn to cope with them when they are young! Bureaucracy can make errors that cause much frustration. Two weeks of trying to prove that he was not the criminal was upsetting.

All's well that ends well. Michael started his new job and moved into his apartment.

Hold on, there is more to this story. His working hours at the restaurant who hired him were not to his liking. He was asked to work odd hours during the day and night and did not get his proper sleep. After one shift of three in the morning until nine AM, he was asked to come back for the 3PM to midnight shift. There were many days like that. It was not what he was told at the interviews. Michael started looking for another job after three weeks of not getting enough rest to function normally.

In order to obtain a job these days, one must persevere and send out many resumes and that's what Michael did before an opportunity rose. He was interviewed by at least eight different people and that process took two months or more. At last he was hired to do a job he really likes with normal working hours. He is a sales representative and loves the job. Since Michael is a rather quiet person, no one expected him to be a salesman. Perhaps some of the genes pass on down through generations.

Frank's daughter, Lori, is also a sales type person who co-owns a photography studio. Lori graduated from Ohio State and is fluent in Spanish and French. She has two good looking children. Frank helps with their care after school some days which I think is remarkable.

CHAPTER 33—Housing Problems

Some of our family has had problems with the deteriorating economy as far as housing is concerned. Some of them have downsized. Selling a house or buying a new one is a great concern at this time and causes some grief. Our son nearby would like to buy another home but feels that his home might not sell and if it did, they would lose the equity.

A lot of the population in the United States bought homes in the past ten years that they could not afford and then were unable to keep up the payments even though both parties worked. People tend to live beyond their means and perhaps expect too much when they are first married. It is also common for both spouses to work until they are sixty-five years old. In my era, it was rare for any women with children to work.

Banks were failing a couple of years ago but the government subsidized them to keep our country from falling into a true depression similar to The Great Depression. Automobile manufacturers were helped out, too, in order to keep the jobs. The jobless are many but each year the economy is getting better. As mentioned before, Ohio has been one of the states hit the hardest as far as unemployment is concerned.

Democrats and Republicans keep trying to find better solutions to a better economy. Since they do not agree on the policies that might work, it may take some time for our country to prosper again but I believe we are on the way.

Health reform and coverage for the poor is so important. Since I grew up during The Great Depression, I sympathize with anyone who does not have a job or enough food to feed their family. People tend to think that those on welfare are not truly deserving of this help but I disagree. Some may take advantage of the system but there are more legitimate cases than not. How can one be at fault if they have lost their job due to cutbacks?

Since I am no expert on politics even though I pay attention to what is going on in the world, I have my own opinion and am not trying to force it on anyone. I watch The McLaughlin Group and This Week and believe there is hope that our country will find a way to better the situation.

What I have observed is that most Presidents, Democrat or Republican, from Thomas Jefferson on down tend to get caught up in a web of politics and, like the spider, sometimes get tangled up in it. Undoubtedly, this happens in any level of political offices, too.

CHAPTER 34—Back to the Past

What could be better at the age of eighty than to take a trip down Memory Lane, back to the year 1939? I had the marvelous opportunity to fulfill that desire when Bobby was visiting us in 2008. He offered to drive Frank and me to Kittanning, Pennsylvania where we had lived for three years. Bob decided that he did not want to accompany us.

I had thought many times about going back to see Kittanning but never seemed to find the right time. My family enjoyed living there when I was growing up, and I retained fond memories of that small town. I had heard that it had not changed since 1939 and I wanted to find out if that was true. Frank also had a hankering to see one of the eleven localities where we grew up. Kittanning was only thirty miles from my birth city of Pittsburgh, so we also decided to visit my cousin Phyllis and her husband Bob who lives on Mount Troy.

It was a rather chilly day for the day before the official start of summer. However, it did not rain. As we leisurely drove there, I was fascinated with the Navigator guiding us, all the while marveling at today's technology.

As we approached Kittanning, I noticed a familiar bridge and hill, but the courthouse looked larger. Like a flash of lightning, I remembered a jail from years gone by that we passed to get to our apartment. I did not see Isaly's ice cream store, nor the movie theaters we loved as children. As we drove down the highway left of the courthouse, I realized we had missed the street where our apartment should have been. We turned around and went back to that street. We could see the hill which we had zoomed down on our sleds as youngsters of nine and five. There were more homes on that hill than years ago.

As we traveled along, I recognized the street where I learned how to ride a bicycle. We were able to find our way to St. Mary's of Guadalupe, the school and church we attended. How beautiful they had been remodeled. We took pictures in front of the church and inside. We ventured to the home next to the church to see if we could get some information. The nun who opened the door told us that the pastor was not home that day. St. Mary's is located on the corner across from the Allegheny River which

has a boardwalk along the shore.

I was determined to find a library to donate the first book I had written which I called SMALL CHANGE (revised as THE ADVENTURES OF FLOSSIE, ROBBIE, AND JUNEY During The Great Depression). The children's book includes a chapter about our life in Kittanning.

We found the library with the help of a passerby. The library had an experienced and accommodating staff. I donated SMALL CHANGE to a staff worker who seemed happy to include my book in their library.

As I was speaking to the volunteer about my book, Bobby was questioning another staff member about past records. She was able to find papers from 1939 which had the names and addresses of the population in Kittanning, and that included our parents' names, occupations and address. We found out that our address was 107 Oak Ave. There had been a gas station across the street where I used to buy a loaf of bread and pay for it later when mother ran out of flour. Now, a house sat there, an unintentional target for cars turning left or right.

We drove back to the main street where we had lunch at Dizzy Lizzy's which had been called Clark's Restaurant when we lived there. We had never eaten at a restaurant when we lived in Kittanning because we did not have the money. Mother baked bread every other day. We lived a simple life and never starved, but there was barely enough to eat because our dad was on the road selling and looking for jobs. His meat packing company he started when we moved to Kittanning had failed because of his habit of extending credit to many customers who did not pay their bills. The Great Depression affected many people. My father was also robbed one day of some of his profits and the culprit was never found.

I noticed that Dizzy Lizzy's was on the corner across from the two hotels where my brothers and I watched a fire once. We also watched tight-rope walkers gingerly trek back and forth from one hotel to another across the connected wires. We were fascinated and loved the entertainment.

After a tasty lunch, Bobby, Frank and I drove to Pittsburgh. As we approached the steep hill and the steps that led to my cousin Phyllis' house, Frank and I grimaced. So many steps to conquer! We were able to make the long climb to the house and were greeted by Aunt Meryl, Phyllis and her husband, Bob.

Aunt Meryl is my deceased Uncle Philip Schmitt's wife. She looks good for the age of 94. We had a pleasant visit with our relatives. They were very hospitable. Their back yard looked like a painting by Thomas Kinkade. Standing on their deck, we could see the steeple of Most Holy Name Church which we attended when we lived on Troy Hill in Pittsburgh. We laughed when we reminisced about the old days and adventures.

On the way home, we hashed over our trip and I thanked Bobby for driving us there to renew fond memories.

CHAPTER 35—Back to the Present

Today is Friday, February 4, 2011. The weather has been worse this winter than most. It snowed more than usual in December 2010. Some days our driveway was impassable and after it was plowed, it snowed again. City snow plows cleared our street occasionally only to deposit mounds of snow at the entrance of driveways. On Tuesday, after I arrived home from my heart specialist appointment which consisted of a heart ultrasound and a heart monitor strapped on me afterwards, I visited Bob. Upon my return home my car became stuck in the accumulated snow and ice in our driveway. The temperatures have been at an all time low and ice freezes into hard packs of precipitation making it difficult to drive uphill.

After calling my friend whom I pay to clear the driveway, he could not navigate my car up the driveway without burning the tires, either. He scraped the snow and ice about five times and finally was able to back my car up our obstacle ridden driveway. There are fences, the neighbor's air conditioner and our small flower garden plot in the way plus a curve and two window wells in our basement windows.

Wednesday was a blizzard type day with freezing ice, snow and sleet. I was supposed to return the heart monitor after twenty four hours and the time was up at 11 AM Wednesday. I unhooked the cumbersome heart monitor and did not leave the house that day. My son-in-law slipped in his driveway that very same day and my daughter in Kansas called to tell me that she fell on black ice as she stepped out her front door. They were not hurt. On Wednesday evening, our niece who lives in Akron was hit by a semi-trailer truck on her way to nursing school. She is recovering from a slight concussion.

Marlene picked me up in her van on Thursday morning to return the heart monitor and to take me to the eye specialist in Stow where the doctor put drops in my eyes. I learned that people with blue eyes take longer to be able to see after the drops than those with brown or green eyes. I spent the day dozing off and on until my eyesight returned to normal about six and a half hours later. Well, not really normal, for I was told that I need to have laser surgery on my right eye to remove the film that formed after my cataract surgery a year and a half ago. That minor surgery is scheduled for March 16, 2011. In order to keep driving, this must be done. Of course, glasses may have helped but they cost a lot of money and I would rather not wear them. The doctor told me that Medicare will pay for the surgery and does not pay for glasses.

Friday was sunny although still very cold and icy. As I stepped out the back porch door, an icicle nearly missed my head and I had trouble keeping my footing because the ice was molded into large and small bumpy lumps. The salt did not work but I forged ahead to water workout, the beauty parlor, to play Bingo at Quirk with two of my friends, and to the care home to see Bob. At the beauty parlor, another patron was talking excitedly about being stuck in her driveway and I empathized with her. However, my beautician said that she had been busy but did not go in to work on Wednesday when the city was practically shut down. Schools were closed and just about everything else.

My friends and I saw Bob in therapy. We watched while he tried to stand up with the bar. It seemed to me that he was doing better but perhaps he was at the same stage as before he had pneumonia. It is difficult to know if his evaluation next Wednesday will be favorable or not.

After I hung up all his clothing that I had tagged, he did not want to push his wheelchair by himself. Since I am not allowed to push him, I urged him to do so. He complied to a certain extent and slowly worked his way up to the television lobby. Two aides noticed and commented that I was doing the right thing because he needed the exercise to keep his circulation moving. After we reached the table and sat down, Bob complained to me that I did not care about him and spent all my time with my girlfriends. Granted, I go somewhere with my friends about once a week, but it does hurt my feelings a little that he does not understand that I have been iced in and had doctor appointments. He also tells our daughters here that all I do is go out with my girlfriends and that I don't like him. He also said that he did not want me to come to see him over the weekend.

This is not what I envisioned about twenty years ago - aging gracefully into the sunset with my husband. Thoughts of holding hands and being treated with respect are not going to happen. Nevertheless, I will carry on with a smile on my face. Bob usually apologizes when he sees that I am not happy with him.

As we were leaving, Bob yelled out at the top of his voice that he loved me. Dementia is very puzzling. I called back, "I love you, too, but you better behave."

When I arrived home, I was pleased that I made it into the garage and was able to scoot over the ice while holding on to the fence and house. Home, sweet home! Thank you, God!

CHAPTER 36—Angel Touches

When Joyce was eight months pregnant, she and Ed returned to Akron from North Carolina. She drove most of the way, while Ed slept through some of the snowstorm. Midnight, their giant black Labrador dog, accompanied them in the back seat. We agreed that they could live with us until they were settled here.

Ed was able to find a better paying electrician's job. I enjoyed helping them and cooking for them. I was thrilled that I would finally have a grandchild here at home.

Two weeks before their baby was born, Bobby and Jan had another baby boy. He was very healthy and handsome, and they named him Eric.

Nichole Marie was born at City Hospital, our first granddaughter. She has always been special to me, the twin who, by the grace of God, made it through all the trauma. I helped Joyce take care of her, bathed her, rocked her, fed her, and enjoyed her immensely the three months they lived with us. She was a beautiful happy, smiling baby.

I gave Joyce and Ed our room. Bob and I slept upstairs and Dave was sleeping in the other upstairs bedroom. Nichole (Nikki) slept downstairs across the hall from Joyce and Ed. One night when Nikki was about a month old, I heard her crying. I knew that Joyce was exhausted that day, so I started getting out of bed to help her. As I put on my robe, the crying stopped, so I assumed Joyce had gotten up to rock her. I heard the rocking chair squeaking on the uncarpeted hardwood floor. Bob and Ed slept through the night and didn't hear the baby or the rocking chair, but Dave heard it.

The next morning as I was making breakfast, Joyce said:

"Thanks, Mom, for taking care of Nikki last night."

I replied, "I started to get up, Joyce, but heard the rocking chair and I thought you were rocking her."

We both thought that Dave must have rocked Nikki. He loved Joyce and Nikki and was always willing to help. When Joyce thanked Dave, he said he did not get up to rock her, either. We have never been able to explain who rocked Nikki, and marvel at this phenomenon. There is no explanation, except to wonder if it was my mother or an angel from above. Ever since Nikki was born, I had thought many times about how much she would have enjoyed seeing her sweet great granddaughter.*

*This story has been published by Joan Wester Anderson in her book The Power of Miracles and also in Chicken Soup for the Soul – Living Catholic Faith.

There have been many other unexplained happenings in my life, so I believe that anything is possible.

The out-of-body experience at the age of seven had a definite effect on my approach to life and I became more devout in my beliefs and felt more compassionate about others instead of myself. I have had no fear of death since then. I know it will be a beautiful, peaceful coming.

Sometimes I think the girl who rescued me may have been an angel, or was guided by her angel to be there at the right moment to save my life. I thank God every day for saving me. I would have missed so much, my husband of sixty-two years, our five wonderful children, our nine bright grandchildren and our sweet great-grandchildren, the opportunity to help others with my books and poetry. I firmly believe that God saved me and blessed me for a purpose, and I feel my angel is watching over me all days and all ways.

When our family no longer had enough to eat, or proper clothing for winter, or a father we could count on to support us the way that fathers should, the deep faith that embodied me after the near-drowning sustained me through all the adversity of the Great Depression and World War II, being abandoned continually by my father, the lack of food and necessities of life.

My wonderful caring mother, who I sometimes think of as a Saint, and I prayed and prayed and we never starved. I kept smiling, unafraid of anything, and my brothers and I worked hard for everything we had. I felt God and his angels were watching over our whole family.

I still feel that way today. I pray, to God, in Jesus' name, mostly for other people. My prayers are answered so much of the time that I am in awe of prayer. God is such a kindly benefactor. Perhaps some of the answers never happen the way I expect them to, but I realize God has plans for me, and answers in His own way. He knows what is best for me, and protects me by sending angels to guide me.

I continually thank Him for the gift of life and health and even pain. He suffered and died for us, and we must offer our sufferings up to Him.

The more positive my belief in Him, the more positive my belief in everything honorable and good. Whatever befalls, I still feel His arms embrace me as they did in the tunnel of light—from age seven to eighty-three and counting.

I am an ordinary person like everyone else, but I have over the course of time experienced some extraordinary occurrences.

Many events that seem like coincidences have affected circumstances in a positive manner. Perhaps these coincidences should be called God-incidences.

A significant event happened two days before my dear mother passed away unexpectedly many years ago. Bob was driving the family car when someone made a left turn directly in front of us, resulting in an accident that must have been meant to happen. Although no one was seriously injured, the car was damaged to the extent we were unable to drive it, so it was towed to a repair garage. We had planned to leave for Fort Lauderdale, Florida with our five children the next day, August 15, 1965 to visit Bob's parents but the trip had to be canceled. We weren't sure how many miles we would travel each day, so did not make reservations ahead of time. Thus no one would have been able to get in touch with us on the way down, a trip which ordinarily would take about three days.

It was such a shock when Mom had a coronary occlusion at 3:30 A.M. on August 16. If not for the car accident, we would have been on our way to Florida and no one could have informed us of her untimely passing until at least three days later. I would have been more than devastated. I loved her so much and never a day passes that I do not think of her and miss the closeness we had.

When I was trying to determine how to raise the money to print my first book instead of using household funds, I won my first poetry prize, and then three athletic board contests with my mother's favorite number, sixty-four. Within a month, I had the $400 needed for the first printing of one hundred books. I was not in the habit of winning so often.

When Aunt Betty passed away at the age of eighty-four from cancer, David and I wanted to attend her funeral and drove the two hours from Akron, Ohio, to Pittsburgh, Pa., on the turnpike, our usual route to Pittsburgh. As we were about to exit the turnpike, we were delayed twenty minutes due to traffic congestion, thus we were unable to meet at Aunt Betty's and Uncle Pat's home as planned. We had hoped to follow him and their daughter, Kathy Sue to the memorial mass, which was to be held at St. Theresa of Avila Catholic church.

David and I had no idea where St. Theresa's was located, but drove down the highway which we assumed was in the vicinity of the church. Since we did not see any signs that would have helped us find the church, we decided to stop at a gas station where the attendant said he never heard of St. Theresa's. We then drove farther south to stop at another gas station to find a map, or make a call to the church. St. Theresa's was not listed in the phone book—how unfortunate! The attendant there said he never heard of the church, either. David looked at a map, and determined we should drive north to reach Lindley St., which intersected Avila. However, we weren't sure whether Lindley was directly off the highway or not.

The mass was to start at ten A.M., and it was already nine-fifty A.M. I was about to panic but prayed instead. It was very important to me to arrive at the church on time out of respect for Aunt Betty and her family.

I insisted that we stop at another gas station. Upon entering, I asked for directions to St. Theresa's, but the clerk and two customers at that station also said they never heard of it. Just as I turned around to leave, I noticed a handsome, well dressed young man, in a suit, with a tie, and a dark topcoat approach the door. I mentioned to David, "I think this young man will know where St. Theresa's church is located."

I asked him immediately upon entering if he knew, and he eagerly gave us the directions. He politely said "Turn left at the light, proceed up the highway, and turn left at the intersection." I thanked him and we proceeded on our way farther north. As we approached an intersection, we happened to be driving in the center lane when suddenly the young man appeared in his car on the right hand side of us, and pointed to the left side of the hill. I waved to thank him and sure enough, about a mile up the hill, we found Lindley Street which connected to Avila; and down the hill was beautiful St. Theresa of Avila. David remarked, "Perhaps Aunt Betty sent that young man to guide us," and I agreed.

It was now ten minutes past ten A.M. as David pulled up to the church entrance so that I wouldn't be too late, while he parked the car. As I entered, I felt a sense of relief and gratitude because the priest hadn't as yet walked up the aisle to start the mass. I said, "Good morning, Father." He replied,

"Good morning, we were waiting." I should have asked him why.

As I walked up the aisle toward the altar, I noticed my cousin Janice and her husband Jerry from Wisconsin and sat with them. David joined us, and we felt that God was with us as the priest walked up to the altar to start the mass.

I really felt Aunt Betty's presence, also, for I believe that she was instrumental to us finding the church on time. Perhaps the young man was an angel, for he looked like he could have been of heavenly descent. I don't believe I have ever seen such a meticulously dressed person, except when I saw the angels as a child.

One of the poets in my group was lonely and rather despondent after his wife divorced him. She would not let him see his children. One day, he stopped at the grave site of my mother in Oakwood Cemetery. His father and sister are buried in the same cemetery. As he knelt by my mother's gravestone and looked into the haunting eyes of the Blessed Virgin Mary on the stone and then lifted his eyes up at the sky, he saw an angel formed in the clouds, and he felt some peace and was in awe, for he believed that my mother could possibly be an angel, too. I had written a poem, THOSE HAUNTING EYES, about the carving of the Virgin Mary in her tombstone, and that is what drew him to this location.

After he walked the four miles home, there on his doorstep was a small kitten, a white Calico with orange markings. He took the stray in and now is not as lonely. He named her Sherbet and they have become close companions as cats and people do. She is a very friendly kitten, and my husband and I love her, too.

THOSE HAUNTING EYES

I watch the parade of life pass by each day
with scintillating sound of laughter and music,
joy and sadness, or tales of woe,
peace and love with outstretched hands
needing, or extending help, to those in distress.
I personally perceive the world through rose colored glasses
But know there is anger, war, waste and fighting.
We remember the veterans and their glorified past
and watch with pride their parades on special days,
Hear reverberating echoes of melodic memories
which lead us to the resting place
of heroes and ordinary people.
I stop at my dear mother's grave site
to plant geraniums and pray,
Mystified by those haunting eyes of the Virgin,
those deep pools of understanding and feeling
caught in the carving of her tombstone.

Yes, the parade of life still passes me by
But I begin to sense some of the enigmas of life
as I tenderly gaze with profound emotion
at those granite illusions.

CHAPTER 37—The Importance of Prayer

For many years now, there has been much controversy about whether The Ten Commandments should be displayed in schools. My thinking is that they should also be followed at home by the parents or parent. Today's morals, like a broken window, are lacking in respect to The Ten Commandments. Society tends to hide from this fact and a child's upbringing could suffer adversely.

Tucked away as if in a drawer of a filing cabinet, it seems that morality, civility, honesty, integrity, discipline, and righteousness have been replaced by a modern lack of spirituality. Instead of following the Ten Commandments, they have been replaced by prejudice, permissiveness, sexual freedom, and political maneuvering. Our message to the children in this day and age is "it's okay to have sex before marriage, it's okay to live together, it's tolerable to cheat in government, it's a right to own guns." I shudder when mass killings take place in schools or elsewhere.

We hear so much hype by the media that nothing surprises anyone anymore. Oh, yes, drugs, sexual abuse, guns and killings tend to be commonplace. Violence and hatred seem to be expected.

Let's get our priorities in order, not like papers scattered on a desk left unsorted. We need to teach respect, morality and manners instead of accepting so-called "attitudes." Let's get back to the way it used to be when parents where in charge in a loving way and children were not always the center of attention, getting whatever they want.

Too much doting on children by parents causes them to rebel because they feel parents do not care how they act or what they do. Children need rules to follow. Parents who have tough love produce children who succeed in life. And for those who feel they must build up their offspring's self-esteem, that is only earned by the child's own self. What a parent says and does is also very important. By living and teaching the Ten Commandments, parents show love. Children feel loved and respected when parents take an interest in their activities, also.

Even if both mother and father have to work, they must take time to guide and listen to their children. They must know where they are at all times, with whom they associate and what they are doing.

Yes, there will still be some abuse in the universe because there are some sick people, but it wouldn't be so prevalent if most parents do not abuse their child in any way. Abuse can be the acceptance or promotion of drugs, sexual and moral decay instead of trying to correct it. It all starts at home.

The daily habit of praying can conquer all things, can restore hope in all situations and is necessary every day for peace of mind. Morning prayers, prayers before meals, evening prayers, and most important, prayers of thanks to God for the gifts He bestows on us each day can make each day a better day. Children who are taught to pray or who read the Bible will be more likely than not to follow the Ten Commandments.

Along with prayer, parents need to limit the time their children watch television and play with all the electronic toys that attract them. Parents also need to make sure their children play outdoors instead of sitting in front of the computer most of the time.

Children tend look up to sports figures. Parents need to be heroes to their boys and girls instead of ill mannered, sometimes violent, so-called sports heroes who get paid beyond expectations. School teachers are heroes in their own way and should be paid more because they teach our children knowledge. However, they cannot be held solely responsible for teaching discipline, morals and manners. That should begin at home at the tender age of one or two years, when the child understands "no" and feels loved at the same time.

Respect for others must be taught at home by parents, no matter what race, color, income or religion. 'Families who pray together, stay together' is an old cliché which works in any era.

I continually thank God for the gift of life and health and even pain. He suffered and died for us, and we must offer our sufferings up to Him.

The more positive my belief in Him, the more positive my belief in everything honorable and good. Whatever befalls, I still feel His arms embrace me as they did in the tunnel of light.

CHAPTER 38—Bob Saves Marlene*

*I think it is important to include the following chapters from two of my short story books because they are all a part of my world, the past and the future. They are in random sequence which is the form of most short stories but I think you will find them amusing and informative in their content.

Nothing unusual had happened in Marlene's life the first six years of school. She had always received top grades and had many friends. The teachers all liked her even though she was a chatterbox. She was invited to many 'girls only' parties.

When she was in the sixth grade, one of her classmates planned a 'girl-boy party'. Marlene was eager to tell me about being invited but had a feeling I wouldn't approve. She was right. I said, "I think sixth grade is too young to have a 'girl-boy' party. I'm sorry, but you will have to skip this one."

Marlene was so disappointed that she told everyone at school the next day that I told her she was too young to attend the party. That turned out to be a big mistake. Five of her so-called friends were infuriated by my decision because they thought their mothers might be influenced by it.

They threatened Marlene, "We're gonna' get you after school." When class was dismissed for the day, Marlene became frightened when she saw the five girls approaching her on the playground. They immediately started to pound on her.

At that very same moment, Bob came out the school door and broke up the crowd and saved Marlene from a beating. The kids had forgotten that Marlene's dad worked part-time as a custodian at the school. He admonished them for ganging up on Marlene and sent them home. The children liked him, and they never picked on Marlene again.

Marlene arrived home out of breath and explained to me what happened. I was glad that Bob saved our lovely child from an undeserved attack and was surprised that the girls became hostile to her remark and my decision. After all, everyone has a right to their opinion. I did not think it appropriate to rush relationships that early. After that happened Marlene curbed her tongue.

She didn't even want to go to the party anymore and agreed these particular girls were wrong to attack her because of my decision. When Marlene was in the seventh grade, I gave her permission to attend a 'girl-boy' party as long as there was supervision. She was actually glad she waited for she felt more mature and able to make the right decisions when confronted by boys. She decided that if she got married and had a daughter, she would not rush the 'boy-girl' relationships, either. Maybe she would even prolong it another year!

CHAPTER 39—Camping?

When Joyce was nine years old, we decided to take her on a on a trip to Cook Forest in Pennsylvania. Our other children were all working that summer.

Our family had never been camping before as a unit. Cindy and Marlene had been to Girl Scout camp and Bobby had been to Boy Scout camp a few times. Bob and I were never interested in camping, so we were rather shocked to see the primitive cabin and inhale its musty odor.

After a restless night's sleep on the lumpy mattresses, we ate cereal for breakfast. We asked Joyce what she would like to do first that day, and she replied, "Let's ride bikes." We rented two bicycles, one a bicycle built for two. Joyce and I had fun balancing the bicycle built for two and followed Bob along the road.

In the afternoon, we took Joyce to a children's amusement park nearby and naturally, she enjoyed the rides. They were especially fun for her because they had nursery rhyme themes which she loved.

Returning to the cabin, I cooked spaghetti and meat sauce in the crude cookware. Since there was no television set, we read, talked and told knock-knock jokes until bedtime. Good old family stuff!

The following day, Joyce went horseback riding along with other tourists, on a special trail, while Bob and I waited for her. We drove around later to look for canoe rentals and found a rental where the river was easy to navigate, or so we thought. You see, Bob had never been canoeing in his whole life, and never even learned to swim. Although I had been canoeing as a teen, I did not think I was capable of paddling the canoe by myself.

Joyce sat in the middle of the canoe while Bob and I made an attempt to paddle. It was obvious immediately that this was not going to work, because we could not paddle in sync. The canoe, out of control, landed on some rocks in shallow water, and try as hard as he could, Bob could not budge it while in the canoe, so the family sat there for a while trying to figure out what to do. There was no one in sight to ask for help.

Bob was wearing brand new fifty dollar shoes, so I suggested he take them off and then wade in the water to pull the canoe off the rocks. But Bob, irritated by the whole situation, stepped into the water with his new shoes, anyhow, and finally pulled the canoe free of the rocks.

Joyce and I could not help laughing about the whole incident, especially when we saw Bob's new shoes drying out on a tree limb in the sun later that afternoon. The shoes were not completely dry by morning, but Bob wore them, regardless. Every step he took was a swish, swish.

However, after the shoes dried out, they were still wearable, although they did not look new anymore. Needless to say, we never went camping again, nor did we want to. Our perception of camping after that was a week at the Holiday Inn.

CHAPTER 40—GRANDPA IS MISSING

The city of Barberton, Ohio, holds its annual mum festival in September every year at Lake Anna. There are many brilliant colors of mums which creates a spectacular view. Other forms of entertainment are provided for three days, a small train ride, a Ferris Wheel and a water ski show.

When our grandchildren, Nikki and Mike, were twelve and ten respectively, we took them to the water ski show

Grandpa parked the car a few streets away from the lake, and later decided to go back to move the car, at least that's what he told Grandma and the kids. There was a huge crowd and everyone enjoyed the flowers and the water ski show.

After the show, the four of us started walking to the car, but Grandpa couldn't find it. They walked around the same block twice, which took about ten minutes. Grandpa finally announced that he did not move the car from the parking spot, but just pulled it up a little.

Then Grandma, Nikki and Mike remembered where the car was parked and invited Grandpa to follow them. He protested, saying they were going in the wrong direction. He went his own way.

Grandma and the kids found the car without any problem and decided to find Grandpa. After Grandma drove around several blocks twice, Nikki and Mike became upset, and Mike started to cry, "Papa's lost, Papa's lost." Nikki was supposed to baby sit in twenty minutes and feared she would be late.

Grandma decided she would leave, take Nikki to her baby sitting job, and come back for Grandpa afterwards. Just as they turned the last corner, there was Grandpa standing there looking bewildered. He got in the car and was embarrassed and angry with himself.

Nikki and Grandma gently lectured him, but felt sorry for him at the same time. Alls well that ends well, they thought, and the rest of the day went great.

CHAPTER 41—The Whiteout

I'm not afraid of very many things, but driving a car or being a passenger in a car is not my favorite thing to do. I'd rather fly in an airplane. Short distances require one to drive, so I drive just where I need to go, avoiding circles and expressways.

One evening five years ago, just before Christmas, my husband and I were driving to the Cleveland airport from Akron, Ohio, to pick up Cindy who was arriving from Kansas for the holidays. Akron is thirty-five miles south of Cleveland.

A light snow was falling as we left for the airport, but soon turned into a whiteout. The windshield wipers did not help at all, and it was as if giant snowballs were being hurled at us. Even our peripheral vision was blocked, and we could not see a thing, except a dim red tail light on the truck ahead. We relied on this red light to stay on the road. Suddenly, the light disappeared as the truck exited the turnpike and then there was nothing to follow. I prayed for another light, and for a safe trip.

As we inched along, something told me that we should stop right NOW. I called out to my Bob, "Stop the car!" which he did immediately. We opened the door to find ourselves perched on top of a deep gully alongside the left lane.

"Thank-you, God and our angels," I uttered. We veered to the right lane and followed another truck's red tail light in front of us. Neither one of us thought about pulling off the highway because we did not want to be late to pick up our daughter.

The snow and blizzard never let up as we followed the light for about ten miles until the truck turned off the turnpike. We were enveloped in the trauma of blindness once again and traveled very slowly a few more miles.

Once again, I sensed that we should stop, and I shouted, "Stop the car, Bob!" We got out of the car to find ourselves on the edge of another deep gully on the left. I pleaded, "Dear God, please, no more."

Greeted by another truck's tail light as we returned to the right lane, we followed it until we approached the airport. It was with a sigh of relief and thankfulness when we embraced our daughter.

The drive home was uneventful because the whiteout had dissipated. We were grateful and happy to enter our driveway safe and sound. The visit could not have been better.

CHAPTER 42—Babysitting Mishaps

From the age of fifty-one to sixty-five, I traveled to Texas at least once a year to help take care of our grandchildren. Our daughter, Cindy, and her husband, Russ, went on a deserved vacation at least twice a year. Our son, Bobby and his wife, Jan lived nearby in Texas. They asked me to baby sit their two children a few years later after their sons were born. At first, I felt relaxed and felt confident; after all, I had raised five children! However, after a series of mishaps, I realized that taking care of our children when I was young was much easier than the responsibility of baby sitting our grandchildren.

The first time Cindy left nine month old Philip in Grandma's charge, he wouldn't let Grandma change his diaper. He cried continuously and crawled away. It took about an hour to change him.

The next few visits went smoothly as planned. However, after Philip's baby brother, Shaun was born three years later, things took a turn for the worse. While I was baby sitting them for the evening, Philip was so excited to see me that he started jumping on his bed. I asked him to please stop jumping and he did, but as he jumped off the bed, he landed on a ball. He actually didn't hit his head hard. However, I noticed he seemed quiet after that. I didn't think anything was really wrong except that he got scared. I put the boys to bed an hour later and they fell fast asleep.

When Cindy and Russ arrived home, they checked on the boys before they retired. All was well. At one o'clock in the morning, little

Philip awakened and proceeded to throw up. Cindy and I got up to see what was wrong. Evidently, Philip had had a slight concussion after he fell on the ball the wrong way. He had to be kept quiet for a day. I felt bad, although I knew I could not have prevented the fall.

The next year's visit, sixteen month old Shaun slid head first into the baseboard and had a big knot on his head, but was all right. Bob and I had been having so much fun with the little boys we loved so much. We never left the boys alone, but Shaun was hard to keep up with, and we both felt that baby sitting was much more difficult than raising our own children.

A few years later, when Cindy and Russ moved to Kansas, Philip underwent a tonsillectomy right before a business trip his parents felt obliged to attend. I was hesitant to stay with the boys at first because I had a premonition that Philip would start bleeding while we were there. However, we agreed to stay to please our wonderful daughter.

The day after Cindy and Russ left for their trip, Philip jumped off a coffee table and started bleeding. We rushed him to the hospital, and by the time the doctor checked him, the bleeding had stopped. We took him home, and once again he began bleeding the next morning. We drove to the hospital once more. The doctor said to keep him quiet for one day and the bleeding would stop. Unfortunately, that day was Shaun's sixth birthday, and the plans we had made for celebrating had to be canceled.

Shaun was so unhappy he ran out of the house without a jacket in sixty degree weather and rode his bike up and down the neighborhood in the middle of the street. I was nearly frantic with worry and disappointment because Shaun would not obey me.

I was beginning to wonder why, through no fault of my own, something unusual seemed to happen nearly every time we baby sat. And more was to come!

We also had many mishaps when we stayed with Bobby and Jan's sons in Texas. One visit when I was baby sitting Ryan and Eric, their dog, Benji, and several cats, I made the mistake of including a red shirt in the same batch with the boys' underwear. Although I usually did not mix colors at home, I had seen others mix some of them. I was exhausted and to save time, I threw a red T-shirt in the load of wash. It was horrifying to see the results—all the underwear turned pink! I soaked all the pink clothing in Clorox and washed them again, to no avail. I was devastated, as was Jan when she saw what happened. It was enough to make a grown woman cry!

I blamed some of my exhaustion on the cats who woke me up every morning at five o'clock to go outside and thus robbed me of sleep. The cats nearly scared me to death one night. The security lights had gone out and being in the dark seemed eerie. Nevertheless, I fell into a deep sleep until there was a loud thud on the bedroom door which would have awakened the dead. Thump, thump, thump, again and again, caused me to think that a prowler was trying to break in. Then it dawned on me that it might be the cats wanting to go outside a little early. Sure enough, they were jumping up on the door because they wanted out. During that visit, one of them also kept walking on the dining room table, much to my chagrin. I loved the cats, but loved Benji much more because he did not cause trouble.

The boys also stayed up late, as was their custom, so that I was overwhelmed every visit, and wasn't thinking clearly. Ryan and Eric wore pink underwear for a couple of years, I understand.

The next visit, two months after Bob had broken his shoulder in two places, we traveled to Texas to stay with Ryan and Eric. We loved them so much, and planned to take them many places, but a bizarre thing happened. We were ready to leave for Toys R Us when we noticed that both Bobby and Jan's automobiles had a flat tire. Since Bob's shoulder was not completely healed, he couldn't change the tires and they could not go to the store. The next day a kind neighbor repaired both flats, so we took our grandsons to buy them presents.

A terrible thing happened another time the grandparents went to Texas. Grandma and Grandpa thought they would surprise Bobby and Jan by cleaning the whole house the day before their arrival home. The old vacuum that I had always used before wouldn't work, and nine year old Ryan told us that he knew how to operate the new one. He told me how much water to pour into the tank. I was hoping he was right. As Grandpa was vacuuming the hallway, we realized that

242

something was burning. Grandma told Grandpa to stop, but he kept running it for a few more minutes. That was the end of the vacuuming, the vacuum, and practically the end of the relationship. Grandma had not used good judgment.

I apologized over and over for breaking the vacuum, and offered to pay for the repair.

Shortly before our last visit to Texas, I fell from a chair and broke my elbow so was not feeling up to par. Bobby and Jan were so kind to let us stay at their condo, and Jan went out of her way to prepare food, delicious spaghetti sauce and a homemade apple pie. Grandma hadn't been able to digest spaghetti sauce since she had her gall bladder removed the year before, but it tasted so good that she ate a large portion. She didn't sleep all night and was shaking all over with nausea and diarrhea the next morning, so couldn't entertain the boys.

Even younger people sometimes have bad experiences when they visit. Cindy feels that something always breaks when she comes home to visit. One time the washer broke after she used it, the next time the garbage disposal quit working and the next time the microwave oven broke.

Although Bob and I would never intentionally do anything to cause trouble, we seemed to attract bad luck whenever we visited. Now all the boys are grown, and somehow everyone lived through it. One has to see the humor in it all, and realize that Grandma's and Grandpa's enjoy their grandchildren, but are always glad to get back home away from the responsibilities of taking care of little children. Having babies and taking care of them is for the young!

CHAPTER 43—Cats We Have Known

Our family loves animals, especially cats. They don't have to be of pedigree, just ordinary household cats, even strays. Two of our daughters have one cat, one daughter has two cats, and one of our sons has owned five at a time.

Our daughter, Joyce, has had many cat encounters in her life. At the age of seven, she had a pretty white cat she named Mama Kitty, who had three litters of kittens, eleven in all. The last litter was born behind our living room couch while a college football coach was recruiting our son, Bobby. This memorable occasion took precedence over the coach's dissertation.

When Joyce was seventeen, unbeknownst to her, a cat crawled up into her motor while she was visiting a friend. The poor creature got caught in her fan belt when she started the motor and the fan belt broke, entangling the cat who finally fell out much to Joyce's dismay. It was too late; not all cats have nine lives! Joyce's friend followed her to make sure she arrived home safely; but this incident was very traumatic, and she fretted about it for days

Years later, Joyce's husband, Ed, brought home a cat from the farm where he installed electricity, and they named her Christie. Christie had three kittens, one they decided to keep. They named her Marble because she was black and white all over. Suddenly, fleas were invading their home and the living room carpet was infested with them. Ed was beside himself because the fleas jumped on him and bit him. Ed took the two felines back to the farm to join the other two kittens from the litter. A few days later, poor little Marble was stepped on and crushed by one of the cows. The family felt so sad.

Joyce, Ed, and their two children, Nikki and Mike, had a pretty little white cat by the name of Yoda, whose claws were clipped and who stayed in the house, so there are no fleas. Yoda loved thirteen year old Mike and followed him around in the morning, meowing only for him. Yoda rolled over on her back, just like a dog, for everyone to stroke and pet her. She was a calm cat who listened most of the time but scratched at Joyce and Ed's bedroom every night to jump up on the bed and sleep across Joyce's feet. She never scratched on Nikki's door. It was if she seemed to know that Nikki needed her sleep, but sometimes she bothered Mike, who will let her in his room to sleep with him.

Our daughter, Marlene, had an unfortunate experience with her cat, Patches, whom she and her daughter, Shelley, loved so much. Patches was outstanding with his black and white long hair and beautiful tail that stood proudly in the air. Unfortunately, he always tried to bite Marlene and sometimes broke her skin, but she loved him to death anyhow. Her husband, Don, had never had a pet, and really wasn't too fond of Patches. Patches constantly meowed when Marlene was on her treadmill machine, and finally quit when she was finished exercising.

On Thanksgiving Day, at two A.M., Patches jumped up on top of the book shelf behind Marlene and Don's bed where he had a habit of sleeping. When Don awakened at seven A.M., he noticed that Patches was sprawled out stiff as a board at the foot of the bed. He woke up Marlene, who became distraught over her loss when she saw that Patches was gone. She and Shelley cried, off and on, all day. What an unfortunate way to start Thanksgiving Day!

Patches was only two and a half years old, so the vet assumed he had a heart problem. They buried him in a pet cemetery. Marlene was distraught over his loss and even wondered if he died because she gave him too many cat treats. She kept crying about Patches, so I suggested that she get another cat to replace him.

She found out from one of Shelley's friends, Laura, that her grandmother had five cats and really wanted to find a good home for some of them. Marlene and Shelley visited the grandmother and fell in love with one the cats, Tofu, a beautiful stray with blue eyes, part Tabby and part Siamese. Tofu replaced Patches in Marlene and Shelley's eyes, and did not bite. He was so affectionate, quiet and listened. When Marlene first took him into their home, she allowed him to sleep on her chest for four hours at a time. He liked to cuddle so she didn't want to awaken him. Even Don enjoyed Tofu and let him sleep across his chest. Tofu had a habit of scratching (his nails had also been clipped) on the center counter in the kitchen under which his food was placed, until one of the family added some water to his food. This lovable cat also rubbed up against the refrigerator, the cupboards, the stairs and even the table legs—he loved everyone and everything.

Daughter Cindy found out that she had such a clever cat, named Spike, (whom Cindy's son, Shaun, named before he realized she was a female). Before Shaun went off to college, he also owned a pretty black cat he called Marvin. Spike was always afraid of Marvin, who hissed at her, and so Spike stayed outdoors and away from him most of the time. However, both cats were compatible with Cindy's dog, Princess.

When Shaun was at college and living in a duplex with another student who owned a cat, named Cleo, there was chaos in the apartment. Marvin awakened at five A.M. every morning, ate, and then attacked Cleo, a daily routine. Partly because of Marvin, Shaun rented an apartment of his own for the next semester.

After Marvin left Cindy's home, Spike came into her own. She loved Cindy, followed her around and meowed when her water bowl was half full. She refused to drink from it until Cindy refilled it to the brim. The funniest and most clever thing Spike did was to jump up on the ledge in the bathroom every morning and meow constantly until Cindy put on her make-up before she left for school, where she taught fifth grade. Then Spike settled down. How extraordinary!

Our son, Dave, doesn't own any cats at the moment, but our son Bob, his wife, Jan, and their two sons, Ryan and Eric, own five. Three are outdoor cats, and two are indoor cats. Jan especially loves animals, so they have taken in strays from time to time that other people have dropped off in their neighborhood.

There are many stories about their cats over the past twenty years. Prissy used to catch mice, carry them to the back porch, and meow. One day years ago, Jan's five year old niece, Tanya, looked out on the porch and noticed Prissy had a mouse in her mouth. She told Jan, "Prissy has something in her mouth! Jan said, "Oh, don't worry, it's just her friend." A few minutes later, Tanya exclaimed, "Prissy's eating her friend!" Everyone laughed uncontrollably.

Their cat, Ebony, stood on her hind legs and reached up with her paws like a child reaching to be picked up. Ebony did back flips with help and always landed on her feet. When Boots wanted to be petted and anyone stopped when he wasn't ready, he swatted them with his paws to make sure they kept petting him. Boots and Grey both hunted mice and meowed on the back porch until the family acknowledged their catch, then watched the cats devour their meal of fresh mice. YUM!

Taboo, thirteen years old, has a stubby tail, with two back legs longer than the front. She looks more like a rabbit than a cat when she runs. When Bobby sits in his office at home to do paperwork, Taboo sits on the chair behind him and licks his neck.

What would we do without cats? They are companions with different personalities, they love us to death and keep us amused. Perhaps everyone should own a cat!

CHAPTER 44—Trips in Later Years

Eighty degree weather and swaying palm trees greeted Bob and me when we arrived in Harlingen, Texas in January, 1998. My cousin, Rob, a Big Band leader, met us at the airport. We waited for his daughter, Janine, who was flying in from Atlanta. He had asked her to sing with his band at a benefit concert for the girls of St. John Eudes, an orphanage in Reynosa, Mexico. We arrived at Rob's winter home at 11:00 PM.

We hadn't eaten any solid food since lunch, only pretzels passed out by the flight attendant so Janine and I whipped up a spaghetti dinner at midnight. I don't believe I have ever eaten spaghetti that late before, but it was delicious and I digested it.

The next day, Rob and Janine both melodiously played the baby grand piano in the living room. Rob practiced his trumpet each day. Janine practiced singing "All of Me" and "I Had the Craziest Dream" every day. Her voice was as sweet as honey, and clear as a bell. Such talent in one family!

Rob had fallen in love with the trumpet at the tender age of two or three. He took lessons and went on the road when he was fifteen years old to help his family. He became Professor of Music at Iowa St. University and formed his own band after retiring.

His friends from Iowa, Mary and Maurice, who also wintered in Harlingen, took him to see the orphanage of St. John Eudes and the fifty-six girls, ages five to eighteen, who resided there. Mary and

Maurice had been helping fund the orphanage. They donated food, clothing, and helped with renovations.

Rob was touched by the smiling girls, some of whom had been abused, abandoned, and some whose families could not take care of them financially. The girls wore uniforms and are taught by nuns. The older girls had many chores to do, and the younger ones made their beds and kept their rooms, large dormitories, clean and tidy.

Rob started playing a benefit concert each January to help the girls at the orphanage. He recruited players of various instruments from the Harlingen area and they practiced together. Every one is a volunteer, including singers and dancers.

Rob also entertained us by taking us on a tour the area. We crossed the Rio Grande to Progresso, Mexico, to buy souvenirs. Little boys about six or seven years old were sitting in front of the stores playing their accordions while their younger brothers were singing or dozing on their shoulders. The hot sun was very tiring.

Two days later, we drove to Reynosa, Mexico, to visit the orphanage. We passed unspeakable poverty, family shacks with outhouses, dirt floors, children sitting on buckets for chairs, and litter was everywhere. Donkeys were pulling wagons. We stopped at a shopping center, which was rather modern, where we bought hard rolls for the girls, and I bought some marshmallows to treat them. Mary and Maurice brought sacks of cabbages in the van. All of the food for the orphanage was donated.

I suspected that the children ate a lot of cabbage, because we passed fields of cabbage, fields of aloe and not much else. We were amazed at the beautiful monuments as we passed a cemetery with artificial flowers on every grave. I got the impression Mexicans honor their dead more than their living. They are a simple people, though, and have an active faith in God to see them through their poverty.

After arriving at the orphanage with its enclosed buildings, we greeted the little girls. They all gave us big hugs and smiles while saying "Alo." There was Cynthia, Lupita, Celia, Breanna, and Flor, to name a few. Their smiles were contagious, and my heart went out to them as they clutched my hand and followed us on the tour of their home.

Their chapel was simple, yet elegant. The nuns teach them manners and morals along with religion. To make money, they sew and sell their wares, such as Beanie Baby blankets, at their store. I noticed that they needed another refrigerator in the kitchen to replace the broken one. Mary and Maurice had replaced the roof of one of the buildings, and intended buying a new refrigerator soon. I passed out one marshmallow to each little 'Nina'. They were so grateful and hugged me tighter. Some begged for more and I managed to sneak a couple to the urchins surrounding me without the other ones noticing. We took pictures and, after arriving home, I thought about those little girls in need when I looked at the photos. I wanted to reach out to them and continue to help them.

The girls traveled by bus the following day to The Triple Star Ballroom near Harlingen to enjoy the concert on their behalf. They sat very still and listened with awe to the Big Band and my cousin's trumpet hitting the high notes. Janine sang like an angel. The concert was free to everyone, and 850 people attended. The donations totaled $2,500.

We flew home to Ohio the next day. I now had a purpose in mind to help the little girls who stole my heart. Now I knew why God inspired me to write. I sent donations from the proceeds of my books each year to help them.

The trip was an eye-opener and a heart warmer, so I decided to fly down once again two years later, even though I had spinal stenosis and hip arthritis and could barely walk. That was the first time in my life that I had to use a wheel chair to travel to the gates at the airport. I thought about helping the girls, and also thought the warm weather would benefit my arthritic condition.

Not so, because it was very cold in Harlengen for that time of year, about 35 degrees at night and reached perhaps fifty in the afternoon, except for one day, the last day, when it was 70 degrees.

That year, Rob's daughters both flew down to visit, and they helped me immensely. I didn't have to do the housework except for one roast beef meal in the crock pot and dishes once or twice. Janine and Karen practically waited on me hand and foot. They drove me into Mexico, and with the help of a cane, I was able to keep up with them for the most part. The fancy acrylic cane drew a lot of attention, but finally, I sat down and waited while they shopped in extra stores. Little boys kept coming up to me trying to sell flowers, and they practically hit me in the nose with them.

Rob's brother, Don, flew down from Wisconsin to sing for the band, also. I hadn't seen him for many years, and he was such a gentleman, opening doors, taking my arm to help me walk. He practiced his songs with the band along with Janine and I realized everyone in Rob's family is musically talented.

The concert was held in a larger auditorium this time, and it was jam packed. Don and Janine sang their songs to the delight of everyone there. The little girls sat in the front row and got up to dance to some of the songs. Three times as much as the usual money was taken in, and later on one of the benefactors promised to help the little girls each month with a donation for food.

What a wonderful time was had by all, and I flew home the next day. I think the lesson I learned at 73 years is one everyone learns at some time in life. When you reach out to help someone, you get rewarded in some way. Perhaps mine was being helped so graciously by my kin while in Texas, and knowing that my small donations have helped these wonderful little girls. Kindness spreads, or pays it forward and I learned there are many extra kind people in this world.

Another memorable trip we took that was when we went to see the musical, THE PHANTOM, which had been playing in Toronto, Canada for many years. It was such a hit that it was advertised all over the United States and other countries. Buses were booked and quickly filled for three day trips from Akron, Ohio. Since the musical, SAIGON, was playing there at the same time, it was an extra popular attraction.

I had always wanted to see THE PHANTOM, and although Bob was not too thrilled about any trips since he was getting older, he reluctantly agreed to go, and I sent in the money for the trip.

On the eve of our departure, we decided to say good-bye to Joyce, Ed, Nikki and Mike. While walking across the freshly mowed front lawn, a bee stung the tip of my toe because I was wearing sandals. When one is allergic to bees, sandals should be restricted. Brushing the bee aside, and taking a Benedryl at bedtime seemed to help the situation and we left early in them morning for Toronto.

We were surprised when we entered the bus to see two of our friends, Agnes and Mary Ann, on the same excursion. When we arrived in Toronto after an uneventful journey, we checked into our hotel room. It was rather small, but we did not expect luxury on a reasonably priced trip. Little did I know that I would spend most of the trip in the cramped hotel room. It was when I took off my shoes that I noticed the swelling in my left leg. Oh, Oh, I should have gone to the hospital last night after I was stung, I thought. Taking another Benydryl made me very sleepy but took away the itching, burning, and swelling to a certain extent. After sleeping for four hours, Bob awakened me in time to board the bus to drive to a restaurant for dinner and afterwards see SAIGON.

We ate, toured a museum on the premises, and then drove to the theater. My stomach was nauseous and I could feel a fever coming on and ate sparingly. Somehow, I managed to sit through the play, which was entertaining, but not exactly what we expected. Meanwhile, my foot and leg kept swelling.

Back at the hotel, another Benydryl helped me sleep all night. In the morning, the group planned to take a tour of Toronto, but I she stayed in the room and slept most of the day. After eating a roll and drinking orange juice, a deep sleep overcame me.

Bob, who originally did not want to go on this trip, had the time of his life touring Toronto with the group. They explored a castle, visited the new sports stadium, stopped for lunch at a nice restaurant, and drove all around the city. When the group returned to the hotel, Bob awakened me because for it was time to get ready for dinner and afterwards to see the musical THE PHANTOM. It was difficult waking up, and horrifying to see my foot and leg puffed up like an elephant's leg. I could not get my foot into my shoe, but was determined to see

THE PHANTOM. Somehow I dragged my shoe across the room with my toes.

As we entered the bus, we found out that a young girl who was on this same trip was ill all day in her hotel room with some kind of virus, and was not able to go to the play. At the restaurant, the peas and mashed potatoes did not look inviting but I ate some of the dinner. When we arrived at the theater, once again I dragged my shoe until we reached our seats.

Well, the play was wonderful, and I managed to stay awake, but at intermission needed to visit the ladies room. Limping along, I entered one of the booths. I put my purse down on the toilet paper holder, and did not notice that the paper was caught in my purse as I left the booth. After crossing the room to wash my hands in the sink that looked more like a horse's trough, I became aware of everyone laughing and turned. Just at that moment, Agnes and Mary Ann entered the rest room and started laughing, also.

They pointed to me and it was then that I noticed that the toilet paper caught in my purse had followed me across the room. It was rather embarrassing, but not the end of the world. I never sweat the small stuff. Chuckling, I quickly tore the paper off my purse, gathered it up and deposited it in the waste basket. It made me realize that taking Benydryl during the day, for whatever reason, was not a good idea.

I returned to my seat, still laughing with my two friends, and they have never forgotten this incident to this very day. Every time I see them at church, it brings back memories of THE PHANTOM. The next morning Bob and I returned to Akron with the rest of the tour. My leg had started to slim down somewhat but I still needed another day to rest.

It seemed wonderful that Bob enjoyed the trip. However, this trip taught me a lesson. Never, ever, go on a trip the day after being stung by a bee, or at least go to the hospital and get treated for the sting before going. Perhaps we could visit Toronto again, so that I could see the sights, and perhaps a different play.

CHAPTER 45—Smoke and Angels

There were times long ago that I believe our Guardian Angels protected us and our home from going up in smoke.

Bob started smoking cigars when he was thirty-eight years old because someone had given him one to celebrate the birth of their son, and Bob decided he enjoyed smoking. Also, my dearest mother told him he looked distinguished when smoking a cigar. What man wouldn't want to look distinguished?

At that time, no one knew the dangers of smoking, so Bob smoked mainly in the recreation room downstairs. He always lit up a cigar at about five o'clock in the morning, right before he left for work, and carried it with him to the car.

On two occasions, our home could have gone up in smoke, and we could have lost our lives, except for one of us waking up. One morning, after Bob lit up a cigar in the kitchen, he thought he flipped the match into the kitchen sink, but unknowingly, it had ignited the curtains by the sink after he walked out the kitchen door. He backed the car out of the garage, and left to start the six A.M. shift at B.F. Goodrich Tire & Rubber Company.

I heard the car backing up, and turned over in bed to see a light shining on our bedroom door although the door was shut. Puzzled, I arose and opened the door to see the reflection of light on the hallway door. Entering the kitchen, I discovered the curtains and the kitchen cabinets on fire. Immediately after awakening the children, I called the fire department and threw pots of water at the curtains and cupboards. The fire trucks arrived in just a few minutes because the fire station is close by. They put the fire out completely but the cupboards were damaged and had to be replaced. Luckily, we had good insurance coverage. Luckily, also, that I saw some kind of light on our bedroom door. Where the angels watching over us? I firmly believe that they were.

A couple of years later, Bob's carelessness started a fire in the recreation room downstairs. After lighting up his cigar, he flipped the match into the ash tray, but missed, before leaving for work. Marlene was aroused slightly from her sleep as the car backed out, thought she smelled smoke, but dismissed it since she knew her dad smoked early in the morning. However, Joyce, eleven years old, in the other upstairs bedroom, awakened to smell the smoke coming through the register, ran downstairs and then down to the recreation room to discover the couch in flames. Joyce ran up the stairs and shouted to awaken me. We both carried buckets of water to put out the fire, called the fire department to make sure it was extinguished, and I thanked God and His angels for waking up Joyce.

Bob was banned to the garage to smoke his cigars from that day on. We also found out how dangerous smoking was for anyone's health, and that the walls of the recreation room stayed cleaner without the smoke buildup.

There were no more actual fires after that, but several other incidents occurred for years. Bob had retired and had extra time on his hands. Although he had never cooked before, he started boiling potatoes on the kitchen stove but neglected to check on them. He was also getting forgetful. I returned home the first time to a house filled with smoke, and burned potatoes and pans which had to be thrown away.

The second potato incident occurred while I was shopping. I was not finished and had planned to go to another store, when something or someone told me to return home immediately. I drove home and was shocked to see and smell the smoke upon entering the kitchen. Bob was downstairs in the recreation room and did not smell the smoke which permeated the entire first floor. Angels again talking to me and guiding me!

I do not drink coffee, but every morning when I awakened to the tantalizing aroma of the freshly perked coffee Bob made, it was a comfortable feeling. Even though Bob was retired, he arose early in the morning and quietly made coffee.

Our life had become somewhat routine after years of being together, and unfortunately, his dementia accelerated. I had a hard time understanding his sudden mood changes, his repeated questions, forgetfulness, or verbal abuse, which rarely happened before when we were younger.

At times, I resented his indifference, although he was occasionally attentive. Once in a while I raised my voice in retaliation against his abusive words, but that really fused the problem. He always apologized after he calmed down. He kept asking the same questions over and over, and even forgot to turn off the potatoes or eggs when he boiled them on the stove. Four times, I came home to find the first floor filled with smoke, burnt spuds and pans. He was either in the garage smoking, or down in the recreation room reading the papers, watching TV or listening to music. I begged Bob not to boil potatoes any more, but he just wouldn't listen.

After I read a book about dementia, I decided that I would make an effort not to yell at him in retaliation anymore, and that helped tremendously.

When I became more or less incapacitated with spinal stenosis and could scarcely walk or bend down for a short period, Bob helped in many ways. He carried the wash upstairs, loaded or unloaded the dishwasher, took out the trash and ran some errands. I was grateful for the help.

All this activity kept him busier than usual, so his mind seemed more alert and he asked the same questions less often, and did not forget to turn off the boiling potatoes. He read two newspapers a day, listened to music, and watched TV, but found time to help Flossie, and for that she was very grateful.

After my spinal stenosis eased, Bob still helped with some of the chores and tried to control his moods. I loved waking up to the aroma of coffee and really do appreciate Bob fully for the good man he is regardless of minor changes. One has to learn how to live with changes in another, in order to keep the peace.

CHAPTER 46—A Future Mother

When Nikki was in the ninth grade, her Child Development class were given a choice of one of their assignments. They could either choose to do community service with children, or to take care of an automated baby doll for a weekend.

Nikki, who loved babies and baby-sitting, chose the baby doll, whom she named Xander and took home for the weekend on Friday, March 3, her fifteenth birthday. The family had planned a birthday dinner at Nikki's favorite restaurant. She couldn't leave Xander home because she had to take constant care of him in order to get an 'A' in Child Development.

The customers stared at her as she cradled the naked baby in her arms. Xander had no clothes as yet because they didn't have time to stop at the store. Every time Xander cried, Nikki pushed a button on his back until the baby was comforted. Sometimes he was hungry, or had to burp, or needed a diaper change, or just wanted to be cuddled. If she didn't respond to the baby's needs, an abuse light was programmed to blink.

That night, Nikki expected that the baby would awaken a few times, but she never dreamed it would wake her up sixteen times. The teacher had used a key to program him, but probably was unaware he would keep Nikki awake most of the night. She had only two hours of uninterrupted sleep and was very tired on Saturday.

However, Nikki and her friend, Ashley, took Xander to the mall to buy him an outfit. Nikki carried Xander and he slept for the hour they shopped. The baby doll started crying nonstop on Saturday evening, but none of the buttons stopped his wails. Nikki had no choice but to push the panic button.

Xander shut down completely. Nikki called her teacher and left her a message because she wasn't home. Xander slept all night and, thankfully, so did Nikki. Suddenly, he started crying again on Sunday morning. When the teacher called, she was amazed that the program was restored after the panic button had been activated. Previously, that had never happened.

Sunday night Xander awakened only six times, and Nikki took good care of him. She didn't mind the baby waking up.

Monday morning, Nikki told her mother that she really wasn't ready to return Xander because she had become attached to him. She could have returned the baby doll to the teacher early in the morning, but opted to carry him around with her to all her classes until the last period.

Some of Nikki's classmates teased her as they walked through the halls between classes, and tried to get the abuse light to blink. However, Nikki protected Xander and didn't let that happen. Nikki was determined to get an 'A'. Her teacher reiterated once again that she didn't understand why the panic button reversed itself. Nikki was happy that it did, for then she didn't have to bother the teacher to come to her home and reprogram him.

Two days later, Nikki mentioned to her mother that she sort of missed taking care of the baby doll. That was not the usual result.

Obviously, the purpose of this experiment was to make the students realize that taking care of a baby is very difficult. However, Nikki didn't mind all the work and planned to be a good mother after she graduated from college and married.

And now she is one of the best mothers I know, very calm with any situation.

Great-Granddaughter Kaleigh.

CHAPTER 47—In Conclusion

No one knows what the future holds. I do not know what will happen with Bob in the care home. Right now, in February 2011, he has a viral infection and is taking an antibiotic. One day at a time will happen whatever befalls. He never seems to lose his sense of humor and that endears him to everyone. All I can do is pray and show him love and support.

Our family will still celebrate all the birthdays the same as we always have. Today is Joyce's birthday. We will hire a bus to take Bob and the family to Chili's for dinner.

Bob and Flossie - Bob's 89th Birthday Celebration at
Belgrade Gardens

As a proud grandmother, I will attend Shelley's graduation Summa Cum Laude in Music Education from Mt. Union University in May. I will follow her career in teaching music. I will delight in the birth of Nikki's second baby. I will continue to attend church every week and continue to pray for others. I will still go to Kansas for a few days in April, the good Lord willing.

Kaleigh and Ava

Flossie holding Shaun

Exercising, eating sensibly, and writing will be on my agenda for as long as I am able. Learning something new each day never stops.

Several years ago, when I asked my dear 98 year old friend, Mary Downing, her secret to a long life, she responded that she exercised for an hour every morning, drank orange juice every day and ate a small piece of chocolate every day. I have been doing the same thing for years.

Mary was one of the most interesting persons I have ever known. She visited 109 countries in her lifetime. She went to the North and South Pole when she was 88 years old and lived to be 100. She liked to help others and left a legacy of good will to others.

All people can learn something new every day just as she did. When my toes tend to curl up from arthritis, I put a bar of unwrapped soap between my sheets. I know, it sounded ridiculous when I first heard this method, too, but it seems to work for me along with 800 mg. of Vitamin E and eating bananas every day. Sometimes it all stems down to believing something will work.

I have found out that smiling helps keep friendships alive and makes others, even strangers, feel better. When I see others smile, it makes me happy, too. Many of my friends remark that I tend to smile regardless of any trauma in my life. Why should I complain and make others miserable?

Thinking positive keeps me going. I try to show respect for others.

And most important for peace of mind is that I like myself. Being kind to oneself and forgiving oneself makes it easier to forgive others.

Forgiveness of others is one of the most important criteria for a peaceful and fruitful life. It can destroy a person if they do not forgive and forget. To meditate each day is always helpful. And remember, no one but God is perfect – we all make mistakes.

Most of my books conclude with a poem, and so shall this book which is basically about forgiveness.

FORGIVENESS

Sometimes ghosts from the past
Live on to haunt in the present
Bad memories seem to last
And make life so unpleasant.

Lies and abuse of any kind
Are hard to forgive for the victim
Banish it all from the mind
Dwelling on it can make life grim.

The wounded fed a fantasy
Tend to believe what was said
Though they know habitual falsity
Are lies that they should dread.

However, one should recognize
For truth and beauty to be at hand
Forgiveness is the path for the wise
And only God can reprimand.

FLORIANA HALL

Forgiveness makes sufferers better
In every way, in everything
Pardon can be a true trendsetter
Frees you from the puppet string.

Like a breath of fresh air
Bear no malice toward others
Even if they were never fair
To all, our sisters and our brothers.

Forgive and forget sins of the past
Live only for joys of the present
God's love surrounds you at last
With the fragrance of only His scent.

Floriana Hall

BIOGRAPHY

Floriana Hall, b. 10/2/27, Pittsburgh, Pa., June 1945 graduate and Distinguished Alumna of Cuyahoga Falls High School, Cuyahoga Falls, Ohio, attended Akron University, married Robert Hall 62 years, five children, nine grandchildren, four great-grandchildren, author/ editor of six nonfiction books and six inspirational poetry books: SMALL CHANGE, self published, out of print; THE ADVENTURES OF FLOSSIE, ROBBIE, AND JUNEY During The Great Depression (2006), published by www.Booksurge.com (now www.CreateSpace. com) ; THE SANDS OF RHYME, poetry, self published, out of print; DADDY WAS A BAD BOY (to be ordered from me); OUT OF THE ORDINARY SHORT STORIES, published by lstBooks.com, taken over by Authorhouse ; HEARTS ON THE MEND (2006), published by www.PublishAmerica.com; FRANCIS, NOT THE SAINT (2008), published by www.Booksurge.com (now www.CreateSpace.com); GATHERING GRACES, poetry (2008) published by www.Cyberwit. net and SELECT SANDS OF RHYME AND REASON, poetry and short stories published by www.Cyberwit.net (2009); FRANCISCO, NO EL SANTO, Spanish Translation of FRANCIS, NOT THE SAINT, (2010) published by CCBPublishing, Canada. Young Children's book SMALL PLEASURES by www.Cyberwit.net (2010). All books may be purchased from www.Amazon.com

Founder/coordinator of the Poet's Nook at Cuyahoga Falls Library, Editor of The Poet's Nook's four books, THROUGH OUR EYES,

POEMS OF BEAUTIFUL NORTHEAST OHIO, (out of print); POET'S NOOK POTPOURRI, TOUCHING THE HEARTS OF GENERATIONS and VOICES IN VERSE, Weaving Words (2008) published by OMNI Book Publishing. Winner of many poetry contests. Published in United States, England, France and India. Poetry teacher, YOU, ME, AND POETRY, for www.LssWritingSchool.com WHO'S WHO IN INTERNATIONAL POETRY, several others.

Contact Floriana: HAFLORIA@sbcglobal.net
Website: http://www.alongstoryshort.net/FlorianaHall.html
www.BooksofExcellence.com

Would you like to see your manuscript become a book?

If you are interested in becoming a PublishAmerica author, please submit your manuscript for possible publication to us at:

acquisitions@publishamerica.com

You may also mail in your manuscript to:

**PublishAmerica
PO Box 151
Frederick, MD 21705**

www.publishamerica.com